Michael Heseltine [illegible] cated at Shrewsbury School [illegible] itics, Philosophy and Ec [illegible] ted President of the Oxford Unic [illegible] ow of his college in 1987 and [illegible] in 1988.

In the 1960s, he hel [illegible] roup and he remains a major shareholder.

He first entered Parliament as the Member for the Tavistock division of Devon in 1966 and, since a redistribution of Parliamentary boundaries in 1974, has represented Henley.

He spoke for the Conservative Party in opposition on Transport during the late 1960s. In 1970 he was Parliamentary Secretary to the Ministry of Transport and Parliamentary Under Secretary of State for the Department of the Environment. He became Minister of Aerospace in 1972 until the Conservatives were defeated in 1974. Again in opposition, he was a member of the Shadow Cabinet holding the Trade and Industry and the Environment portfolios.

He served as Secretary of State for the Department of the Environment from 1979 to 1983 and then as Secretary of State for Defence until his resignation in 1986.

He is a member of the Council of the Royal Zoological Society, an appointment which stems from his life-long interest in the conservation of the natural environment. He is creating an arboretum.

He married Anne Williams in 1962; they have one son and two daughters, and the family divide their time between homes in London and Northamptonshire.

MICHAEL HESELTINE

The Challenge of EUROPE

CAN BRITAIN WIN?

Pan Books London, Sydney and Auckland

First published in Great Britain 1989 by
George Weidenfeld & Nicolson Ltd

This edition published 1991 by
Pan Books Ltd, Cavaye Place, London SW10 9PG

9 8 7 6 5 4 3 2 1

ISBN 0 330 31436 X

Printed in England by Clays Ltd, St Ives plc

To my mother

Contents

	Acknowledgements	ix
	Introduction	xi
1	Our History: a Question of Identity	1
2	Creeping Federalism	15
3	The Budget: Whose Money?	38
4	Europe's Economy: Falling Behind	58
5	A Market Solution	76
6	Our Agenda: Britain's Opportunity	95
7	Education: Raising Our Sights	126
8	Environment: a World Without Frontiers	155
9	Defence: the First Responsibility	178
10	The Future: a Tory Vision	207
	Index	217

Acknowledgements

I have received generous help from many people in preparing this book. The staff of the House of Commons library provide a unique service. I cannot thank them enough. To the many others who gave generously of their time, I am profoundly grateful. They belong to the growing number of people who believe that Britain must pursue a leading role in Europe with energy and conviction, and have helped me to say so.

Introduction

'If one does not know to which port one is sailing, no wind is favourable.' So said Seneca, Roman statesman and philosopher, in the first century AD. He might have been describing Britain's predicament, some 2,000 years later, in her relationship with her continental neighbours before and since the birth of the European Community.

This is a partial book, in both senses of the word: if it stretched to a dozen volumes, it would still be incomplete, and its judgments are necessarily mine alone – British naturally, Conservative certainly. It surveys the landscape of Europe through a highly personal lens. From both sides of the Channel, the popular picture of Britain in Europe is too easily coloured by the latest political squabble or the complaint of a special interest group. Each of us in a sense is partial, too close to our own self-interest to see the whole, too preoccupied with the present to stand back and consider the future. Of course, we must be certain of our advantage in all this, but if the politician is to persuade the British people to rise to the European challenge, it is to their imagination that he must finally appeal.

As I wrote each chapter, one theme emerged at every turn. The growing speed of change and the gathering concentrations of power in the modern world force the same choice again and again upon the British people: whether to cling to the sovereignty we know and value, exercising it, even as it shrinks, with all the resourcefulness we can find; or to strengthen that sovereignty by sharing it with others, acknowledging the hazard in order to grasp the greater opportunity. It is often a choice between looking forward and harking back. Time and again, through the chronicles of the post-war years, the British habit of making the wrong choice – at The Hague in 1948, in Paris in 1951, at Messina in 1956 – can be seen now with a clarity which is painful but instructive.

Have we at last learnt? I profoundly hope so. We have clung too long to past achievements and failed to anticipate the unfolding of a new Europe and our need to find a place in it. We know now the price we have paid for allowing others to design the mould and to pour into it their own driving self-interest. We have seen how our misjudgments forced us on the defensive and turned victor in war into supplicant in peace. One lesson learned is that hesitancy, like confidence, can feed on itself. By the time Britain was accepted into the Community in 1972, we had denied ourselves the chance to share in the strong collective growth of its first fifteen years of life.

In increasingly competitive worldwide markets, the Europe of the 1970s was among the least effective regional players; and within Europe Britain was among the least effective countries. The slower growth of the 1970s gave heart to those who, either blind or hidebound, wished to reopen the argument that we had been, and might again be, better out of Europe than in. By the 1980s there was a new recognition of the value of more open competition, and Conservative Britain led the way. It came to be understood that the engine of sustained recovery would have to be the one which the Community's founders had designed and embodied in the Treaty of Rome in the first place. The single European market – the true common market – had become indispensable. The work of constructing it had to be taken up afresh, but this time completed. Now the British people's representatives are at last in a position to play their full part. But we must avoid the hesitancies which historically have proved so catastrophically ill-judged.

Can we accept the changed circumstance of Britain's place in Europe and of Europe's in the world? The questions are really the same, because the two circles are concentric. Europe's chance of attaining her full potential in this generation as a civilizing, enriching force can only be enhanced by Britain's willingness to contribute all her talents.

Urgent questions follow. To some there is no answer. How can we compete in Europe if our people are educated and trained to standards which even now do not match the best of European endeavours, let alone those of Japan or the United States? To others, the answers are encouraging. How precious is this Europe to its inhabitants? Europeans are concerned about the quality of their lives and their concern for the environment knows no national boundary. They thoroughly understand that we pollute each other as easily as we pollute ourselves. No single country of European size can exert decisive influence on the environment alone, but together the Community can move the world.

What of Europe's economic potential? The world believes in it, and both the richer and the poorer countries are watching our growing ability to set the pace of economic change. Already Europe matters too much for them to shrug aside our standards and, as a source of aid and investment, for our wishes to be ignored. The Community is a triumph for capitalism. Its member countries are among the richest on earth, its mainspring the dynamic of enterprise and reward. As the national frameworks of law, practice, regulation and subsidy are replaced by common rules essential to forge twelve markets into one, the ideas that have transformed capitalist Britain must also enthuse the common capitalism of Europe.

What particular talent has Britain to offer her European fellow citizens? It is not immodest to believe that Britain's political skills and our tradition of constitutional government must be of value in the common pool. British parliamentarians have heard their continental colleagues affirm it often enough and my survey of the Community's institutions has convinced me they are right: as the federal elements of these institutions become more pronounced, so the need becomes plainer for a new infusion of democratic control.

We have something to defend, a rich inheritance – the very core of Western civilization – so benevolent that for all mankind's sake we know we must be vigilant in its defence and staunch in its support. To defend Europe's values we must defend its soil and this is something that Europe quickly understood after 1945. It was in NATO that we first discovered the habit and the wisdom of European co-operation. We learnt that, for the purpose of common defence, Britain's place was in Europe; and so long as the Conservative Party has any strength that lesson will be remembered. For me and, I believe, for most of my generation the ambition to build Europe makes no sense without an equal determination to defend it.

Can Britain win? Does she look likely to be to the fore between now and 1992 in the work of completing the single market, and has she the economic strength and the political will thereafter to remain one of the leaders of the Community, directing its course into the coming century?

I have no doubt that our country must take its place on the bigger stage. I want to see us boldly spreading our influence across the world of tomorrow; and while we have no entitlement to any prize, there are plentiful opportunities – risky to reach for, certainly, but rash to let go. We should always remember that to pick and choose in Europe is to lose; it is to fail to grasp – as Britain has sometimes seemed in danger of doing – that all the strands of the Community's life are interwoven within a wider tapestry.

The framework of the European Community is indivisible and if we have not understood that, we are wasting our efforts and deceiving our partners. If we do understand, then we can help to give it form, not just because we have ideas and experience to contribute but because our very conviction is a key to the opening of doors. I yield to none in my pride in Britain's past; it makes me the more impatient to build on it. Britain's genius is a treasure which I am willing to share with others, provided they will do the same. I will never grudge them any benefit if we too can share that benefit but I would resent their advantage if the British people were left drifting in their wake as our partners sail ahead. The tide of history has carried us close to Europe's shore. We should accept that destiny; the wind will never be more favourable.

CHAPTER
1

Our History: a Question of Identity

Britain's past is tightly spun into the history of Europe and it is this web of influence that makes us what we are today. The relationship goes back to the origins of the British people and has lasted in spite of long periods of mutual neglect.

To assert a common European inheritance is not to deny our nationhood. Britain's national identity was forged earlier than that of most of her European neighbours. British history has been a constant process of absorption, and at times rejection, of European influences but the periods of national isolation have rarely lasted long. Until 1815 the peoples of Britain – with English and Scots sometimes allied, sometimes opposed – were regularly engaged in continental wars. England's unwavering interest was in maintaining the balance of power, although Scotland's recurrent concern for 300 years before the union of the Crowns was to keep English power in check. Then, after a century of relative detachment from continental Europe during which an overseas empire absorbed most of their energies and attention, the British people found themselves, twice in the space of twenty-five years, fighting to prevent the dominance of a single continental power. From the shocked aftermath of those two catastrophes, and the determination on the part of the belligerents that they should never recur, sprang the European Community.

We are, of course, an island nation and thus physically separated from the continent. But, formative as that fact has been in our national make-up, the whole history of mankind has been one of transcending such barriers. And Britain's history has been no exception.

The English, Scots, Welsh and Irish are descended from continental Europeans – Celts, Anglo-Saxons and Danes. The Romans imposed an initial unity which brought us within the European civilization of imperial Rome, a heritage revived, as in the rest of Western Europe, during the Renaissance. England's modern history can be traced back to the social structures established by the Saxons, the political unity imposed by the Normans and their Angevin successors, and the culture disseminated throughout these islands by a Church which embraced all Europe until the sixteenth century. Even the Reformation, which in many ways set England and Scotland on a different course from large parts of the continent, was an experience common to all Northern Europe. Underpinning it all there was – and is – an intellectual vigour, a philosophical outlook that is the common gift of the Greeks to us all. Thus the intellectual, religious, artistic and cultural heritages of British and continental Europeans are linked and shared. So now are our economic and political destinies.

Britain was made part of modern Europe by the Church and by the Normans. We became part of that great ecclesiastical network which in the Middle Ages was called Christendom. Christianity gave Europe that distinctive cultural unity which lasts to this day. As the poet T. S. Eliot put it, '... the common tradition of Christianity has made Europe what it is.... It is in Christianity that our arts have developed; it is in Christianity that the laws of Europe have been rooted. It is against a background of Christianity that all our thoughts have significance....'

From earliest times the enrichment of Britain and continental Europe was reciprocal. The Christian faith and learning brought by Augustine and Columba in the sixth century were carried back by English scholars and missionaries in the eighth century, when Boniface was busy converting the German tribes, Bede was established as Europe's foremost historian and Alcuin was in charge of Charlemagne's revival of classical learning.

If unity of faith was a common bond throughout Western Europe in medieval times, dynastic considerations meant that continental politics were never far from the thoughts of English rulers. With William the Conqueror, England also become a part of a political power which embraced a great tract of France. Thereafter the intermingling of the history of France with that of England and Scotland, both dynastically and culturally, continued for some 500 years. Economically too there was a constant traffic between this island and many parts of mainland Europe – when wars did not inhibit it. The drovers' trails which began in the pastures and hills of England ended in the markets of France, Italy and the Low Countries, and by the late Middle Ages the wool merchants and clothiers were amassing great fortunes through their continental trading links.

In the sixteenth century, one ideal of a united Europe took shape among humanists. Humanism was brought to Britain from Italy by men who had gone across to the continent to study. Theirs was a vision of a united, revived Roman Empire but not a *politically* united Europe. They believed in separate kingdoms – bound together in a cultural unity and subject to the same legal code. Hence the powerful revival of Latin studies and the adoption of Roman law in many of the countries of Europe, including Scotland. Ideas spanned Western Europe; Erasmus felt as at home in his rooms in Oxford, debating with friends like Thomas More and Dean Colet of St Paul's, as he did anywhere in his restless wandering throughout the continent.

The unity of Catholic Europe was shattered by the Reformation and the consequent division between Catholic and Protestant states. Intermittent warfare made travel and trade difficult. But ideas still crossed frontiers freely and books were translated. Many a sixteenth-century English library had its copy of Machiavelli, although he was banned in both Catholic and Protestant countries. The development of learning in Britain went hand in hand with its development in the rest of Europe. Scholars, even from geographically remote Scotland, attended the universities of France and Holland. The great names of European letters and thought are the common possession of all our peoples, although not all reputations travel equally well. (The genius of Shakespeare, and later of Goethe, was for a long time appreciated only by their fellow countrymen.)

The mingling of cultural influences continued. Late sixteenth-century 'Scottish baronial' architecture reflected the style of the French château. The seventeenth century saw the ideas of Locke and Newton take firm hold, especially in France, while many of the artists and craftsmen employed by British patrons during the seventeenth and eighteenth centuries were born on the continent. The Hanoverian kings brought to Britain German music and a notable Hanoverian musician in Handel. Italian painting, sculpture and architecture dominated British taste for centuries. The Enlightenment was a pan-European phenomenon which fully embraced both England and Scotland. In the eighteenth century the Scottish philosopher, David Hume, enjoyed a Europe-wide reputation, while Robert Adam influenced domestic architecture as far afield as the court of Catherine the Great of Russia.

A kind of constructive tension – waves of opinion creating their own reaction – took place in Europe from the sixteenth century onwards. For England there was a continual struggle between a sense of belonging and a sense of separation. During the Enlightenment – the age of Voltaire, Montesquieu and Adam Smith – there was a ferment of thought and imagination which touched all of Europe. There then followed a reaction. The Germans revolted against French culture. The Russians revolted against the decadent West. But this reaction, like the Enlightenment itself, was evidence as much of Europe's unity as of its diversity.

The English Reformation did, of course, diverge from the path taken by the followers of Luther and Calvin, and that, coupled with a period of domestic political turmoil, meant that for much of the seventeenth century, until 1689, England was less involved politically with continental Europe. Such ventures in the European theatre as were made were purely defensive or accidental, such as the acquisition of Dunkirk and Tangier. What was taken was soon surrendered. The inhabitants of the British Isles were seen by their fellow Europeans as a bizarre people locked in extraordinary revolutions which few could understand.

With William III's accession, there was renewed involvement in European affairs. Indeed, they became a party issue. The Tory Party continued to be isolationist and regularly attacked the Whig Party for indulging in foreign entanglements – though these were inevitable, given that successive monarchs right through the eighteenth century were either Dutch or German. The Tories then regarded involvements with foreigners, particularly Europeans, as a disastrous Whig invention, like the national debt, expensive wars and the rise of the mercantile interest in politics. But European politics in the eighteenth century were a shifting kaleidoscope of allegiances and rivalries, and Britain was an active player in the game, which was played out not only on the continent but also in far-flung parts of the globe as colonial interests became increasingly important to national economies.

Trade boomed during this period. 'Wealth is power' was the cry, and manufacturing and mercantile interests increasingly influenced political decisions. From the 1660s to the late 1820s, the exclusion of Dissenters by law from government and public affairs prompted many nonconformists to channel their energies into industry and business. Thus Britain grew industrially and developed a strong trade in manufactured goods ahead of the continental countries through a driving force that was not state-inspired.

What trade might have brought together, the violent upheaval of the French Revolution conspired to drive apart. Napoleon conquered much of continental Europe and imposed upon it French Revolutionary political institutions and a new legal code. It is a legacy in which Britain never shared.

At the same time Britain was beginning her rapid industrial advance which, during the first half of the nineteenth century, carried her to a position of economic supremacy over the continental powers, comparable to that which, a century later, the United States developed over Europe. Economic change, once in motion, gathered its own momentum. Confidence in the future became self-sustaining. Optimism knew no bounds as growth and prosperity continued at an accelerating rate. Rapid industrialization was greatly helped by Britain's strength as a maritime power, which guaranteed easy access to imported raw materials, especially cotton. Foreign export markets were crucial and even during Napoleon's European blockade the colonies provided expanding markets. Two-thirds of the cotton goods produced were exported.

Ultimately, thanks to her success in the global conflict with the French, Britain succeeded in creating an empire which came to demand the greater part of her energies and attention. From 1815 onwards, for almost 100 years, Britain moved steadily away from continental Europe, although on the world stage the competition for empire among the great European powers continued without respite – a competition from which Britain emerged pre-eminent.

During the nineteenth century the Foreign Office and successive Foreign Secretaries – Castlereagh, Canning, Palmerston – kept watchful eyes on Europe but as the Victorian era unfolded the British people increasingly looked beyond their own continent to their colonies in Australia, Canada, Africa and, above all, to their empire in India. It was left to our own royal family, together with the other royal houses, to maintain and foster the historic relationships – mostly by intermarriage.

Ironically, it was a continental inheritance which at this time helped to sunder us from continental ideas. Britain's devotion to the supreme value of a classical education differed from trends in the rest of Europe. By the nineteenth century, the classics had become the principal means to make the British ruling class fit to govern the multiplying colonies, providing them with an ideology of empire. But it also became a bastion against the encroachment of science into the public schools. There grew up a determination that education should be academic and not designed to prepare people for a job. It was meant to form character rather than to train scholars, to produce a rounded man equipped to govern the Empire, with his mind on a rather higher plane than that of commerce. This classical tradition was unique to British education. In French and German schools, where science became increasingly popular, the teaching of the humanities continued to include science after the two cultures had become separate in Britain.

In 1914 the British people were, temporarily, dragged back into continental politics and conflict, but in the twenty years after the Treaty of Versailles of 1919, they showed signs of a longing to return to their 100 years' detachment. It was in 1939 that our destiny finally became inseparable from Europe, although a whole generation had passed before this became widely recognized. The reasons for this are worth examining.

During the Second World War the experience of Britain and the continental nations, who were to found the Community, had been very different. The latter were *all* occupied. During those war years, in prisons and camps, men and women from all nations had been thrown together and had dreamt of a new and better world. The nation-state, they felt, could no longer provide stability and peace for its citizens. In these same years the British people, through experiences no less profound, had been confirmed in their established view of their country's position in the world.

Britain had experienced her finest hour when, totally alone, she had held out against Hitler. Links with the continent had been severed while those with the Commonwealth and the United States had become stronger. In the post-war world, it seemed natural to the British to stand apart from Europe. Their country was undefeated, their industry was relatively intact and the Commonwealth and Empire who had fought at their side – a natural market and above all a source of raw materials – seemed guarantees of economic strength.

At the same time, never had British prestige been as high on the liberated continent as it was in 1945. Forbidden news from the BBC, and Winston Churchill's voice, had for years given hope to the inhabitants of the occupied nations. Many on the continent asked themselves who but the British could lead Europe out of the chaos and destruction of war. Even France, the only major power left in the Western half of the continent, seemed weak in comparison. Her economy, already stagnating between the two world wars, had been severely damaged, while a strong Communist party threatened French stability.

From these different experiences and perceptions grew many misunderstandings which kept Britain and the original six countries of the first European Community apart for nearly twenty years. In the Benelux countries and in France there existed two opposing schools of thought. The first, which in 1945 was the stronger, wanted a thoroughly weakened Germany, strictly controlled by the victorious powers. De Gaulle wanted the Saarland for France and, if possible, all the territory up to the Rhine, together with international control of the Ruhr – the heart of Germany's industrial power. Even the Netherlands wanted large stretches of German land, preferably without its German population! The other school, in the minority at first, was composed mainly of those who did not believe that a repetition of the policy of domination, as postulated in the Treaty of Versailles, would bring the changed and better world they had dreamed of and hoped for during the darkness of the occupation years.

As the rift between the Soviet Union and the West became deeper, more and more people argued, as Keynes had argued in 1919, that the restoration of Europe would be impossible without the renewal of Germany's economic and industrial strength. Although France continued to insist on the original policy, she did so with less force after de Gaulle, its strongest advocate, resigned. (It was only after his return to power in 1958 that he became one of the architects of the Franco-German reconciliation.)

In his speech to the United Europe meeting at the Albert Hall in May 1947, Churchill put the case for the economic reconstruction of Germany in a characteristically robust way: 'Germany today lies prostrate, famishing among ruins. Obviously no initiative can be expected from her. It is for France and Britain to take the lead. Together they must bring the German people back into the European circle.'

There were, of course, sound practical reasons for restoring the economic life of Germany. Britain and the United States were responsible for the most densely populated and most devastated part of occupied Germany. In the reconstruction of the German economy they saw a way of ending their heavy financial burden.

In 1947 General George Marshall, the United States' Secretary of State, launched his plan – the uniquely generous and wise offer of financial support for the reconstruction of Europe. America insisted on West Germany's inclusion as a beneficiary, in order to keep Germany out of Soviet hands. To rebuild Europe's economy, Germany had to become part of that very reconstruction, but the crucial question was how to keep the German people from reviving their hated hegemony once they had been brought back into the European circle.

In 1948 the Soviet Union fired the first shots in the Cold War. This was a crucial stimulus to any who were hesitant about European co-operation. The Russians renounced their agreements with their former allies, closed the road and rail corridors to Berlin, which had been occupied and divided by the Four Powers, and proclaimed Berlin the new capital of East Germany. The western allies united, kept a life-line to West Berlin through a massive air-lift and, through united civil and military effort, faced down the Russian threat.

From this series of events the North Atlantic Treaty Organization (NATO) was born in 1949. The United States thus committed herself to the joint defence of all the western European nations, together with the twelve founder members. West Germany, of course, was not included as she had been disarmed and was still occupied, which focused more sharply the question of her place in the new Europe.

In 1950 that great Frenchman, Jean Monnet, initiated a proposal intended to resolve this dilemma. As a young man, during the First World War, Monnet had played an important part in organizing Anglo-French economic co-operation. When the Second World War broke out, the British and French governments had asked him again to lead their London-based organization for economic co-operation in their common war effort.

Monnet's breadth of vision and constancy of purpose have made this unelected economist and lobbyist perhaps the leading figure in post-war Europe. Not the least of his gifts was an understanding of the British character. And although British politicians took a long time to understand the potency of his ideas, Monnet's eventual influence on British national policy in the second half of this century may one day prove to have been greater than that of any other figure.

In 1943 Monnet drafted a *note de réflexion* about the peace that should follow victory over Hitler's Germany. This, he thought, could only be achieved through an entirely new organization embracing the European nations and their economies. This note contained many aspects of the proposals he was to submit in 1950 to the then French Foreign Minister, Robert Schuman. These proposals, known as the Schuman Plan, gave birth to the first of the European Communities, the European Coal and Steel Community, which pooled the iron, steel and coal industries of France, Germany, Italy and the Benelux countries (soon to be known as the Six) under the first supra-national body, the High Authority – forerunner of the European Commission.

The other five nations had the common experience of German occupation and control over their industry. Since the German industrial complex had been centrally directed to the war effort, there had been considerable co-operation between all six nations, especially in resistance to the demands which were being made on them by Albert Speer, the Nazi industrial supremo. Grounded in part, therefore, on their recent experience, the coal and steel industries of the continent were a natural first step for formal collaboration. The founding treaty of this first Community was signed in Paris on 18 April 1951.

Monnet's timing was opportune. With the exception of Greece and Yugoslavia, the Soviet Union had forcibly turned all the Eastern European nations, including East Germany which it occupied, into Communist-controlled satellites. The remaining continental democratic nations felt severely threatened, so it was natural for Monnet to urge Robert Schuman to turn to the leaders of Italy and Germany, Alcide de Gasperi and Konrad Adenauer, as obvious partners.

Schuman's parents had come from Lorraine, which they left in 1871, when Lorraine was incorporated into the German Reich, to settle in Luxembourg. But he returned to Germany in order to study and, being a German citizen until Lorraine became French again in 1918, his German was as fluent as his French. De Gasperi was born in that part of Italy which belonged then to the Austro-Hungarian Empire and, as an active politician there, he spoke German effortlessly. Adenauer was a Rhinelander who, during the inter-war years, had worked, albeit in vain, for Franco-German reconciliation. All three came from border areas which had suffered from the vicissitudes of European wars, which to them had been civil wars. All three were convinced Catholics and leaders of Christian Democratic parties.

The establishment in 1951 of the European Coal and Steel Community, with Monnet as President of the High Authority, was the first step on a road which Britain was most reluctant to take, despite encouragement from the United States. Dean Acheson, US Secretary of State, later wrote: 'Despite my most earnest arguments, in the next few days Britain made her great mistake of the post-war period by refusing to join in negotiating the Schuman Plan.' It was not that British statesmen were indifferent to European unity, but that those who supported it – most notably Winston Churchill and Ernest Bevin – had never intended the United Kingdom to be an immediate participant. During the first year of the Second World War, there was a flash of apparent interest in federal forms of co-operation between France and Britain. It was again Monnet who formulated the proposal made by Churchill to organize a total fusion of the governments and parliaments of Britain and France. This came to nothing when Petain took over the government of France and concluded a separate armistice with Hitler's Germany. Succeeding events did nothing to encourage the British to tie themselves more closely to the continent.

In Zurich, in September 1946, Churchill appealed to the continental nations and especially to France and Germany to work together towards a united Europe. He declared: 'If we are to form the United States of Europe or whatever name or form it may take, we must begin now.' But in common with most of the British people, he saw Britain as being within three circles: the Commonwealth, the Anglo-American bond and Europe. We could never belong exclusively to any one of those three circles but we could, it was assumed, move independently and with confidence within all of them. In the last forty years our influence in each has shrunk dramatically and the part which Churchill foresaw for Britain has been rewritten.

After the launching of the Marshall Plan, Ernest Bevin, Foreign Secretary, took the lead in bringing the European nations together in what was then called the Organization for European Economic Co-operation (OEEC). But Bevin and his colleagues, like their Conservative opponents, saw the OEEC as a temporary measure necessary to organize the United States' generous assistance in the material reconstruction of Europe and help promote a long-term commitment, but not as a step towards an economically and politically united Europe – though the

United States made it clear that it favoured this.

It is clear that Bevin thought deeply about relations with continental Europe. He acknowledged that Britain was a part of Europe and felt that Europe would not be able to go anywhere without her. He also believed that Britain's relationship with America and with the Commonwealth made it difficult, if not impossible, to reconcile our position with that of France and Germany, which he regarded as unencumbered by wider responsibilities. Bevin looked for future co-operation, particularly in the fields of defence and economics, but argued that because of Europe's weakness neither was possible without the involvement of the United States.

In 1948 those who sought a new form of European co-operation met in an atmosphere of great enthusiasm at a congress in The Hague. It was boycotted by the Labour government but Churchill and other Conservatives played a prominent part. The congress led to the establishment of the Council of Europe but it soon became clear that the Conservative Party did not intend at this stage that it should be much more than a place for the exchange of ideas.

Monnet, with his many British friends, knew all too well that few of them shared his vision of Europe. But he seems never to have doubted that Britain would one day change. Shortly before the birth of the Coal and Steel Community, Stafford Cripps, the Chancellor of the Exchequer, asked Monnet whether France and Germany really intended to go ahead without the United Kingdom. Monnet replied: 'You know how I feel about Britain. Europe needs Britain. However, I know that, as long as a United Europe is a hypothesis, your country will not join the enterprise. Once it has become a reality you will join, and we will welcome you.'

Those who knew Monnet best doubt whether he expected the British absence to last as long as it did. After 1950, misunderstandings between Britain and the Six increased, while the Six made what now seems headlong progress, though there was an early set-back. The Korean War brought a demand to incorporate the defence potential of West Germany into NATO. The French government proposed the formation of a European Defence Community to achieve this, but their National Assembly refused in 1954 to agree. To resolve the problem Anthony Eden, Prime Minister of Britain, proposed the formation of a Western European Union (WEU) to guide and co-ordinate common European defence interests, and this came about by the revision of the Treaty of Brussels in

1954, which also set the scene for the re-armament of West Germany. The case for German accession to NATO was becoming overwhelming, and they were admitted as full partners in 1955.

In 1956 the Foreign Ministers of the Six met in Messina, Sicily, and decided to plan in earnest the creation of a common market. There followed the Treaty of Rome on 25 March 1957 and the establishment of the European Economic Community. The British government, to the disappointment of many on the continent, even declined the invitation to send an observer to Messina.

Several British initiatives to form a link with the Community were understandably seen by its member states as attempts to impede development. The most obvious example was when, at the end of 1957, as a Common Market between the Six was seen to have become a reality, the United Kingdom proposed the formation of a free trade area, consisting of the Community and the other member states of the OEEC. The British Prime Minister, Harold Macmillan, even threatened to pull out of NATO unless the EEC agreed to negotiate a free trade agreement. But de Gaulle, with whom he argued this in June 1958, and Adenauer were not moved. So in 1959 Britain organized EFTA, a free trade area consisting of seven Western European countries outside the EEC. Thirty years later, it can be seen simply as a defensive alliance – the latest of a series which the rulers of England had for centuries put together, almost by instinct, against any continental combination which seemed likely to grow uncomfortably strong.

There followed two more years of hesitation while defence links with America became even closer. Then in July 1961, the Conservative government under Macmillan opened negotiations with the Six to see if Britain could negotiate satisfactory arrangements to enter the Community as a full partner. 'We in Britain are Europeans,' Macmillan at last felt able to declare, although there were those in his party who contradicted him. 'That has always been true but it has now become a reality which we cannot ignore,' he explained, adding: 'I believe that our right place is in the vanguard of the movement towards the greater unity of the free world, and that we can lead better from within than outside. At any rate, I am persuaded that we ought to try.'

It was indeed an all-important reality – one forgotten by the British people, or hidden from them, for 150 years but one which they could no longer deny. Macmillan's choice of words read like a deliberate endorsement of Monnet's prediction to Cripps. But the reciprocal welcome to Britain, which Monnet had predicted, was to be delayed for another ten years.

Despite the protracted – and in large part successful – negotiations led by Edward Heath, the British attempt to join was summarily blocked by de Gaulle's veto on 29 January 1963. Under Harold Wilson, the Labour government tried again to join in 1967, but it too was baulked. This second British application was left on the table and pressed again in 1970, this time successfully, thus earning Edward Heath, by now the British Prime Minister, his place in history.

I cannot know what was in the minds of my colleagues as they voted in October 1971 to commit Britain to the European Community. But I myself was painfully aware that as a nation we had misjudged time and time again the determination of our continental neighbours in the post-war world to move closer together. Our miscalculations had obliged us to pay a high price – a price we must not pay again. I knew, too, that the divisions of Europe had in our own century, in our own lifetime, been responsible for destruction on a scale never experienced before. For too long the politicians of Europe had been committed to their separate nationalities, some to the point of obsession.

I was also struck by the decline of Europe's position in the world, and by its increasing political and economic weakness. By the beginning of the twentieth century, leadership in industry, innovation and cultural influence had already begun to pass from Europe to the United States. The countries of Europe were finding their future defined for them by others until, by the 1970s, it was clear that a divided Europe would grow more impotent with every decade. Britain, West Germany, Italy and France, each with fifty or sixty million people, faced a world of 260 million Soviet citizens, 220 million Americans, 900 million Chinese and 115 million Japanese. It was a world which made any European country standing alone look very puny indeed, and it was clear that, separately, the European states could never again be the powers that they once were. But together they could recover both strength and influence. (The twelve nations of the Community number 320 million people, roughly the size of the population of the United States and Japan put together.) In voting for Britain's accession to the EEC, I had no doubt that I was both protecting British self-interest and enhancing Britain's ability to influence tomorrow's world.

What was clear in 1971 is even more so today. The conditions which made it possible for Britain to be semi-detached from Europe for so long have vanished for ever. There is no empire to sustain us; we are no longer an industrial super-power; we can no longer pretend that Britain is in any sense an equal partner of the United States. There is nowhere for us to go except as part of a European consortium. In 1989 few British citizens would, I think, deny this truth.

For myself, Britain's still novel position as a full partner in Europe is a constant stimulus. We are challenged by the course of our history to learn a new role and our survival will depend on the skill with which we play it. There are those who fear that in moving closer to Europe, Britain will lose her identity. On the contrary, I believe that within Europe she will find a much greater one.

CHAPTER
2

Creeping Federalism

While the original six nations of Europe worked to create a common market during the 1950s which reflected their own national self-interests, Britain stood apart, if not aloof. Officials from the Foreign Office, or sometimes from the Board of Trade, attended the discussions and many of the negotiations, but it became increasingly apparent that we were bystanders while the others were players. We had our reasons – or so we thought. Our leadership of the Commonwealth, our Atlantic alliance, our worldwide friendships and, uniquely, the vivid recollection that for a brief but unforgettable moment we had stood alone among the European foes of Germany, had forged in us a self-image which was ill suited for a venture founded on the conviction that national sovereignty was no longer a sufficient force on its own to shape the post-war world.

British officials sat, without instructions, witnesses to a process that was growing visibly more confident, powerless to stop it and prevented from supporting and thus influencing it. As Rab Butler was to say years later, 'We just thought it wasn't going to work. That's where we were wrong.'

The countries of continental Europe did not of course approach this historic occasion with like minds. The debate about how to achieve greater integration was as alive then as it has remained. The federalists in Europe argued the need for a great leap forward but they set targets that for many were inconceivable. In the event, practical politics demanded a gradual approach that might over generations, and with experience, unfold into greater things.

This divergence of approach is reflected in the dilemma which faces Conservatives today, as it has from the outset. Ringing phrases about ultimate objectives proclaim a goal of economic and monetary union. Every national leader within the Community has signed up to them. But the detailed contents of the communiques are of an altogether more seemly modesty. The gradualists have in practice been winning. Yet a capacity for at least the occasional leap in the dark has been shown, for example in the creation of the European Monetary System in March 1979 – with the British Prime Minister, James Callaghan, taking Britain's reserved seat on the touchline.

What has become of the vision of the 1950s? No one today should doubt the scale of it. Compared with the central state institutions of our principal competitors in America and Japan, the Community's endeavours may seem weak and diffuse. But, given the legacy of centuries of strife, the present coherence of Europe is a miracle. Against all the odds, European democracies have willed the creation of a fledgling political, economic and judicial infrastructure which our grandfathers would never have believed possible.

The Treaty of Rome committed the six founding nations in the long term 'to lay the foundations of an ever closer union among the peoples of Europe' and, more immediately, to achieve a customs union as a stepping stone to the ultimate objective. These commitments were made by far-sighted statesmen because they felt them to be necessary; they were not the result of clear popular demand. They stand as splendid examples of leadership, and proof that pragmatism and vision are not incompatible.

On 1 July 1958 a target date was set for the establishment of a customs union; it was achieved eighteen months ahead of schedule in 1968. All duties between the Six were abolished and a common tariff wall was created around the Community, which in the previous year had adopted a common value added tax throughout the new market.

Essentially the guiding strength of this new Europe lay with the national governments. National departmental ministers were to meet regularly on behalf of their governments in a Council of Ministers to deal with matters relevant to their specialities. The Ministers of Agriculture, Transport and Finance did so from the start but all such groups together formed the Council of Ministers, which was, constitutionally, indivisible. In the main they could resolve their business but failure to do so could lead, as in the normal way of governments, to reference to heads of government for ultimate resolution.

This led to irregular summits – three times in ten years – for heads of government, which, in 1974, became formalized in thrice-yearly meetings of the European Council. (The 1986 Single European Act gave legal recognition to the European Council and it was agreed then that it should meet twice a year.) It was always envisaged that the Commission would be at one remove from the Council of Ministers, possessing powers to initiate legislation, to administer the workings of the Community and to defend its commitments once enacted. Once decisions were taken by the Council, the Commission would have executive responsibility for implementation. To ease the workload of the Council, national civil servants were seconded to make up specialist teams, under a committee of permanent representatives – the ambassadors to the EEC – enjoying the collective title of COREPER. Management and advisory committees were also established to assist the Commission and were manned by civil servants appointed by member states.

Administration by delegation was the order of the day but the system had both strengths and weaknesses. The coming together of experts on the operation of national policies in particular specialist fields ensured that the emerging European proposals were more likely to take account of different national practices. So far so good, but an over-assertive civil servant was often well placed to block progress.

All too frequently nothing happened. Delay was endemic and, without the exercise of political will to produce effective management of this central bureaucracy, progress was limited. It was an early example of the evolving European dilemma: to what extent, having willed the means, are national politicians also willing to make the agencies they create work properly, or to ensure that the European Parliament acquires the authority to do what ministers will not do?

The Commission today consists of seventeen members. Two are nominated by each of the larger members of the Community – the United Kingdom, France, Germany, Italy and Spain – and one each by the seven smaller members. Each Commissioner has his own portfolio, often allocated after much horse-trading at the start of every four-year term of office, but each in addition accepts collective responsibility for the policies of the Commission at large. Decision-making is collegiate, and by simple majority vote.

Where the treaties require the Council of Ministers to legislate, the Commission submits draft proposals to the Council, and (as the treaties and practice require) consults the Parliament as well as the Economic and Social Committee. The Economic and Social Committee is a body appointed by the national governments from representatives of industry, the trades unions and the professions. Under the terms of the treaty, it must be consulted on certain matters before decisions can be taken, but its opinions have never been of much influence and what influence it had has been gradually eroded. The Commission then carries out the decisions of the Council. The Commission has legislative powers of its own under some treaty provisions and delegated powers entrusted to it by the Council of Ministers in other fields. This is similar to the practice of secondary legislation in the form of Statutory Instruments in the British Parliament. It also acts as a law-enforcement agency, being able to bring member states before the European Court of Justice for breaches of treaty obligations.

If we stand back and examine the substance of the Brussels Commission, two important strands emerge. First, it enjoys power that is real. Its power has increased because, over forty years, the member states have willed it; and on any rational forecast it will further enhance its position. The tensions caused by its steadily developing power were clearly shown by the outcry which its President, Jacques Delors, provoked in Britain when he warned the European Parliament in July 1988 that, within ten years, 80 per cent of economic legislation 'and perhaps even of fiscal and social legislation as well' would be 'of Community origin'. The fact that Lord Young, British Secretary of State for Trade and Industry, gave his view that the figure would be perhaps fifty per cent, a few days after M. Delors made his remarks, only served to show that the debate was no longer about what was happening but about the speed of change.

National parliaments often adopt Community proposals as their own without any general awareness that they originated in Brussels. (The classic example is perhaps the Employment Bill, presented to the House of Commons on 30 November 1988, which was reported in the press as a further stage in the government's radical approach to the supply side of the economy but was in fact largely the implementation of the principle of equal treatment for men and women as regards employment, working conditions, vocational training and promotion, expounded in the EC Directive of 9 February 1976.) It is also the case that much of the work in Brussels actually originates in national capitals: the Commission drafts the detailed working papers but usually only after consultation with national governments.

The other notable characteristic of present political arrangements is that they are about as ineffective and as unaccountable as they could be. This is for one overriding reason: too few of the politicians of Europe will acknowledge the scale and significance of the forces for change which they have set in motion, and the institutions themselves are totally incapable of adjusting to that change. We have federalism by stealth, whether because national electorates cannot be told the truth or are not trusted to understand it, or because their elected leaders have failed to comprehend what they have assented to.

The general fear, particularly in the United Kingdom, appears to be that public opinion would react against what is happening and try to stop it if it did understand. So we let matters drift. Little by little, the Council of Ministers transfers power to a largely unaccountable Commission. Slowly, a European Parliament, regarded with profound suspicion by its national rivals, is flexing its muscles.

There is no escaping the fact that a fledgling federalism is emerging, however the dictionary definition of this emotive word may be stretched to pretend otherwise. Many may not like it but it cannot be wished away. It would be better to understand and come to terms with the changes which have already come about, and which continue apace, if we are to safeguard those interests most important to us in Britain, such as influencing Community expenditure by demanding value for money.

Responsibilities are not always clearly divided between Brussels and the twelve national capitals but the Commission now negotiates for the countries of the Community in external trade matters; takes the lead on internal trade and competition policy; administers and plans most agricultural and all fisheries policy; and is assuming a growing role in environmental and conservation policy. National governments retain responsibility for foreign and defence policy, economic policy (although there is provision in the Rome Treaty for encouraging 'convergence' of economic policy), education, health, social security, housing, law and order, and the administration of justice.

Responsibility for regional policies, overseas aid and transport is shared with national governments. Apart from this, a range of policies is administered by what one might call 'Eurangos', European autonomous non-governmental organizations, a mutation of that dangerously prolific British growth, the quango, sixty-six of which I killed off in 1979 when

I was at the Department of the Environment.

The European Parliament consists of 518 members, elected since 1979 by universal suffrage. The role of the Parliament is limited; it can offer opinions, which the Council can disregard – though the Council cannot act without seeking its opinion. There are two exceptions to this generalization, provided that a two-thirds majority can be secured. First, the Parliament is empowered to dismiss the Commission. (Although there has been much talk of such a dramatic gesture, it has never in practice happened.) Second, in the last resort, it can reject the Community budget. On several occasions it has done just that and arrangements have had to be made for the Community to limp on from month to month on a system of emergency financing.

Within clearly defined limits the European Parliament can also alter and increase the budget, so that over the years the budget has become their most effective way of influencing policy. The Parliament's members have used it as a weapon against the Council and year after year they have succeeded in pushing spending beyond the limits proposed by that body. But they have never really exploited their potential as a public accounts watchdog because they have always been more concerned with volume of provision than the effective use of resources. And that, as we have learnt to our cost, is the socialist formula for disaster.

The European Court of Justice in Luxembourg (which is distinct not only from the International Court of Justice in The Hague but also from the European Court of Human Rights in Strasbourg, with which British newspaper commentators too often confuse it) exists to rule on Community legislation and to give final judgment on the interpretation of the treaties that govern the working of the Community. It is open to any government, the Commission or the Parliament to invoke its powers if the rules of the Community are in dispute.

The Court consists of thirteen judges, assisted by six advocates-general whose task is to make detailed submissions on cases brought before it, in order to help the judges make their decision. The judges are chosen – one from each country plus one other – from 'persons whose independence is beyond doubt and who possess the qualifications required for appointment to the highest judicial offices in their respective countries'.

Community legislation, when passed by the Council of Ministers, becomes part of the national law of the member countries. It is then the duty of national governments to ensure that these laws are upheld. Our

European Communities Act 1972 allowed directly applicable Community law (such as regulations and certain directives) to become part of the law of the United Kingdom without needing the prior approval of Parliament. The UK as a member state is bound to implement such proposals, once approved by the Council of Ministers, although the form and method of implementation are within its discretion. On occasion the courts have been asked to decide whether the legislation in question did properly implement the directive concerned.

The founding fathers recognized the complexity of the task upon which they had embarked. It was one thing for governments to commit themselves to the generality of the European intention; it would prove quite different to compel compliance in detail, as vested interests would resist the pressure to conform with Community directives and laws which threatened them. Governments themselves might avert their gaze, the Commission might blunder in the drafting of legislation, so sanctions would be essential to enforce whatever policing arrangements were devised. If national law officers failed to bring transgressors to book, there would be need for a judicial long-stop. Over the years the Court has proved a formidable force for political and social change – for example, in the case of equal pay for women. It is the most 'federal' of the Community's institutions and could be described as the most effective locomotive of European integration.

I wonder if those who in the 1940s first started to build the new Europe from the rubble of the old order could identify in today's structures the vision that led them on. Is the Community a bureaucrats' paradise, impatient for unrestrained power, voracious in its consumption of taxpayers' money, ambitious to push its frontiers outward in an ever widening circle of detail and directives? Is the Community wise enough to know the measure of its success and of its shortcomings, and confident and energetic enough to reach for the next dimension? Are the ambitions proclaimed in the Treaty of Rome still realistic?

There can be no simple or final answers to these questions yet; but the balance of evidence must favour the visionaries. No leading politician in Europe now wishes to undo, in any fundamental sense, what has been done; nor is there any mainstream political party offering the alternative of a purely national destiny. The concept of a Europe moving ever closer together has achieved overwhelming general support, even though its evolving form remains the subject of deep and sometimes contentious debate. The stronger we feel that that form must be inspired by capitalism, the more determined and energetic we must be in influencing its evolution.

The visionaries will take further heart from the attitudes of those countries which are close to, but are outside, the Community. There is a reappraisal in Finland, Norway, Sweden, Switzerland and Austria, whose people feel overshadowed by the Europe of tomorrow. A clutch of Mediterranean countries feels the same unease. Profound economic and political questions are posed for these countries on the periphery. It is worth remembering that the Community still trades more with the former EFTA countries than with the United States and Japan put together. As I shall discuss elsewhere, similar questions will also arise in Central Europe if parts of Mr Gorbachev's changing empire seek links with the West.

Despite the rhetoric with which politicians seek to allay domestic anxieties about the growing influence of Europe, the governments of the Twelve are now moving more decisively towards fulfilment of the European Community's purpose than at any time since its foundation. Behind the headlines, beneath the flamboyant national gestures, there is a relentless momentum. No one should be surprised. The organizations that I have described are made not of steel and brick but of human beings ambitious for their own convictions, driven by their own sense of purpose to achieve results within the duration of their careers.

The first specific objective of the Treaty of Rome was to create the Common Market; but by the 1980s it was apparent that the voting structure within the Council of Ministers doomed it to make progress towards that first objective only at the pace of the slowest or more obdurate members in those areas where the treaty required unanimity. Although the original treaty provided for majority voting in respect of a number of articles, the Luxembourg Compromise of 1965 – demanded by de Gaulle so that France could not be outvoted on major issues – was on occasion used to counter that provision.

The resolve of all governments to strive towards creating 'a real common market' resulted in the decision to amend the founding treaties by the Single European Act of 1986. This episode again illustrated the essential difference between our approach to political change and that of our partners. Britain was dragged reluctantly to the conference table, protesting that what was needed was not a constitutional innovation but the political will to make existing arrangements work. The continentals felt the need for a legal and political framework for the new phase of EC development and at the European Council in Luxembourg in December 1985 this majority view prevailed. Our partners proved right: the Single European Act has set in train a period of rapid decision-making. Britain, still displaying the same reticence towards monetary union, should be able to see, having lost such an argument once, that a similar conflict should not be provoked unless there are good grounds for believing that the change would be fundamentally inimical to our national interest.

In signing the Single European Act, the British government has put its name once again to the central purpose which everyone on the continent understands. In the preamble the signatories declared they were moved by the will 'to transform relations as a whole among their states into a European Union, in accordance with the Solemn Declaration of Stuttgart of 19 June 1983'. The preamble also recalls that the 1972 Paris summit 'approved the objective of the progressive realization of economic and monetary union'.

The Act was given a second reading by the House of Commons on 23 April 1986 by a majority of 159. Only a handful of Conservative anti-Marketeers joined the Labour Party in voting against. Britain was the first of the major European countries to ratify it on 19 November the same year. In so doing, we endorsed for the second time the principle of qualified majority voting, explicitly defined in the Treaty of Rome, and accepted a weakening of the safeguard of the Luxembourg Compromise by limiting the areas where unanimity would be required. This was as comprehensive a redefinition of national sovereignty as we have ever known. But the case for adopting the Act was overwhelming – to achieve the advantages and opportunities of a single market, which would be the largest in the industrial world.

One can argue about the significance of the extension of majority voting for measures necessary to complete the internal market. The House of Commons Foreign Affairs Select Committee concluded in 1986 that in practice, faced with the hostility of the European Parliament, the Commission and a majority of European states, the discretion left to the British government could be minimal. But the British government takes a more realistic view. Some major matters are still reserved for unanimous decision. These relate, in particular, to fiscal provisions, the free movement of persons, and the rights and interests of the employed.

With the adoption of the Single Act, legal constraints are now heavily stacked against a member country wishing to hold out against the majority. But sophisticated politicians in reaching collective judgments will always gauge the sticking point beyond which a member nation cannot be forced to go. They will be mindful, too, of the resourceful way in which different member nations have played the Community card in their own domestic political games, where a plea of *force majeure* can often prove convenient.

The Single Act added two further powers to the Parliament. Its formal agreement by majority vote is now necessary for the admission of a new member to the Community or for an association agreement with an outside organization or country. But the more important change is the role provided in the legislative process known as the co-operation procedure, which the Single Act introduced in respect of a number of important treaty articles. Hitherto the Commission put its proposals for legislation to the Council of Ministers, which obtained an advisory opinion from the Parliament and then adopted them with or without amendments. Now the Council adopts a common position. This is put to the European Parliament, which considers it and, by absolute majority of its members, may reject or amend it. If the Parliament suggests amendments to the common position, the Commission reconsiders and submits fresh proposals to the Council, taking account, as it sees fit, of Parliament's views. The Council of Ministers can only amend proposals from the Commission by unanimity – a fact of considerable advantage to the Commission in its influence over events.

Parliaments should be a check on bureaucracies as well as on executives: so should the European Parliament be on the Commission. In fact they are often natural allies. Both Commission and Parliament are 'federal' institutions which define their power in relation to the Council of Ministers – the authority which represents national interests. Since the passing of the Act the collusion between the Commission and the European Parliament has been more and more evident – Commissioners seeing the European Parliament as a force to be called upon to augment their strength *vis-à-vis* the Council of Ministers. Of course, officials in Brussels will find the European Parliament as tiresome as bureaucrats always do find elected institutions but at the end of the day they need the Parliament as a court of appeal against the Council.

It is easy to disparage the European Parliament but a Westminster MP should exercise some caution before doing so. The scrutiny of legislation by a European Parliament committee – multi-party and unwhipped – can be detailed and effective. Governments will be disinclined to encourage this: they naturally dislike scrutiny. Conversely, the examination of legislation in a Westminster standing committee can be farcical, both before a guillotine (because the opposition blathers and the government side sits quiet) and after it, when large chunks of legislation may not be discussed at all. If the European parliamentarians perfect the art of scrutiny, their example might begin to make ministers uncomfortable at home.

In the way it goes about its business, the European Parliament is closer in form to the United States Congress than to Westminster. Its power lies in committee; its collective function is more symbolic. Westminster is the opposite. Not the least of the advantages of the Single European Act is the way it has directed the European Parliament into legislative action and relieved the pressures caused by its previous tendency to see power merely in terms of increasing Community budgets. The 1988 EC budget of 45 billion ecu* (£29 billion) is small beer by national standards – the United Kingdom budget that year was £170 billion – but it is still taxpayers' money.

A major defect in the machinery of Europe is the inability of national parliaments to influence events. Ministers may be held accountable to the House of Commons but only *after* the votes have been cast in the Council of Ministers. The European Parliament is not yet able to provide an all-weather check on the Council of Ministers but it is far better placed to do so than the national parliaments, from which ministers in theory derive their authority but which are altogether outside the decision-making process.

Under the Treaty of Rome the Council of Ministers has no executive power. The only executive power resides in the Commission. What has happened over the last twenty years is that the Commission has presided over a *de facto* transfer of a significant amount of its executive power from itself to a network of committees. It is within a myriad of bodies staffed by the civil servants that much power now effectively lies; but it is power without adequate scrutiny, although the Parliament is making a limited attempt to rectify this. The United Kingdom Parliament finds it hard enough to exercise effective control over its own government. It would be idle to pretend that it has any influence over the institutions of the European Community. It is equally unrealistic to believe that it could *ever* have effective control, or that other national parliaments,

*Exchange rate: £1 = 1.57 ecu at the time of going to press.

singly or acting together, could create an effective control mechanism.

The electors of Europe therefore have either to resign themselves to the steady accumulation in Brussels of power and influence beyond the reach of democratic control, or see to it that the European Parliament is galvanized into improving upon the lack of will which has dogged its existence so far. It now has new constitutional powers with which to assert itself. However, without a career structure for its members, without the influence which the US Congress bestows on seniority or the power which it accords to committee chairmen, the European Parliament has yet to be seen as a mainstream political force. Partly this is because in Britain there is virtually no lateral movement of politicians between the national and international scene. The unspoken belief that a British politician elected to the European Parliament 'goes native', with all the overtones of treachery implied in such a suggestion, is unlikely to commend him to the selection committees that control the road to Westminster. Patronage lies at home.

Furthermore, until very recently Euro-MPs were not thought to matter. (There are those, including many Westminster MPs, who still hold that view.) The structures of Europe from the start had something of the aspect of an imperial outpost, its Commissioners remote, its British-born representatives eccentrically submitting to exile in Brussels or Strasbourg, while public opinion was encouraged by the national media to see Europe as 'them' and Whitehall and Westminster (though only by contrast) as 'us'.

The British are not the only people in the Community to find difficulty in seeing themselves as European. There are few policies, if any, upon which Europeans look to the Community institutions for guidance. If a debate took place about the sort of Europe we want to see, the direction in which it should evolve, the policies it should pursue, the chief interest in each of the constituent democracies would be in the implications for its own nationals and not for those of Europe as a whole. This is hardly surprising. But it is often convenient to allow unpopular decisions to appear the responsibility of others, and governments exploit the perceptions of difference: enjoying taking credit for their successes whilst encouraging their supporters to divert the blame elsewhere when things go wrong. The European Commission – remote, foreign, bureaucratic, unelected – might have been designed specially for the purpose.

All manner of political games can be played between the Parliament and individual member states. I would not seek to define the future pattern of evolution but it is now apparent that votes in the European Parliament are going to matter. Coalitions of interest are emerging and will be reinforced. Trade-offs will become the means for delivering votes. The need to build alliances, and to create good will, will not only involve national governments and their Euro-MPs. The Commission too will have to work harder at maximizing support if it wants to carry its legislation. Time is always short. There are all the familiar pressures which affect legislatures worldwide. It will often be easier to compromise, to make a concession, than to fight for more ambitious targets. The Parliament has already begun to learn some new tricks with the powers granted to it by the Single Act.

At the first reading procedure in the period between July 1987 and October 1988, the Commission accepted 558 out of 768 of the European Parliament's amendments (72 per cent). The Council accepted 206 out of 487 amendments (42 per cent). At the second reading procedure in the same time scale, the Commission accepted a further 48 out of 91 amendments (52 per cent), whilst the Council accepted 15 out of 70 amendments (21 per cent). These figures may not tell the whole story but they are evidence of real influence.

The frustrations of national parliaments will, however, grow as they feel power slipping away. How can they be turned from anxious or resentful sceptics into active and influential partners of the European Parliament, helping to direct events rather than being swept along by them? This question is of such fundamental importance, and the potential for conflict is so great, that this flaw in the Community's democratic machinery warrants the closest examination.

No one would wish to deny our nationhood but it is the case that, from the moment Britain threw in her lot with that of her European partners, no logical alternative has existed to the transfer of some power to the European institutions. Many of those who were opposed to the original decision remain unconvinced today and to them what has come to be known as the democratic deficit is a weapon with which they continue to fight old battles. Others watch as events unfold which seem inevitable but which naturally arouse anxiety and sometimes conflicting loyalties. The existing order is changing, and change is unsettling. We must look more closely at what in practice is happening, or can happen, if we are to determine to what extent Parliament has been left out and how we might improve matters.

The European Commission initiates proposals. It knows that, at the end of the day, it has to secure approval and support from the Council of Ministers. In this sense it is in a very similar position to a Whitehall department. The rest of Whitehall may not know of the first gleam in a minister's eye but discover it as soon as the consultative processes begin. To try to bounce departments into unexplored and hasty decisions generates much resentment and is not easily forgiven. So, political animal that it is, the Commission begins early to consult the bureaucracies of the national governments and the interest groups involved. Ministers are tested for reaction, national responses emerge and these are fed back into the Brussels machine. At this stage national governments have a clear idea as to what the issues are and the Commission has a good idea where each government stands. The House of Commons may remain ignorant of events or hardly touched by them unless it suits a pressure group, a vested interest or a minister to alert MPs to what is happening. The Commission will meanwhile have calculated how to proceed and will formulate its proposals, adding to them its judgment of how far it can accommodate the various national views.

After a draft legislative proposal has been adopted by the Commission, it submits it finally to the Council of Ministers and publishes it. At this stage it becomes available to each national parliament. It is easy to see how the preparations can cause resentment, although the procedures are very similar to those whereby British governments draft White Papers or legislation without formally involving Parliament. Nearly always someone will claim that Europe is riding roughshod over national interests. Certainly any group which feels that its representations during the consultative process have been ignored will invariably deny that there was any effective consultation at all. To listen to the reaction of the Opposition, of local authorities or of trade associations to proposals presented by the British government is to appreciate the pitfalls.

But that is not by any means the end of the matter. Every draft proposal for European legislation sent by the Commission to the Council is submitted to member countries' parliaments. The Select Committee on European Legislation is the forum in which proposals are first considered in the House of Commons. (Many other national parliaments also have arrangements for looking at drafts.) The Select Committee is an all-party committee which scrutinizes the draft proposal and reports to the House its opinion as to whether the proposal raises issues of legal or political importance.

The House of Commons could perhaps benefit from the more general approach adopted by the House of Lords. Their Lordships become involved in a formal sense at the same stage as the Commons but the terms of reference of the two committees are different.

The Commons Committee is asked to consider draft proposals and other documents and to say if it considers that these raise questions of legal or political importance; to give its reasons; to report what matters of principle or policy may be involved and what possible effect there may be on the law of the United Kingdom; and to make recommendations for further consideration by the House. By contrast, the Lords take a more general approach. Their Committee is appointed to consider Community proposals, whether in draft or otherwise; to obtain all necessary information about them; and to make reports on proposals which it believes raise important questions of policy or principle, as well as on other questions to which it thinks the special attention of the House ought to be drawn. The Lords are thus in a position to deploy their time more effectively, by exploring what they regard as the more important issues, than the Commons Committee which is bound by the duty imposed on it to patrol every inch of its territory.

Their Lordships have other advantages. They start with a range of experience denied to the Commons. Among their ranks are former permanent secretaries and Treasury mandarins more than willing to turn their skills to outwitting their former colleagues. Captains of industry are there to bring to bear the heavy barrage of their business experience. In addition, their Committee not only draws on some ninety members of their House as opposed to fourteen in the Commons but has the power to co-opt experts from elsewhere within their House, or from outside, to raise their fire-power. The quality of their reports reflects the talent available to them. It would be quite within the power of the Commons to enable its Select Committee to adopt a similar approach. They would then be able to make more use of sub-committees to examine specialist subjects. (The party balance need not be upset if co-opted Committee members were not permitted to vote.)

The Commons Committee has the difficulty of working to a tight deadline, seeking to complete its scrutiny in time for debate to precede adoption of the legislation. (The Lords take a more contemplative approach.) The Commons Select Committee summarizes the proposals (or documents) and recommends whether they should be debated and, if so, suggests whether on the floor of the House or in one of the specialist Standing Committees on European Documents. Following a resolution of the House on 30 October 1980, the government has undertaken, except in unusual circumstances, to hold such debates before it has to reach a conclusion in the Council of Ministers.

For the record, in the 1987–8 session of Parliament, 117 recommendations were made by the Select Committee for debate on the floor of the House and in Standing Committee. In the same session of Parliament twenty-nine debates took place on the floor and fifteen in Standing Committee. (It is not possible to reconcile the numbers of recommendations with those of debates in the same session, since a recommendation in one session will often lead to a debate in the following one.) In order to ensure that any MP can participate in the work of these Standing Committees on European Documents, even if not appointed to it, any member is free to attend and participate. During the 1987–8 session, six members took advantage of this opportunity. As has been stated, there were fifteen debates in Standing Committee, and there are more than 500 members of the House who are not in the government. It might be concluded either that members are content with the arrangements, or that they are simply ignorant of the whole procedure, or – worst of all – that they feel that their participation would change nothing and therefore do not bother.

The reality is that power rests with governments – through the whipping system – and the bureaucracy that serves them. There is not the slightest sign that any government will surrender this power or that Parliament has the will or the resources to redress the balance.

We in Britain have had hundreds of years to develop our institutions, and our instinct is to let them evolve naturally and to be suspicious of constitutional blueprints. But we must always be watchful of those who are quietly accumulating real power while leaving elected representatives with no more than the trappings. The British have a strong instinct against 'Eurocracy' and that instinct is sound. The more remote the exercise of power, the more we need to make sure that it is controlled by those who are answerable to the electors.

The collective ability of the twelve nations of Europe to wield power is formidable and it should not surprise us that those who have a hold on that collective power do not want to let go. Rather than allowing our attention to be diverted by arguments about words such as 'federalism', 'European Union' or 'national sovereignty', we should take a look at how power is exercised in practice and then try to find the best way to make that power democratically accountable.

No one in Britain believes that the present system works well. The average citizen knows that Europe is too remote. The British members of the European Parliament are answerable to the electors every five years but have only limited influence. The government is represented on the Council of Ministers and at the European Council and is answerable to Parliament at Westminster but ministers do not always have the time or the continuity of attention needed to follow a line through to success. The powers of the Council are limited: it can dispose but it cannot propose – only the unelected Commission can do that. So the Council lacks one of the essential characteristics of government, the power to put forward legislation.

Members of the Council of Ministers are too busy to spend more than 5 to 10 per cent of their time on the Council's affairs. In Britain they must represent their constituents in Parliament, oversee their departments and defend the discharge of their ministerial responsibilities. Any business they do in the Council of Ministers must be secondary to most of what crosses their desks in London. They fly in, read out their speech, listen wearily to eleven other speeches, then frequently find that it is too late to come to a conclusion, and take the next plane home.

It is not in any sense a Council as we would understand it: a group of people who had grown to know each other and to develop enough trust for the give and take of genuine bargaining. The minister with whom you tried to bargain yesterday may be represented by his deputy today and by an ambassador tomorrow. Before the next meeting there may have been a domestic reshuffle or an election and a new minister will appear who knows little, and likes less, of the previous arrangements. Only the Belgian ministers live in Brussels, so there is none of the backstage informal contact in twos and threes which can so often overcome difficulties; there is little enough contact even with the national officials based in Brussels upon whom the flying visitor is so utterly dependent.

Nor in fact is there one Council. There are half a dozen major bodies. *The* Council is the Council of Foreign Ministers, which in theory should exercise a supervisory role over the others but in practice cannot do so. For instance, ECOFIN (which looks after economics and finance) and the Agriculture Council seldom agree with one another but the Council of Foreign Ministers has no power to knock their heads together. The repeated crises over the farm budget therefore remain unsettled until they are referred to higher authority, the half-yearly meetings of the heads of government.

The absurdity of the present system is seen in the attempts of twelve heads of governments in the space of a two-day summit to negotiate – ostensibly in private but with frequent excursions to the nearest television studio to prevent their natives becoming restless – unresolved details such as dairy quotas. Summits, according to those who attend them, are something between a farce and a tragedy. I have even heard it suggested, on the best authority, that not all European leaders master their briefs.

No one setting up a company would put effective power into the hands of a group of constantly changing part-timers, whose main interest and enthusiasm lay elsewhere, to be chaired and directed by a different person every six months. This system puts the real power into the hands of permanent officials. All of us who have held ministerial office know how hard it is, even for a hard-working full-time minister, to keep control of the permanent bureaucracy. 'Yes Minister' is not wholly an illusion. So what possibility can there be of a minister – who is rarely there – sensibly pitting his judgment against that of a diplomatic 'Sir Humphrey' smoothly running on the inside track, with a self-confidence won through years of steering nervous politicians through international negotiations?

The Council of Ministers meets behind closed doors. The European Parliament can ask questions but those who answer do not want to put at risk agreements negotiated with difficulty, so they say as little as possible. When ministers go back to be questioned by their national parliaments, there is the same enormous pressure not to rock the boat. Members of Parliament know that they can only accept or reject and they have to take the minister's word that the agreement struck was the best available.

This is a brittle arrangement. It requires, before any controversial but necessary political changes can be made, that all possible options must be examined. There needs to be public discussion, open argument and some give and take. It does no good for relations between the Community and the member states, or between governments and parliaments, if controversial legislation has to be pushed through late at night when no one is looking. And it makes ministers hesitate before proposing the kind of changes which, however difficult, may be strongly in the national interest.

Naturally the members of the European Parliament do what they can to explain European issues in their home country. The Danish *Folketing* has a market committee and the Danish MEPs brief their party members. That regular briefing created an informed opinion which helped the Danish government to win the referendum on the Single European Act in spite of the anti-market majority in the *Folketing*. The German *Bundestag* and the Belgian parliament have special committees which include their MEPs. In Britain we have nothing at all like this, which only serves to widen the gap between the parliaments. Only in 1988 did Members of the European Parliament obtain their own security passes to the Palace of Westminster, a facility available for years to the lowliest research assistant. Now MEPs can dine in the canteen – but not in the dining room.

Most national parliaments are not content to be on the sidelines. Our capacity to keep some control over the executive, and over others whose actions affect our constituents, has to derive from our sovereign rights if it is to be really effective. So I doubt whether the real answer to the power of an ineffective Council is an increase in the countervailing power of the European Parliament. Any proposal to increase power there should stand on its own merits. What we need is the democratic authority of national parliaments brought to bear upon the institutions of the European Community.

I have all the respect for MEPs due from one parliamentarian to another. They do the best they can with very limited power. The whole idea of 1992, the complete liberalization of trade within the Community, was led by the British Conservative MEPs, including conspicuously Basil de Ferranti, MEP for Central Hampshire until his untimely death in 1988, who was one of the first to see the advantages of the internal markets and to organize to secure their completion. The European Parliament won the support of the Council, of the Commission and, in the Single European Act, of all twelve national parliaments. Its own powers have thereby increased and may increase further.

But MEPs are thin on the ground. There is in Britain only one MEP to every eight MPs. They have to spend a great deal of their time out of the country and away from the lobby journalists who write the main political stories and make politics come to life for the average voter. More power would certainly bring them into more prominence but so long as the MPs who dominate the political discussion remain at arm's length from the workings of the Community, there is a real danger of friction between the European and the national parliaments, which would leave more power than ever in the hands of unelected officials.

Britain is not the only country in which MEPs are thinly spread. We at least have single-member constituencies no bigger than an American Congressional district. In most other Community countries the MEPs are elected on regional lists and 'represent' one and a half million voters apiece or even, in some countries, five million. In other countries there are national lists. Continental MEPs really are remote from those who elect them and have a worse problem than their British colleagues. They too need a solution. Ten years' experience of direct elections shows that the present arrangements are, if anything, divisive rather than cohesive. If national and European interests are to be reconciled to the benefit of all of us, then we badly need something more. One suggestion which has been canvassed to remedy the democratic deficit is the election of the European Commission but I see no prospect of either national governments or national parliaments being willing to contemplate so dramatic a shift of power.

There is, however, another way in which democratic control might be better exercised and it has an excellent precedent. Just over 200 years ago the thirteen founding states of the American Republic decided that they could no longer carry on with the original Continental Congress, which was rather like the present Council of Ministers, a continuous process of difficult intergovernmental negotiation. Although the present United States is very different from the European Community, the relations between the original thirteen states were not so different. There were the big four, Massachusetts, New York, Pennsylvania and Virginia. Rhode Island was tiny, like Luxembourg today. And the views of the states differed radically on many questions. But, to keep their internal trade open and to avoid domination in external trade and currency by a powerful Europe which was playing them off one against another, they had to create a more effective political system to manage their affairs.

The Convention which opened in Philadelphia on 14 May 1787 came close to breaking up before agreeing on a compromise which distributed power in a manner which large and small states deemed fair: in the new Congress, with two chambers, the states would be represented in the lower House according to population but given equal representation – two from each state – in the upper House or Senate. From 1787 until 1913 the Senate of the United States was elected from the assemblies of the individual states. From the day the Senate was founded no one has doubted that each Senator speaks for his state or that the Senate speaks collectively for the United States of America.

Europe is not America. The Community does not have, nor does it need, the same institutions as the United States. It has no responsibility for defence or home affairs. Nor are the old states of Europe the same as the new states of America were then, but here is a precedent that we should explore. Features of the United States constitution have been adopted or adapted in the making of many later constitutions, especially of federal states. And a particular feature is often the second chamber designed with the main purpose of ensuring that the concerns of constituent areas or provinces are clearly expressed at the centre. The United States Senate should be examined as a model for an upper tier of the European Parliament. The West German upper chamber, the *Bundesrat* (Federal Council), consisting of members of the *Länder* governments, is a model nearer home. Such a system, adapted to our own use, would be incomparably better than the present arrangements, for which there is absolutely no successful precedent – nothing to show that it can ever be made to work or, even less, subjected to anything resembling democratic control.

The direct involvement of national parliaments in the democratizing of the Community can be effected by creating an upper House of the European Parliament *from within the membership of our national parliaments.* I would however depart from the American precedent by having an unequal distribution of upper chamber seats, based on already established proportions. At present, larger countries such as Britain have 10 votes on the Council of Ministers, where there are 76 votes in all. This system of weighted voting, together with the right of even the smallest member state to nominate a Commissioner, ensures a satisfactory balance of power between the weaker and stronger members. On established proportions Britain could have 20 'senators' in a 'senate' of 152 members – larger than the 100-strong United States Senate but roughly in proportion to the larger size of the Community's population. The position of the new bi-cameral Parliament in relation to the Council, the Commission and the Court would remain unchanged.

Such an innovation would mean a shift of power from national governments to national parliaments but, since power has been shifting steadily in the other direction for a long time, this would be no bad thing. Governments should be reminded from time to time that it is not they who are sovereign but parliament. If the British House of Commons can find twenty or so members to make up a Cabinet, it could just as easily find from its ranks twenty 'senators' to watch over its sovereign interests in the European Community.

There is no special virtue in a minister going off to Brussels on the morning flight. Parliament has no say in his appointment, no chance to weigh his qualifications before he sets off and, when they try to question him, he can hide behind collective government responsibility and say very little. If, however, the senate and its committees consisted of nominated members of national parliaments, the picture would be very different.

There are several ways in which nomination could come about, ranging from election (under any one of several systems) to government selection: and national parliaments would rightly insist on choosing independently. In Britain, a system of nomination by Parliament, similar to the appointment system for the existing specialist select committees, would probably command support. The wishes of the government would be met. The whips would influence events, as they do in every nook and cranny of parliamentary life – but only in the initial setting up. Thereafter members would serve for a parliament at least, and would be representative of and answerable to Parliament rather than to government. But governments would be wise to use their patronage judiciously, for those despatched will need skill and experience to win for Britain in the European corridors of power.

The new senate would enjoy the same power as the existing European Parliament; its agreement would also be required for European legislation. This would again enhance the influence of national parliaments.

Information is power and governments have power because ministers have the back-up of their departments. But it would be a foolish government which withheld information from a senator when he needed it. Our twenty senators would need access to as much national information as possible; but, being permanent, they would also have access to the stream of information upon which European decisions are based. They would be an integral part of the informed political life of the Community and of the domestic parliaments as well.

Above all, such a change would bring European affairs into the mainstream of national political life. The debates in the senate would be open. European political decision-making would not only become the concern of Westminster but would also in consequence begin to attract the fuller attention of the media and would be much more widely understood. Public opinion would be given a better chance to form its own views on what was going on and would be better able to judge the wisdom of political decisions.

There is another step, which has a sound precedent, this time in British practice, to which we should revert and which would enhance parliamentary accountability while going some way to remedy the weakness of departmental ministers who are available only part-time for their European responsibilities. The Foreign Secretary has overall responsibility for Britain's relations with the Community but no member of the Cabinet is under greater pressure as he travels the world attending to British interests. A second Cabinet minister should therefore be appointed to support him in the Foreign Office but with responsibility for the Community. Such an appointment would serve several purposes: the minister would represent parliamentary opinion in the round to other governments, could keep watch for any unnecessary delay in the ceaseless negotiations and would take an active interest in the development of European policy and in the detailed expenditure of our money.

From little acorns, great oaks grow. By treaty we are committed to the European Community and, in 1986, we gave a powerful new momentum to the business of making it work. That was our free choice, as it was for all of our European partners. Each of them will exploit the multiplying opportunities to the full. The rules to which we have all subscribed are scrupulously fair. The treaties allow each signatory the same opportunities; what they cannot do is prescribe the extent to which the member states, separately or jointly, will exploit those opportunities. That is for us.

CHAPTER
3

The Budget: Whose Money?

'Get hold of the figures!' I was told as a brand new articled clerk with the famous chartered accountants, Peat, Marwick and Mitchell; 'that's the starting point.' They had sent me to audit the accounts of the Fatstock Marketing Corporation and their sound advice rang in my ears as I searched the streets of Islington with growing bafflement for the Corporation's slaughterhouses. Finding the figures would be simple enough, I was convinced, if only I could find the building. That was in 1955 but both the memories and the message remain with me.

Let us join a rather more experienced accountant arriving today at 200 Rue de la Loi, Brussels (the address of the European Commission) to inspect the European accounts. Working from the figures in the Community's budget for 1987 we see that it stood at 36 billion ecu (£25.2 billion at the 1987 exchange rate) – over 95 per cent of which was redistributed among the member states. This amounts to only just over 3.14 per cent of the total of all member states' budgets and though double the size of the 1973 figure, it is still less than 1 per cent of the European gross domestic product. (To put it in some perspective, it is equivalent to the total 1989 UK public expenditure on health alone, and our contribution in 1987 was 1.1 per cent of British government expenditure.) The increase, over the years, reflects both a higher percentage of national tax bases and an increase in the size of those bases. But the EC is far from the profligate monster of popular myth.

The Community in 1988 had just under 21,000 officials, half the number employed by the city of Paris and no more than the Belgian Ministry of Finance. Despite the rigorous control of manpower exercised by successive Chancellors of the Exchequer, the UK Department of Customs and Excise alone employs 27,000 people.

Where did Europe's money come from in 1987? Mostly from a 1.4 per cent value added tax levied across the Community (65 per cent of the budget in 1987) and customs duties on imports into the Community, accounting for 25 per cent of the budget. Levies on agricultural products imported from non-member countries account for a further 4.5 per cent. The Community also imposes levies on imported sugar and certain types of glucose (4 per cent). The rest of the 1987 budget was made up by sundry payments and non-repayable advances from member states.

And where does it go? Sixty-seven per cent of the Community budget in 1987 was allotted to the European Agricultural Guidance and Guarantee Fund. This section of the budget accounts for nearly all of the Common Agricultural Policy (CAP) funds. The purpose of the Guidance part of this fund is to speed up improvements in agricultural methods and encourage rural development. The Guarantee part of the fund gives price support for agricultural products. The disproportionate share of the budget devoted to agriculture is explained by the fact that it is in this area that Community financing has taken over most clearly from national financing. The proportion has fallen over the years as the overall budget has increased and new policies claimed a growing share. The 1979 figure was as high as 76 per cent but this is forecast to fall to about 59 per cent by 1992.

Two other funds reflect the pressure within the Community to recognize the different stages of development of the national economies. Their purpose is to enable the weaker members to develop faster in return for allowing the richer countries access to their markets. The Regional Development Fund (7.6 per cent of the budget in 1987) has two main objectives: to build up backward regional economies and to redevelop declining industrial regions. The Social Fund (7.6 per cent of the budget) deals with the human dimension of the regional economic differences, through policies designed to counter increasing unemployment, particularly among the young and the long-term unemployed, and in the use of vocational training and education.

Development co-operation accounted for 3 per cent of expenditure and is intended primarily for food and development aid for the countries of the Mediterranean, Asia and Latin America. In addition, the Lomé Convention provides for financial and technical assistance to sixty-six African, Caribbean and Pacific countries, totalling 8.5 billion ecu between 1985 and 1990. This assistance is financed outside the budget by the European Development Fund, to which the countries contribute, and by means of loans from the European Investment Bank. Research, energy and technology absorbed a further 2.6 per cent of total expenditure. Finally, the administrative costs of the Community itself amounted to approximately 5 per cent of the budget.

Those were the latest actual figures for revenue and expenditure available at the time of going to press. Let us now look at the projected figures for the latest budget in greater detail. The 1988/89 Budget proposals are laid out in Table 3.1 and the basis on which revenue is collected from each country in Table 3.2.

It is readily apparent that there must be winners and losers in the process of collecting and disbursing funds on this scale between twelve very different economies. If the driving force that brought the twelve members of the Community together is enlightened self-interest, a glance at Table 3.3 – showing the net position of the twelve members – makes it apparent that for some of the Community enlightenment begins, like charity, at home.

In total, contributions exceed receipts as some items cannot be apportioned to individual countries: the overheads and administration, overseas aid and trans-European research. Such expenditure benefits the whole Community, as is shown in Table 3.4. This Table also shows that the budget is heavily skewed towards agricultural spending.

From the outset the United Kingdom had expected to run a heavy deficit in its account with the Community. Britain was bound to find herself paying levies based on high imports from third countries but her ability to benefit from the European support system was limited by her relatively small UK agricultural base. The problem had become acute by 1979 because the terms originally negotiated in the accession treaty did not provide for any long-term reconsideration of this position, only for gradual incorporation into the 1970 'own resource' system over a five-year transitional period, 1973 to 1977. These terms were nominally but ineffectually 'renegotiated' in 1975 by the Labour government. The incoming Conservatives had had enough: an effective and enduring adjustment to the budgetary arrangements had to be found.

Table 3.1 Preliminary Budget Proposals 1989 (in ecu)*

Administration	
Expenditure concerning personnel	1,006,379,000
Buildings, equipment & miscellaneous	286,097,500
Expenditure resulting from special functions	133,136,548
TOTAL	1,425,613,048
Operations	
Agricultural market guarantees	28,190,000,000
Guidance (agricultural structure)	1,599,000,000
Fisheries	361,100,000
Regional development & transport	4,946,550,000
Operations in the social sector	3,688,255,000
Energy, technology, research, nuclear safeguards, information market & innovation	1,773,677,600
Repayments & aid to member states	2,993,050,496
Co-operation with developing countries	1,303,207,000
Other expenditure	1,005,000,000
Operations: TOTAL	45,859,840,096
Commission: TOTAL	47,285,453,144
Other institutions	736,165,134
GRAND TOTAL:	48,021,618,278

(Source: The Community Budget: Facts and Figures, 1988, Office for Official Publications of the EC, L-2985)

For several years after the Conservatives were elected in 1979, the budget question overshadowed all the government's dealings with its European partners. The unfairness of Britain's position had become overwhelming. In 1980, her net contribution was £1.13 billion in 1988 money terms. Britain had improvidently imposed upon herself this expense by allowing, indeed obliging, the other Europeans initially to form a European club without regard for the interests of late arrivals like us. But something had to be done – and it was.

Between 1980 and 1984, the government negotiated a series of direct rebates amounting to some two-thirds of Britain's net contributions,

* The final adoption of the 1989 budget was 44,837,799,585 ecu.

Table 3.2 Revenue 1988 (in £s)

Member State	Sugar and isoglucose levies	Agricultural levies	Customs duties	Financial contributions		VAT own resources		Total
				Previous financial years	Current financial year	Previous financial years	Current financial year	
Belgium	97,200,000	207,000,000	489,600,000			25,678,000	800,292,645	1,619,770,645
Denmark	41,580,000	12,150,000	181,890,000			6,578,000	545,722,624	787,920,624
Germany	358,380,000	140,940,000	2,515,680,000			77,783,000	6,499,707,200	9,592,490,200
Greece	10,800,000	22,500,000	93,240,000			−72,250,000	280,168,877	334,458,877
Spain	68,760,000	202,050,000	404,460,000			−2,479,000	1,923,686,345	2,596,477,345
France	436,500,000	112,500,000	1,168,470,000			333,435,000	5,649,136,788	7,700,041,788
Ireland	16,650,000	5,400,000	108,810,000			−21,894,000	170,880,941	279,846,941
Italy	159,480,000	349,470,000	829,800,000			107,629,000	3,953,600,000	5,399,979,000
Luxembourg	—	180,000	6,750,000			3,456,000	57,068,134	67,454,134
Netherlands	111,420,000	115,830,000	763,740,000			97,036,000	1,297,109,217	2,385,135,217
Portugal	90,000	66,240,000	91,080,000	1,206,000	207,905,434	—	—	366,521,434
UK	85,050,000	200,700,000	1,941,660,000			−206,178,000	1,821,407,147	3,842,639,147
TOTAL	1,385,910,000	1,434,960,000	8,595,180,000	1,206,000	207,905,434	348,794,000	22,998,779,918	34,972,735,352

(Source: Budget 1988, OJL 226, 1988)

Table 3.3 Member States' Contributions to or Receipts from EC Budget and GDP 1987

	Contributions to EC		*Receipts from* EC *(b)*		*Net contributions*
	£ million (a)	*% of total*	*£ million (a)*	*% of total*	*£ billion*
Belgium	1,186.4	(4.8)	686.6	(3.2)	499.8
Denmark	588.6	(2.4)	797.3	(3.7)	−208.7
Germany	6,539.2	(26.5)	3,164.7	(14.8)	3,374.5
Greece	237.2	(1.0)	1,307.8	(6.1)	−1,070.6
Spain	1,190.6	(4.8)	1,383.0	(6.5)	−192.4
France	5,107.5	(20.7)	4,699.4	(21.9)	408.1
Ireland	235.2	(1.0)	1,002.0	(4.7)	−766.8
Italy	3,617.5	(14.7)	3,662.5	(17.1)	−45.0
Luxembourg	51.2	(0.2)	8.4	(0.0)	42.8
Netherlands	1,648.8	(6.7)	2,013.9	(9.4)	−365.1
Portugal	238.2	(1.0)	509.6	(2.4)	−271.4
UK	3,990.9	(16.2)	2,175.1	(10.2)	1,815.8
TOTAL	24,631.3	(100.0)	21,410.4	(100.0)	3,220.9

(a) Converted at average 1987 exchange rate of £1 = 1.4351 ecu
(b) Payments allocatable by member country only

(Source: Annual Report of Court of Auditors for 1987, OJC 316, 1988)

reducing them to £802 million by 1984. A more permanent solution was reached at the Fontainebleau summit in June that year. The package for the Community budget itself raised the Community VAT rate to 1.4 per cent in 1986 and to 1.6 per cent from 1988. But for the UK, it provided a refund (the word 'abatement' has been used to distinguish this from past refunds) of two-thirds of the difference between UK's VAT payments to the EC budget and its receipts from the budget. According to the 1989 Public Expenditure White Paper, total 'abatements' payments since the Fontainebleau agreement in 1984 amount to £4.5 billion. And that would feed a lot of chickens! After all these changes the cost of Britain's smaller share of a larger budget stood at around £1.3 billion in 1988.

The package of measures approved at Fontainebleau led to annual

Table 3.4 Community Budget Payments 1987 (£ million (a))

	Total expenditure	*Expenditure allocatable by country*	*Shortfall £m*
Administration:			
Commission	765.5	–	765.5
Other institutions	407.6	–	407.6
Agricultural guarantees	15,993.2	15,990.7	2.5
Other agriculture	619.2	601.5	17.7
Fisheries	110.0	53.4	56.6
Regional Fund	1,766.4	1,766.0	0.4
Other regional measures & transport	106.1	–	106.1
Social Fund	1,892.1	1,892.1	–
Other social policy	95.6	–	95.6
Research, energy etc	627.3	–	627.3
Costs incurred in collecting own resources	549.0	549.0	–
Other repayments	1,129.5	558.0	571.5
Co-operation with developing countries	553.1	–	553.1
TOTAL	24,614.6	21,410.7	3,203.9

(a) Converted at average 1987 exchange rate of £1 = 1.4351 ecu

(Source: Annual Report of Court of Auditors for 1987, OJC 316, 1988)

cuts in the real value of price support and this, with the assistance of other measures, has begun to transform the situation. Significantly, a new concept of stabilizers was agreed, the effect of which was to reduce unit support as production exceeded announced targets, thus removing the risk that extra output automatically pushed up the subsidy bills. The skimmed milk mountain shrank from 775,000 million tonnes in 1986 to a barely visible molehill in 1988. The butter mountain slithered from 1.3 million tonnes to 250,000 tonnes. The grain mountain has sharply diminished, helped by the severe American drought of 1988. The beef mountain remains high but the wine lake and the surpluses of Mediterranean products are at last being tackled.

But if a combination of circumstances, including self-imposed

Table 3.5 UK Contributions to and Receipts from the Community Budget

Gross contribution (£m)	*1988*
Agricultural & sugar levies	203
Customs duties	1,429
VAT own resources including VAT adjustments & before abatements	2,844
UK abatement of VAT	−1,598
Inter-governmental agreement contributions	619
TOTAL	3,497
Receipts	
Receipts other than refunds	2,362
Own resources refunds	77
UK negotiated refunds	0
TOTAL	2,439
NET CONTRIBUTIONS	1,058

(Source: Statement on the 1988 Community Budget, CM 525, 1988)

restraint and a more buoyant world demand, has removed some of the pressure and saved significant cost, there is no cause to relax. Community agricultural productivity continues to rise by 2.2 per cent a year, outstripping increases in consumption. There is therefore every prospect that food surpluses may again begin to pile up. The hunt is on for 'imaginative solutions' to prevent or reduce them. In practice, solutions will owe more to political acceptability and the timing of national elections than to imagination, of which there has been no shortage over the years. Much has been suggested; much has been resisted.

Today, it is hard to understand how crucial agriculture was to the European economy forty years ago. By the end of the war much of Western Europe was close to starvation. As the dream of European unity became a reality and politicians added up the large number of peasant proprietors on the electoral rolls, it is hardly surprising that agricultural policy acquired such pre-eminence. Any British politician who remembers that a constituency at that time needed only to sprout a blade of grass to attract the establishment of a branch of the National Farmers Union will understand. Life moves on; today it is the house-builders who fight for those blades of grass.

The most striking feature of continental agriculture is its fragmentation. Primogeniture on the continent has lacked the status accorded to it in Britain; estates were parcelled out among children who were often absent and remote. In post-war Italy fewer than half the farms consisted of one consolidated property; 68,000 of them actually comprised more than twenty parcels of land. The average size of half of Italy's farms was ten acres. In Germany west of the Elbe there was a long tradition of small, family holdings. Peasant smallholdings were more pervasive still in France where in the nineteenth century there were five to six million smallholders, the overwhelming majority of whom owned fewer than 100 acres. By comparison, there were fewer than a million landowners in Victorian England.

Secondly, most of the continent escaped Britain's business-minded revolution of agrarian enclosure until the end of the nineteenth century. With a peasant class resistant to change, and extensive mountainous regions, productive large-scale cereal farming was and is impossible in much of Western Europe. Of course, there were efficient continental farms, economically run: in Prussia, where powerful landlords had large labour forces; in the rich corn and beet producing areas of Northern France; and in the Po Valley. Yet in most of western and southern Germany and in the Midi of France (where, as recently as the early 1950s, nine million out of twenty million lived in little farming communities) small, reasonably prosperous peasant proprietors were the norm. In Italy, land reform in the nineteenth century broke up the estates of absentee landlords in the south and contributed still further to the fragmentation of ownership.

Today much of the criticism of the CAP is justified but it is worth recalling the aims of the early 1950s: to eliminate once and for all the spectre of food shortage in Europe; to ensure that incomes in the agricultural community were maintained at a 'fair' level; to stabilize markets; and to improve productivity. (In Britain, Parliament passed the Agriculture Act of 1947. The preamble defines its purpose in broadly similar terms.) In continental Europe policies were tailored to the needs of the European farming communities and those of the politicians they elected.

One important feature of continental agriculture was and remains that most countries, with their larger acreages per head of population, can produce a higher proportion of food than the UK. Having the capacity to feed themselves – and at times the need – they have done so behind tariff walls with the consequent high level of food prices. It was no surprise to find a higher proportion of their populations on the land – for this and other reasons. As late as 1972, 12.6 per cent of France's working population was engaged in agriculture, 17 per cent in Italy and 24 per cent in Ireland, though only 7.5 per cent in West Germany. In the initial horse-trading between France and West Germany, during the creation of the Community, a deal was struck that gave France a high external tariff to compensate for her relative industrial weakness, and Germany high guaranteed agricultural prices to protect her less competitive farmers. The farming lobby may have shrunk, but in 1958 there were nearly seventeen million in the EC engaged in agriculture. By 1986, in an enlarged Community of twelve member states, this had fallen to ten million or 8 per cent of the working population but in Britain the farming population in 1987 was around 600,000, making up only 2.6 per cent of the working population.

But, as the CAP evolved, West Germany acquired an interest in the policy disproportionate to its share of farms; farmers vote chiefly for the Free Democratic Party which in recent years has played the pivotal role in West German governments. The West Germans have a deep attachment to what are described as 'hobby farms', which is a misnomer because they provide families with second incomes. But these farms are seen as an essential ingredient of a policy to keep up the rural populations. Hobby farmer or rural voter: either way, farm prices matter. Thus an understandable goal – that of European self-sufficiency in food production – was underpinned by a huge political interest.

But subsidy is not a word for which Brussels carries the patent. The OECD has studied the level and trend of agricultural subsidies over recent years. Adopting a common unit – the Producer Subsidy Equivalent (PSE) – it measures how much farmers would have to receive to compensate for the withdrawal of all subsidies and then expresses that amount as a percentage of total farmers' income. Its survey 'Agricultural Policies, Markets and Trade 1988' is revealing (see Table 3.6). From a position in which the Community was well above the average, the situation is less exceptional today. It is simply not true that EC policy is in a subsidized world of its own.

American agricultural subsidies cost approximately the same as European subsidies – around £3 billion a year. The Americans operate a loan-rate scheme by which cut-price loans are extended to farmers and

Table 3.6 Subsidy Percentage of Total Farmers' Income

	1979	*1986*
Australia	8.1	15.3
Austria	37.2	n/a
Canada	23.7	45.7
EEC 10	44.3	49.3
Japan	64.3	75.0
New Zealand	14.9	31.1
United States	14.7	35.4
Average	32.6	47.0

the government guarantees to buy part of the production to keep up the level of prices. That way the loans get repaid! State subsidies are paid on top of considerable federal subsidies. In Japan, intervention-buying to sustain small farmers – who have kept a powerful political voice despite a decrease in their numbers – leads to a level of subsidy that is around two and half times that of Europe as a percentage of GDP. At its most extreme, Japanese crop producers receive ninety-two per cent of their income by way of subsidy.

Although President Reagan argued in the GATT negotiations for a world policy to eliminate distortions in agricultural trade, his deeds have their own eloquence: the OECD survey shows the true American picture. The reality was clearly acknowledged in a speech by the chairman of George Bush's agricultural policy advisory group in 1988: 'Of course, farm programme costs can be permanently reduced by getting the government out of agriculture. However, this is not a realistic alternative. Such a course would be politically impossible, economically irrational and socially disastrous to rural America.'

The politics of agriculture have proved resistant to effective reform. The advanced world in one way or another supports its agriculture at large cost and with serious consequences for the less advanced parts of the world, many of which in an unsubsidized world would have an economic advantage in primary production.

If Britain in the 1950s had accepted Europe's invitation to play a leading role in devising the Community, the framework would have been different and the emphasis on agriculture no doubt less. (By the

1960s de Gaulle's desire to consolidate French agriculture appears to have been one of his reasons for vetoing Britain's application to join.) But there is not the slightest shred of evidence that Britain, if left outside the Community, would have followed a policy of agricultural *laissez-faire*. We were not doing so in the 1950s, when our agricultural support took the form of a deficiency payments system. Under that, the government made up the difference between what farmers were paid at the farm gate and what it was estimated they should be receiving to ensure a fair level of return on the products they sold. In its last year of operation the cost was about £1.5 billion, at constant 1983/4 prices, and by then the policy had been heavily modified, partly to prepare for entry to the EEC and partly to contain the cost of agricultural support. Food prices were kept low at the taxpayers' expense. This firmly entrenched support system is sometimes forgotten by those who, in criticizing the CAP, find the centrally organized farming policies of Europe such a convenient target. If Britain went back to a deficiency payment system as an alternative to the present European support system, it is possible to calculate the cost only within a wide margin of error. One estimate by Christopher Tugendhat, when a European Commissioner in 1982, was of £2 billion – or in today's money £3 billion – per annum.

The cost of the Community's system of intervention-buying of products in order to push the price up to target levels rose steadily to more than £3 billion in 1983/4 and is only now being reduced significantly. Food prices in Britain were bound to rise upon our entering the Community but, after the initial increase, they have risen consistently below the rate of inflation and in some years have actually fallen. Over the past ten years, retail food price inflation has been running at an average of around 70 per cent of general inflation and farm gate price inflation at less than 40 per cent. The change-over from deficiency payments to intervention was intended to transfer the cost of support from the taxpayer to the consumer. The cost of storing Community surpluses has, however, created a situation in which both are paying.

The old system of farm support was a recognition of the necessity for some stability and forward planning in an industry which was subject to the vagaries of the climate and which in the 1950s produced shortages as often as surpluses. Another objective was to increase British self-sufficiency in food for strategic reasons. It used to be a farming maxim that Britain could only produce enough food to feed itself at weekends; the other five days' consumption had to be imported. Nevertheless,

Britain's farm sector was efficient by Western European standards: by the time of our joining the EC in 1974, British farm output had more than doubled in thirty years and the average farm was some four times the size of its Western European equivalent. British farming could expect to serve a higher proportion of Britain's home market once within the Community, and it did. It also benefited from higher Community prices. In the early 1980s some products – barley and lamb in particular – found export markets.

The great drawback of the CAP for Britain was that, as the cost of agricultural support soared, we found ourselves obliged to pay a disproportionate share of it. It became increasingly indefensible among British citizens in particular, as the policy turned shortages into surpluses which were expensive to store or had to be exported cheaply to third markets (thus undercutting their own producers). Selling subsidized butter to the Russians at a fraction of the high street price was not likely to polish up the more visionary aspects of Europe, or any other aspect for that matter.

Britain's agriculture ministers shared with some of their European counterparts the problem of agricultural interests which were widespread. Diversity of product and farm – from barley baron to smallholding, from intensive livestock to marginal hill farming – presented Britain's ministers of agriculture with a ceaseless stream of negotiating difficulties. Fighting on so wide a front, they have found it hard to make clear-cut gains with which to satisfy all parts of their domestic constituency.

In seeking reform of the agricultural policy, we should be aware of the complex political calculations which lie behind it. In recent years, increases in agricultural subsidies to farmers have helped persuade the poorer countries of the EC to open up their protected markets. Given that the EC's social and regional funds have been so small, the agricultural policy's social dimension, as a mechanism for compensating these countries, has had considerable value. A harsher comment would be that the agricultural budget has served as a slush fund. If the objective is to build up Europe's strength by negotiated agreements among its members to the benefit of them all, then a certain *douceur* may prove justifiable. But it would be better if the EC's structural funds were used for such ends rather than CAP funds.

This upward pressure on agricultural spending highlights another political truth which reformers must bear in mind – that political machinery needs lubrication. The Community's machinery conforms to this rule. Twelve national ministers, negotiating matters of critical national importance to all of them, have each to return home as winners. Only alchemists have yet found a way of dividing up an even smaller cake so that everyone gets a larger slice, and thus the Community cake has always grown to accommodate the compromises. Too often achievement has been bought at a price: today's agreements have to be paid for tomorrow but there is always hope that tomorrow will be someone else's problem. And so the budget has grown.

So how is reform of the CAP to be tackled and in particular how is the spectre of the reappearing surpluses to be laid to rest? First, there is little prospect that any alternative uses of agricultural products – except the conversion of grain to fuel for energy – can absorb the Community's steadily increasing agricultural output. Much research is going on into the industrial use of agricultural products and into bio-fuels other than cereals but no one expects significant short-term results. To avoid the return of surpluses, therefore, reduction in output is required. There are various ways in which this might be accomplished.

The milk quotas introduced in 1984 have gone a long way towards resolving the problem of surpluses, albeit at painful cost to some of the dairy farmers concerned. Quotas indirectly benefit large, cost-efficient producers, and therefore consumers, but at the expense of small farmers. In every case a balance has to be struck, so in milk, for example, a quota system has proved administratively viable, while in other sectors farmers are being offered payments to set aside their land from productive use. Support schemes for small farms are on the agenda but such schemes are the least likely to help Britain's relatively large-scale farms. Only the more starry-eyed environmentalists would prefer Britain's upland and pasture to be turned into a wilderness for ramblers; the survival of the family farm is essential to the health of British rural areas.

A new dimension to the enterprise culture offers potential in the fields of tourism and of high-quality craft and cottage industries. Farmers are being encouraged to earn from new sources without damaging the environment and now half of the income of Community farmers arises from non-farming sources. Tax incentives and development grants should be designed to encourage this further.

Paying farmers to do nothing is controversial. However, the principle of redundancy payments is well-established in industry and the registration for set-aside grants by British farmers since the scheme was introduced by the Community last year has been higher than expected. The actual take-up of the scheme is much lower. Farmers are not yet convinced, but they prudently hedge their bets in case they want to go ahead in later years. The land remains available for reuse if weather patterns, world shortages, environmental assumptions or simply inaccurate forecasting create unforeseen demand. But at the bizarre extreme this must be the first time in history that the richest in the land have been paid to convert their productive farms into pheasant coverts.

A ban on the use of certain fertilizers would help to cut surpluses produced by the most intensive farms and would be beneficial to the environment. But such a measure would be hard to enforce, would increase food prices and attack the problem at the point of maximum efficiency.

The CAP's difficulties necessitate constant monitoring and the use of selective instruments to achieve a balance between farm incomes and social and environmental needs. Their solution does not lie, as some advocate, in a 'repatriation' of the CAP to member states. In such an event, member governments would soon find themselves obliged to support their farmers at the highest prevailing Community level, unless narrow protectionism forced up the frontier barriers again. High economic growth will continue to divert the energies of the rural population into economically more viable and better paid activities. But this will take time and perhaps have awkward political consequences.

The treaties establishing the Community were drawn up at a time of low unemployment and, not surprisingly, concentrated on creating a common labour market rather than on measures to create jobs. Nevertheless, the EEC Treaty did provide one such measure. The European Social Fund was created in 1960 and is the Community's prime instrument of social policy. Its objectives are to combat long-term unemployment and to facilitate the occupational integration of young people; to promote stable employment and to develop new opportunities for those who are or may become unemployed.

The Community's Regional Fund, encouraged by British pressure, was introduced in 1975, by which time regional unemployment had become a serious problem. It is designed to help underdeveloped rural areas, whose economies depend for the most part on agriculture, and those areas whose former prosperity was founded on industries which are now in decline, such as coal, steel, shipbuilding or textiles. It provides finance for programmes to improve infrastructure development, grants to industry, crafts and services. Through this means the Community, in partnership with member states, helps to stimulate development in the poorer regions and to redress regional imbalances. The enlargement of the Community to include the southern countries of Greece (1980), Spain and Portugal (1986) led to the Integrated Mediterranean Programmes, which further developed the principles of the Regional Fund.

These funds will help to channel resources to the development of poorer regions. Most of these will be allocated to regions whose GDP per head is less than 75 per cent of the Community average. Such regions include the whole of Portugal, Ireland and Greece; parts of Spain, Italy and France; and Northern Ireland. It is essential that the regions are held accountable for the use to which they put these funds. The attitude of strict economic responsibility, which this Conservative government has done so much to encourage in the UK, must be developed all over Europe.

National governments must also learn that they cannot have their cake and eat it. Too often governments earmark Community structural funds for projects that they would have financed anyway with national resources. Britain, like some other EC countries has included EC spending in its public expenditure totals in order to contain the overall level of public expenditure: thus an increase in EC spending on a regional project has resulted in a corresponding decrease in national public expenditure on another project. It is important that the increase in Community funding for regional development does not lead to such corresponding reductions. The 'structural funds' are to be almost doubled over the next five years and without the principle of 'additionality', Community funding will become a farce.

To its credit, the British government agreed in 1988 to a reform of the regional and social funds, which allows for more programme and project-based expenditure and gives the EC scrutiny of the effects of its regional spending and prevents 'non-additionality'. If a country does practice 'non-additionality', the Community will retaliate by reducing its expenditure in that country.

The Brussels summit of February 1988 agreed that the budget for the structural funds would be increased from nearly £5 billion in 1988 to £9.17 billion in 1993. Member states have never been equally poor or rich, nor have all their regions had equal possibilities to create new opportunities for enterprise and wealth. The price demanded by the nations with the poorer regions to bring the Community together is that sufficient Community resources are made available to areas distant from the main centres.

The interdependence of Europe's disparate regions was recognized in the treaties and given renewed emphasis both in Lord Cockfield's 1985 White Paper on completing the internal market and, more specifically, in the Single European Act. Whereas the main thrust of Community policy must be to provide the legislative framework which will allow the unfettered growth of industry and services, the more affluent regions must expect to pay a small but necessary price for the overall success of the single market.

The inhabitants of South-East Britain or North Rhine-Westphalia might at first resent this but governments cannot escape the responsibility of providing for those areas that do not possess their natural advantages. The West of Ireland, the Italian *Mezzogiorno*, the Greek Islands and Southern Spain, by their very location, will suffer handicaps of inaccessibility, poor infrastructure and a poorly trained labour force. In supporting this commitment to reduce regional differences, we should be aware of the dangers. Funds of this sort, as with most subsidies, can have the effect of supporting existing patterns of low-grade employment or sheltering declining communities from change that, though difficult in the short term, would, if encouraged, prove ultimately beneficial.

There is, therefore, a need for discipline as well as for proper concern. It is important to be sure of what we are trying to achieve and to hesitate before throwing money at the first schemes presented. Those presenting the schemes may themselves be products of a dependency culture. With perfectly proper motives the leaders of economically backward or threatened regions seek the cash for their communities and their natural instinct is to sustain them in their present form. It would be better to question why the communities are backward in the first place and to concentrate help on removing the underlying causes. The most common problem is simply that, for cumulative reasons, the weaker regions are unable to compete. A host of characteristics can prevent or repel economic activity. The structural funds must address the causes of the problem not just the consequences.

Some countries of the Community retain close links with a number of their ex-colonies. Nearly a third of EC exports go to developing countries and an estimated ten million jobs in the Community depend on them. The Community is also the main customer of the African, Caribbean and Pacific states, absorbing some 40 per cent of their exports.

Most of their exports enter the Community tariff-free, apart from agricultural products. Official Community aid to the third world, counting all national and Community sources, exceeds that of Japan, the United States and the Soviet Union combined. The bulk of the aid is national: aid from Brussels amounts to only one-fifth as much as that collectively given by individual member states.

The main vehicle for Community aid is the Lomé Convention, more than half of whose members also belong to the Commonwealth. This provides for preferential trade and aid agreements that allow certain countries access to Community markets (special arrangements exist for Commonwealth countries in the export of sugar, rum, bananas, brandy and, of course, New Zealand butter) and also substantial aid.

The Mediterranean Agreements, which began in the early 1970s, were set up to provide special terms for poor countries of the Mediterranean basin not in the Community. These, however, are being wound down and Britain has consistently argued that these countries do not require special EC assistance as they are not among the poorer developing countries.

A small aid programme (the Non-Associated programme) exists for those countries not in the geographical areas covered by the Lomé Convention. This programme, introduced after British pressure, gives priority to countries of the Indian sub-continent and Central and South America. The small sums given (around £200 million a year) are in complete disproportion to the populations of the countries involved and reflect the rather fragmented approach to aid policy. The European Development Fund provides cash for long-term development programmes in developing countries. Nearly 40 per cent of the projects funded are in the field of rural development, nearly 20 per cent in communications.

The Community has a good track record in both long-term development projects and emergency relief. However, there are serious shortcomings. First, the CAP works against the third world by denying third world countries access to Community markets for their cheaper produce and sometimes undermining third world producers through the dumping of Community surpluses. Second, since the bulk of aid is administered by national governments and not by the Community, there is overlapping and competition. If the EC apportioned to particular member states the job of administering aid to specific countries, it might be done more effectively and the scale of European aid to the third world more fully appreciated.

Third, the EC has no institution like the World Bank through which to advance its interests while helping the third world. If, as many believe, the outcome of the third world debt crisis will be to channel further lending through official institutions like the World Bank, the need for a European Bank will become all the more pressing. Such a bank might have powers, as the World Bank has, to raise money on the international markets and channel it towards sensible lending in the third world (unlike the irresponsible bank lending of the 1970s).

The coming of the single market will have a number of consequences for the Community's trade and aid policy. The present haphazard aid policies, which grew up out of the collective colonial obligations of the Community of Six in the 1960s, will look increasingly outdated. The many separate programmes of the Lomé Convention, the Mediterranean programme, the Non-Associated programme, and the programmes of food aid and national aid, will need rationalization if they are to give the most effective help to the recipients, as well as securing wider policy objectives – most importantly, environmental improvement.

After 1992 we will have to ask whether it would not be more appropriate to have a single integrated Community aid programme, conducted in partnership with national programmes and reaching to all countries which were felt to be in need. There could still be countries regarded as having prior claims on the Community, though humanitarian and political considerations would also have to be taken into account.

If we stand back from the details, what picture appears? Where do British interests lie? The Community was founded without us and its structure accommodated the agricultural and industrial interests of others. That structure is still there and only as the size of the Community budget has grown has the proportion devoted to agriculture declined. The balance of the Community's priorities is only gradually changing.

Britain's first interest as the Community evolves is the pursuit of world prosperity by unremitting work to keep markets open and trade free and expanding. That will mean avoiding frictions which provoke protectionist measures throughout the trading world. Our second interest is to secure European agricultural support policies and regional policies which do not diminish the EC's international competitiveness and which are fair to our regions and to Britain's high-output, efficient farming.

It follows that we want value for money. Too much of Europe's past agricultural support has been about subsidy rather than investment. Future investment must be directed towards reducing costs and improving quality rather than into extra output. At the same time, however, the CAP as a European policy has to respond to many different national agricultural problems. Some part of it must be used to help the poorer farmers (unless we can find some other panacea for them) or they will not support the Community and their own politicians. It will be easier to persuade the other Europeans to limit the Community's agricultural support in periods of high growth, because of the scope for diverting workers from agriculture into urban jobs, but that is not the case in Britain.

Finally, we have to manage the politics of land use. The pressures of lower agricultural output, burgeoning property values and a continuing technological revolution which offers new styles of working and living together raise new and awkward political and environmental questions. The picture is not uniform and, where communications are poor or climate inhospitable, the agricultural downturn still has a harsh effect. But anyone who represents a rural constituency in a prosperous part of southern Britain is aware of the wider pressures. Planning policies will remain critically important and highly controversial in the 1990s. The Conservative Party would do well to trust its instinct and to remember its historic concern for the countryside. It is not just the rural voter who is concerned but a growing number of urban dwellers who see the countryside as an asset in which they too have a share.

CHAPTER
4

Europe's Economy: Falling Behind

A story is told of two Welsh brothers who submitted a tender to build the Channel Tunnel for £1,834.56. Equipped only with two barrows and two spades, they were questioned by politely sceptical civil servants about their plan to divide their modest workforce so that one could start from Calais and the other from Dover. Could they be sure of meeting in the middle? 'Don't worry, boyo,' the elder brother explained. 'If we miss, you'll get two tunnels.' A little confidence will help most human enterprise along, and the grandeur of the brothers' language has a recognizably European ring. But the member states of the Community have learned that the rhetorical flourish will take you only so far; practicality also has its uses.

The Treaty of Rome committed its signatories to monetary and economic union. The same words were repeated in the Single European Act. The European Council meeting in Hanover in 1988 established a committee to examine the steps which might be taken. It might have seemed to the detached observer that there was a common purpose. Nothing could have been further from the truth. There is agreement neither about the desirability of the objective nor the significance of what it means. It follows that there can be no agreement about the speed of progress.

If the steady drawing together since 1945 of the European Community had depended solely on the memory and dread of war, the passage of time might have dimmed the vision and slowed the march. At times this has seemed to happen. And although the Russian threat served as an urgent reminder of the need for strength in alliance, there was no equivalent economic imperative. The 1950s were good times. The future then seemed set fair as the boom of post-war reconstruction with its massive investment programmes began to fill the pockets of the people.

A serious check to the community's progress was the crisis over majority voting in 1965 and by the time it was resolved the following year by the Luxembourg compromise – imposed by de Gaulle – the Community's progress had been reduced to the speed of its slowest or most obdurate member. But by the end of the 1960s renewed pressures for European economic unity were emerging. The evolution of worldwide markets exerted forces of scale and speed which were unprecedented and called into question old notions of national sovereignty. Within a world economy, regional markets formed; and among them the regional market of Europe failed to keep pace. Europe was out-performed.

A wave of technological innovation assumed the pace-setting significance in opening new markets that the smelting of iron, the harnessing of steam and the invention of the internal combustion engine had achieved in former times. But the costs were high, stretching the resources of even the richest states. And as Europe's regional economy fell behind, Britain's reputation as the sick man of Europe deservedly grew. The oil crisis and the currency instabilities of the 1970s were to jerk Britain and all of Europe into a new understanding of their weakness and of the changes that had made them so vulnerable.

What had gone wrong, and what are the worldwide changes to which the Community has had to adjust and must continue to adjust? In the business world, national frontiers are losing their significance and markets are becoming increasingly global. Visitors to the capitals of the world see the same brand names, the same cars, the same soft drinks. Many companies have an interest in reinforcing this trend by their marketing strategies. It would never occur to General Motors or Ford to develop wholly separate product ranges for different nations. With global branding go worldwide strategies. Macdonalds is now the largest restaurant chain in Japan; Wimpy packs them in in Moscow; Coca Cola is a best-seller in Peking. Alternatively, the same product can be made to satisfy local taste with only cosmetic changes, sold throughout a number of different countries but packaged and advertised distinctively to meet the specific market. Franchising makes a high street of the world. There are some markets, however, in which national differences in taste still predominate and multinationals have to learn to design them into their production runs.

Larger markets can sustain larger companies, whose profits in turn can help them achieve an even wider market penetration. The scale of many of today's developments necessitates the deployment of huge resources, demands ever more sophisticated and expensive technologies, larger and larger launch costs increasingly affordable only by the biggest companies, who in turn must be able to sell worldwide in order to cover their overheads. Governments, through public procurement programmes, accentuate the process, especially in the high-technology areas.

Large companies seek wider international markets but need a strong home base from which to exploit more effectively their export potential. But there is another side to the coin: free competitive markets of large scale may sustain several giant concerns at the top of each sectoral pyramid but at the base are a myriad of small firms. Only the giants can compete on a world scale but their skill is as much about harnessing and organizing the products of countless sub-contractors and suppliers as it is about controlling their own production lines. I well remember a particular torpedo contract negotiated by the Ministry of Defence: although the contract itself had gone to a monopoly supplier, 90 per cent of it had been broken out into competitive opportunities. Innovation and enterprise are at their most acute as small firms fight to hold their position and new thrusters attempt to break into the market place. New ideas and services crowd in as competition surges through open doors and gives that lift to the performance of the overall effort. But when it comes to developing export markets, God is on the side of the big battalions. The risks are too high and the resources of small companies too low to assume we can build our fortunes on their backs.

Within the trend to global markets, changes in the financial sector have moved faster and more comprehensively in the 1980s than in manufacturing. Particularly is this so in Britain. In 1979 exchange controls were removed. This was the most radical move announced by Sir Geoffrey Howe during his period as Chancellor of the Exchequer. Abolition of all controls, without exception, allowed British firms and individuals to move their money wherever they desired in the world without hindrance; a freedom few had known before.

Money chases around the world wherever there is daylight and active trading. The convenience of time zones – and the presence of existing financial expertise – made these markets settle primarily in New York, London and Tokyo. As brokers went to bed in one time zone they would hand over within tight constraints their trading positions to partners in the next one; twenty-four-hour financial markets were born. They soon bred a host of different 'instruments' – options, swaps, futures in currencies, bonds and commodities. What it meant, in effect, was that the financial reserves of a corporation or a rich individual could be moved at a moment's notice anywhere in the world.

During this revolution came the British 'Big Bang' – the reform of the City and the sweeping away of anti-competitive restrictive practices that had lasted for generations. Many of the great names of City stockbroking were taken over by financial institutions with larger capital bases, most of them foreign. European, Japanese and American financiers became at least as important as Londoners in the City of London itself. The world of money had undergone a quantum change which, though politically encouraging, soon leapt far ahead of any national political control.

Shrinking distances and accumulating resources may have pushed companies towards a world market but within that market national markets were fusing into regional groupings. Proximity, traditional relationships and new shared interests reinforced the trend. The Canadians found themselves in 1988 engaged in a general election in which the principle issue was the consolidation of the Canadian domestic market with that of the United States. The Pacific Basin may consist of many markets and countries in various stages of economic development but they grow steadily closer together and increasingly the area is coming to look like a regional market dominated by Japan.

Europe itself is as powerful as any regional market. It is by far the world's largest trading bloc: EC countries in 1987 had a 40 per cent share of world trade, compared with Asia and Australasia's share of 12 per cent, the United States' 14 per cent, the rest of North and South America's 13 per cent and Japan's 8 per cent. The total value of EC exports to the rest of the world was $559 billion in 1987. From such a powerful regional base European companies should be able to develop the muscle – in terms of corporate strength, exploitation of public procurement and the maintenance of an effective competitive home base – to compete in markets on a global scale.

But these statistics lack realism. There is no European economy; there is not even a coherent European market. There are twelve different countries, each with its own sovereignty, practices, institutions, currencies. Each has traditionally been as preoccupied with the local European competition as with the problems posed by the huge scale of American and Japanese competition. With Europe's economic strength thus divided, the capitalist world is dominated by the currencies and companies of the United States and Japan. Of the world's twenty largest banks, twelve are Japanese. They are in a league of their own; of the fifty largest companies listed in '*The Times* 1,000' in 1986, eighteen are Japanese, fourteen are American, seven West German, three Italian, two British, two British and Dutch combined, one Dutch and one French.

In 1987 (at 1987 exchange rates/prices) the output of the United States was $4,473 billion and that of Japan $2,377 billion. The output for the European Community was almost as large as that of America – $4,287 billion. With Europe divided, the true story is very different. The largest of the European economies, West Germany, has a GDP only one-quarter of the size of the United States and half the size of Japan. The smallest of the European economies would hardly register on the Richter scale of world finance.

Within this pattern of global markets and regional divisions, the challenge for Europe is to maximize the opportunities available in an enlarged domestic market place, for a dual purpose: that of ensuring growth and that of matching world-class competition not only in the European market place but throughout the world. Self-evidently, no single European nation can hope to command the resources or the clout of the American or Japanese economies. But even as the barriers to the formation of a single European market are removed, we will deny ourselves its benefits if that market continues to behave as it does today. Without change, the market amounts to twelve independent centres of economic decision-making, trading in twelve currencies in twelve different sets of economic circumstances.

Apart from the hidden costs of frontiers and trade barriers, a heavy price is paid in wasted resources, duplicated research, excess capacity, overprotected services, uncompetitive procurement in many fields and short production runs. Inevitably costs are high, innovation low. It takes time and is expensive to transmit money through the complexities of the different banking systems. Exchange rate uncertainties are discounted in higher prices.

The EC consumers' association, the *Bureau Européen des Unions de Consommateurs*, has demonstrated what everyone knows who has tried it: that moving money between European countries is inefficient. It says that, although the average time taken to transfer cash is five days, this covers a range of anything between one day and five months, and a small number of transfers are simply never completed. No doubt large companies manage more efficiently and cheaply by knowing the ropes but small and medium-sized companies can easily be deterred from even attempting cross-border transactions.

It is little consolation to know that the situation is almost as bad between some districts of the Federal Reserve Bank in the USA, where financial regulation has hindered the development of nationwide banks. Europe should be able for once to learn from America's mistakes. Banks enjoy the substantial sums which accrue from delays in money transmission but the customer suffers – and pays. As a graphic illustration, try taking one pound sterling and solemnly converting it through the currencies of each of our European partners on a circular journey from London and back. By the time your pound had completed its trip, it would have vanished and your bank manager would have approached you for £15 or more in bank charges. Send £1,000 on the same journey and the result would be equally inhibiting though less dramatic: it would lose between £50 and £70 of its value on the way round. In the United States, the buck that started in New York is still a buck when it reaches Los Angeles.

Twenty-five years after resolving by treaty to combine their economic strength, the countries of the European Community found themselves in the early 1980s still falling behind. Between 1975 and 1980 the EC increased its industrial production by 17 per cent. In the same period the United States achieved a 25 per cent increase and the Japanese, at 42 per cent, an increase of two and a half times as great as Europe's. In 1988 the Japanese economy grew by 5.8 per cent compared with the OECD average of 3.9 per cent. The EC trade deficit with Japan between 1975 and 1980 increased tenfold to $10.5 billion a year by 1980. European car exports between 1970 and 1980 fell by 23 per cent as car exports worldwide increased by 426 per cent.

Europe as a regional market had to adjust to new patterns of world demand caused by the movements in oil prices. The increases in oil prices in 1973 diverted £12 billion and in 1979 £24 billion worth of purchasing power from Europe, mostly to the Middle East. Slower growth rates in Europe were an inevitable consequence as the local economies adjusted; but the oil price increases alone do not wholly explain the sluggishness of the European economies.

Historically, company development has followed the technological advances which made new products and services possible. The steam engine found rapid application in manufacturing industry, giving eighteenth- and nineteenth-century Britain a distinct competitive advantage. In Europe the construction of railways across the continent, particularly in France and Germany, opened up continental distribution. Air transport has been a critical force in opening world markets. In 1987 passengers flew billions of miles on thirteen million scheduled flights.

Information technology is the touchstone of today's industrial revolution. Its applications are for the world market and the players there are giants. The commercial spoils will go to the nations which most swiftly and effectively harness it. The more we move – as Britain has increasingly been moving – towards supplying services rather than producing manufactured goods, the more important electronic communications become. Consider the fax machine: numbers in the UK doubled between 1986 and 1987 from 87,000 to 173,000 and more than doubled again by the end of 1988 when there were over 370,000. The UK is third in the world in its use of the fax, behind only the USA and Japan. For the first time, small and medium companies can open up easy, quick and relatively cheap worldwide communications.

But if the excitement and opportunity is immense, so too is the competition. In the micro-electronic revolution, which is now a crucial driving force, innovation has intensified this competition. Japanese companies which twenty years ago were primarily satisfying Japanese demand now dominate markets at a world level, demonstrating the unrivalled capacity of Japanese industry to develop technological excellence within a protected economy and then to export it worldwide. Today, of the top ten electronics and telecommunications companies, five are Japanese. Although Siemens in West Germany and Philips in the Netherlands have done well and are fifth and sixth respectively in the top ten, with turnovers of over some £15 billion each, they are only half the size of IBM or General Electric. There is no British company in the top ten. Other European conglomerates, such as Thorn-EMI in Britain or Thomson in France, have simply not matched the vitality of the Japanese in exploiting the products of innovative technological research as their companies faced growing Asian competition in export markets.

Excellence at the frontiers of technology has a further advantage for the market leader. When change occurs, it can be surprising how quickly the *status quo* yields. The successful company can outstrip the official standard-making process by designing products of such a quality that they set new *de facto* standards which then become official standards. IBM has dominated the market in computers to such an extent that it can largely control emerging standards and thereby feed its own growth. Powerful businesses impose standards on their suppliers and sub-contractors, denying market penetration to outside competitors – a common feature of Japanese practice. Standards can also be used to lock out competitors; nations as well as companies play this game.

Congress has always nurtured American-developed technologies and restricted their transfer abroad. The promotion of computer technology by the American Air Force resulted directly in the creation of the robotics and computerized machine tool industries. Most important of all was the creation of DARPA (the Defence Advanced Research Projects Agency), set up in response to the Sputnik launch of 1957. It focused its funding on new computer technology but not on particular military applications; it was committed to supporting basic research of long-term importance (projects with a life of 10 to 20 years). Its clear aim was to accelerate the technological development of the US commercial computer industry on the basis that defence projects were a major user of computers.

One of the European anxieties about the Strategic Defence Initiative was that so large a public programme at the frontiers of so many emerging technologies would give American industry an enormous technological boost. The SDI development contracts placed by the Pentagon around the world were relatively small in value but critical in technological content, with the result that, whenever a foreign company or country was thought to be ahead of American technology, a joint venture in that specific field was offered. The consequences of so comprehensive a transfer of technology to American industry and of the increase in its competitive ability are incalculable.

There are two important points: first, that although individual companies in each country undoubtedly gained from generous American reciprocity, only American industry was at the heart of every deal, thus guaranteeing American industry's pre-eminence at the frontier of all the technologies involved; second, that most of this investment in R&D was funded by the American taxpayer through the programmes of the Pentagon.

In 1984 Congress was prepared (in the Joint Research and Development Act) to alter anti-trust laws to enable American companies to undertake co-operative research, in the face of Japanese government policies promoting pre-competitive work in fifth generation computers. And faced with the aggressive challenge from Japan, America has found it necessary to fund through public programmes half of its total R&D effort. In Japan, government and companies act together with single-mindedness to ensure success. The Japanese Ministry for International Trade and Industry (MITI) co-ordinates the industrial effort. Its latest investment is the Regional Research Core Concept, approved in 1986, which aims to establish research centres in 28 regional cities to strengthen R&D on a joint industry/academic/government basis. These Research Core cities will be eligible for tax benefits, insurance guarantees and financing loans from the Japanese Development Bank. Japan's strength in R&D in recent years lies behind her competitive ferocity; her competence in market-creating product design stems from a heavy commitment to R&D. It is a matter of pride to the President of Honda that his company has a reputation 'for putting technology first and not thinking about money first': and we know what the Honda scale of values did to the short-sighted British motorcycle industry.

With R&D expenditure now a main determinant of economic growth, what is happening in Europe? Only Germany of all the European countries invests in R&D on a scale anything like the United States and Japan. But whatever percentage of GDP each European country may achieve, in absolute cash terms each is a minnow. Furthermore, the R&D spending of each of the European economies competes with that of the others: German and French wheels are reinvented in British laboratories. The aggregate output of all the R&D conducted separately within the several national companies of Europe in a particular product line is not likely to match that of a single Japanese or American competitor. Only by concentrating our efforts will our R&D yield its full potential and effectively challenge the big players.

Against this background of increasingly international markets with their regional subdivisions, how has Britain fared? Relatively weakened by years of exclusion from the Community, Britain encountered the economic storms of the 1970s at a disadvantage compared with the

Fig. 4.1 R & D as a Proportion of GDP

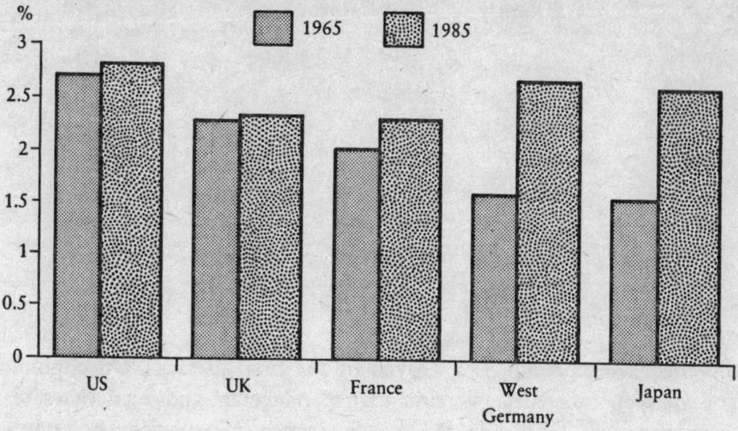

(Source: OECD 1988)

countries who were about to become her partners. One of the many motives for President de Gaulle's much discussed veto in 1963 was the belief that the Macmillan government was facing defeat, that Labour would weaken the economy and that by the time the Conservatives were able to renew their bid for membership Britain would be less able to compete in Europe. In this he was proved right.

During Britain's ten-year wait for membership, our Commonwealth trade diminished, their markets gradually shifting as they sought new trading alignments. By contrast, the six founding members of the EC enjoyed successive fat years of extraordinary expansion. First Germany, then France, overtook Britain in investment, output and exports. The cumulative effect of the trends shown at the top of Table 4.1 contributed to the outcome de Gaulle had hoped for.

Britain through the 1960s and 1970s achieved barely half the growth rates of the two largest European economies. Labour governments, careless of the need for renewal and more concerned with the division of wealth than its creation, were busy from 1964 to 1979 with their proclaimed task of making Socialism in Britain irreversible, with only a brief interval in which a Conservative government's attempts to reverse

Table 4.1 Historical Comparisons of Growth (%)

Year	*UK Rate*	*German Rate*	*French Rate*
1950–60	2.6	6.5	4.5
1960–73	3.2	7.9	5.6
1973–75	−0.8	0.5	1.7
1975–80	1.6	3.6	3.2
1980–85	1.2	1.3	1.1
1986	3.2	2.5	2.1
1987	4.4	1.9	1.8

(Source: PA Cambridge Economic Consultants)

direction were promptly destroyed by the first oil crisis. Uneconomic activities, characterized by inadequate management and restrictive trade union practices, were indulged in at the taxpayers' expense. High taxes, squeezing until the pips squeaked, destroyed a generation of independent family businesses and with them provincial prosperity. There was little innovation and only a slow start-up rate of small firms.

Britain failed to compete. Her world share of exports of manufactured goods at the turn of the century stood at one third; by 1938 it had declined to a fifth; by 1960 to 16.5 per cent; by 1970 it stood at 10.6 per cent. The steep rise in oil prices, and the wage explosion which followed the 1973 miners' strike, left Britain in 1976 with a share of 8.4 per cent. The International Monetary Fund's discipline then forced the Labour government to change direction and by 1980 the British share had recovered to 9.7 per cent, mainly through increased exports to Europe. A manufacturing revival seemed to be on its way but by 1987 our share was back to 8.1 per cent. Between 1977 and 1988, the UK's balance of trade in manufactured goods moved from a surplus of £5.9 billion to a deficit of £14.4 billion. Part of the decline can fairly be attributed to the emergence of new industrial powers but during the latter period West Germany has actually increased her share: from 19.9 per cent in 1980 to 21.5 per cent in 1987.

The Labour government's incomes policy, imposed in 1976, hit both skilled and public sector workers hard and James Callaghan's 'winter of discontent' in 1979 triggered a 25 per cent wage explosion. At the same time, with Britain now a major oil producer, the oil-backed pound rose by 20 per cent. As a consequence of this double catastrophe, our share of world trade dropped again so that by 1984 it was at its lowest level of 7.6 per cent. Nearly a quarter of Britain's exporting capacity had been wiped out. Unemployment crossed the threshold of three million people.

By the late 1970s the 'British disease' had gained world notoriety: inefficient nationalized industries, chronic industrial relations and restrictive practices, high taxation, over-regulation, poor management and so on. Yet Europe as a whole has been no stranger to many of these problems. West German industry has long been hampered by over-bureaucratic social regulations; in France, the role of the state, particularly in the banking sector, until the partial re-privatizations of the Chirac government in 1986–7, has always been significant. Italy has been plagued by an unwieldy patronage-based state sector and a powerful trade union movement.

Of the major Western European economies, West Germany came through the crisis of the 1970s best, largely thanks to the consistent policy of the Social Democrat government of Helmut Schmidt and its successor, Helmut Kohl's Christian Democratic administration, both of them subjected to the discipline of an independent central bank. France, by contrast, after years of largely successful technocratic economic policies, ran into serious trouble during the early years of President Mitterand's Socialist administration and spent much of the next five years recovering. Italian governments sought to weather the oil price increase through continued economic growth and suffered serious inflation as a result. (When efforts were belatedly made to control this, unemployment rose.) In Spain severe monetarist policies, adopted to cope with the economic crisis of the immediate post-Franco years, certainly succeeded in controlling inflation but at the cost of pushing unemployment up to the highest level in Western Europe.

The disease of unemployment was not unique to Britain. The figures show how all of Western Europe suffered in this respect from the economic squalls of the 1970s. Unemployment in Britain nearly doubled from 6.4 per cent in 1980 to 11.3 per cent in 1982, before falling back by early 1989 to around 8 per cent. Over the same period in West Germany it doubled from 3 to 6 per cent, where it has stayed; in France it rose from 6 to 8 per cent and has since climbed to over 10 per cent; in Italy the rate rose from 7.5 to 8.5 per cent then up to 10 per cent in 1988; in Spain it rose from 11 to 16 per cent and by 1989 had reached an alarming 19 per cent; and in Holland it rose from 6 to 11.4 per cent, falling only slightly to 10 per cent in 1988. Britain's unemployment rate, which was a couple of points above the EC average in 1982, was 2 per cent below the EC average by 1989. The adjustment in Britain was as painful as any in Western Europe but the tough leadership of the Conservative government after 1979 yielded better results.

The rate of investment in new equipment is as important to the competitive ability of modern industry as it is to the fighting capacity of a modern army. Without products at the leading edge of technology no company can hold its market share. The figures for fixed capital investment in British manufacturing industry reflect the squeeze on its cash flow. Investment in new hardware only recovered to the peak at which it had been running when Britain reapplied in 1970 to join the Community in 1989, and is expected to fall again. The gross fixed investment of British manufacturing industry in 1970 (constant 1985 prices) was £10.6 billion. After the first oil shock in 1973 it dropped sharply, to recover somewhat by 1980 to £8.76 billion. But the profligacy of the late 1970s unleashed inflation and the second oil shock sent the investment level spiralling down again to £6.4 billion by 1982, the lowest point. It was 1987 before it recovered to £9 billion.

The first oil shock hit Britain hard, since we were not at that stage a large enough producer to benefit from the rising oil price. But other Community members were also severely affected as their costs rose steeply. Their growing awareness of the exposure of their individual currencies, and of the damage which differential currency movements could do to the Common Market, drove them back to the drawing board for a new plan of advance.

Although their manufacturers were hurt by the first oil shock, the original six members had entered the 1970s with a much stronger industrial base than Britain. None the less, they determined that the Community should have stable money and, to achieve that, should organize its own currency system. The European Monetary System (EMS) was conceived in the crisis year of 1978. At its heart was an exchange rate mechanism (ERM) designed to limit fluctuations between the currencies of the members by keeping them linked to each other within narrow bands.

As early as 1970, the Werner Report had called for economic and monetary union by 1980. The oil price chaos of 1973 undermined the first attempt – the so-called 'snake' – but the debate was reopened by Roy Jenkins, as President of the European Commission, in 1977. British ministers, fearing that any attempt to fix sterling too closely with European currencies would fall victim to our rapidly escalating wage costs, coined the oft-repeated explanation that the time was not right. Today, constant reference to joining the EMS is confusing, since Britain formally joined the EMS in 1978, by depositing a fifth of its reserves with the European Monetary Co-operation Fund, but Prime Minister James Callaghan refused to join the Exchange Rate Mechanism in December of the same year and the ERM began without us in March 1979. Little did anyone then foresee that all the market pressures would be in the opposite direction. For six years the upward pressure of oil upon the sterling exchange rate was too high to allow a sensible entry to the mechanism. It would not have proved possible, for the ERM could not hold sterling at a rate significantly out of line with the judgment of the market. The government's policy has remained 'to join when the time is ripe'.

The ERM has succeeded in holding steady the currencies of the eight full member states throughout the gyrations of the dollar in the 1980s. As British industry fought for its life, the rest of the Community was able to sustain recovery with steadier, more competitive currencies. Imports from the Community continued to take an increasing share of the British domestic market.

The pound strengthened, peaking at 5 DM in early 1981. (The British exporter was by then demanding 20 per cent more from his German customers for the same product than he had been in 1980.) Thereafter the pound slowly declined to an average of 3.78 DM by 1985. In 1986, however, after six years of an oil-hardened pound, the oil revenue dropped sharply and the pound fell to an average of 3.18 DM.

With the pound now more competitive, the leaders of British industry in search of stability called for it to be brought within the ERM. The currency movements had reduced the attraction for British companies of investments which industries in other Community countries had been able to undertake with more security. Industry could also see that the EMS had helped to stabilize continental wages and interest rates; it had imposed new disciplines on industry. But there remained the question of how Britain, with a long history of higher inflation than her competitors, would be able to afford to fix sterling firmly in the ERM without first conquering inflation.

The British government has not been alone in facing problems of wage pressure. The French have tough unions, so have the Belgians, the Danes and the Dutch. But, since their currencies are fixed to the deutschmark, their workers know that government cannot adjust the currency to compensate industry for excessive wage claims, as they once did. And the anchor currency, the deutschmark, is stable not just because the Germans are disciplined but because the *Bundesbank* is independent of the Federal government, which therefore cannot print money to pay for wage increases that outstrip productivity. Unions then become conscious of the threat to employment of inflationary wage settlements. The value of such a discipline is well understood in the British Treasury. As the Chancellor, Nigel Lawson, said in a speech at Chatham House in January 1989: 'Close co-operation [between independent states in the European Monetary System] can bring greater stability of exchange rates and reinforce their efforts to bring down inflation.'

Most opponents of full British participation in the EMS sooner or later argue that it would cause an unacceptable loss of sovereignty. But can governments be sovereign in today's financial world? Stacked against them in the money markets, with fingers poised to shift billions at the speed it takes an electrical impulse to cross the exchange-floor, are the money dealers. A twenty-three-year-old whizz kid in a City dealing room may have discretion to buy or sell pounds sterling in tens of millions. There is only one sovereignty in which he is interested – the sovereignty of a strong, well-managed economy. Stability demands the tight management of the monetary side of economic affairs: the end to which the Conservative Party is committed and upon which it was elected. The *Financial Times* is pink in appearance only. Its editorial of 27 January 1989 described the monetary sovereignty upon which Britain based its refusal to become full members of the EMS as 'a licence to depreciate the currency'.

The fact is that the EMS has been more successful than could have been hoped or imagined in achieving its primary objective of exchange rate stability and sustaining confidence in the currency markets. All the ERM currencies have fluctuated much less against each other than against the American dollar. In contrast, the British currency has enjoyed no such stability. Over the last decade the pound appreciated to $2.45 by 1981 – pricing British exports out of world markets and contributing to a 20 per cent contraction in our manufacturing industry – then dived to $1.04 in 1985, bringing inflationary pressures as the price of imported finished goods and raw materials rose.

Detractors of the EMS point to the low growth rates in the states which are full members of it. Growth rates have to reflect the capacity of the economy to meet them. Over-acceleration brings balance of payments troubles as imports make up for the failure of the home industry to keep pace and this inevitably leads to a reining back by government of overall demand. The continental Europeans have enjoyed more stability and, in consequence, lower inflation.

Others argue that sterling, as an international and petro-currency, is subject to special pressures that preclude Britain from joining the ERM. This is an overstatement of a vanishing truth. British oil production as a proportion of GDP is shrinking as world oil prices and the yields from the North Sea fall. Indeed, oil accounted for only 2 per cent of Britain's GDP in 1986/7 and 1.5 per cent in 1988. In the first quarter of 1986 the price of oil plunged by over 60 per cent but the trade-weighted value of sterling dropped a mere 3 per cent.

The internationalist argument maintains that sterling's unique position as a widely traded currency renders regulation futile. But, like the petro-sterling argument, it does not correspond with today's reality. The pound, once the second most widely held currency in the world, has fallen behind the US dollar, the deutschmark, the yen and the Swiss franc. In 1986 the ecu had become the third most used currency for international bond issues, after the dollar and deutschmark.

Pegging the pound to the European currency bloc would not eliminate fluctuations against the dollar and the yen but this is not an argument for the UK alone to stand outside the ERM. In any case this argument overlooks the realignment which over the past decade has seen Britain trading more and more with her European neighbours – a process which will only accelerate after 1992. Figures 4.3 and 4.4 show vividly the steadiness of this convergence. The ERM would provide currency stability for half our exports.

The assertion that the time is not yet ripe for full British membership becomes less and less persuasive. Sir Geoffrey Howe, who as Chancellor and Foreign Secretary has acquired as good a grasp as any British minister of the potential advantages for Britain, told the Scottish Conservative Conference in Perth in 1988 with a touch of exasperation: 'We can't go on saying that for ever.' If we do, any British manufacturer with a significant business in Europe will have a strong incentive to relocate some of his capacity there. After ten years the protestations should now be dropped and Britain should take a step which will strengthen her economic armoury and intensify the fight against

Fig. 4.2 Percentage of Total UK Exports from EC and non-EC Countries

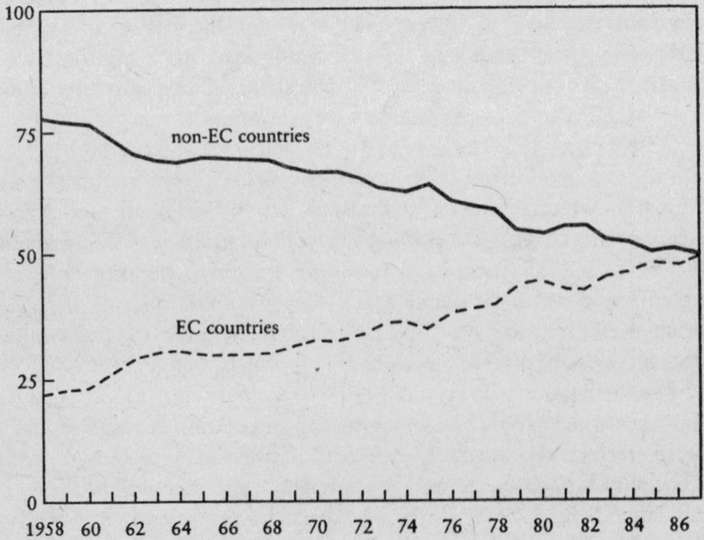

(Source PA Cambridge Economic Consultants)

inflation, as well as advance the unity of Europe.

European governments are in the middle of a searching re-examination of the Community, undertaken because of a belated realization of how unsteady its achievement was and how essential it had become to turn into reality the long-standing paper commitment to a competitive and effective market. The resounding preamble to the Rome Treaty – about eliminating the barriers which divided Europe and pooling its resources – had acquired a hollow ring. It was time for deeds to give effect to the words. The world had changed dramatically since the foundation of the Community.

The men and women upon whom we depend for the creation of Europe's wealth have to run a daily race over hurdles, while their rivals from Asia and America canter easily beside them on the flat. It is a brave fight but no contest. It is high time that the rules were changed. The position was summed up in a Chatham House Report, 'The EC: Progress

Fig. 4.3 Percentage of Total UK Imports from EC and non-EC Countries

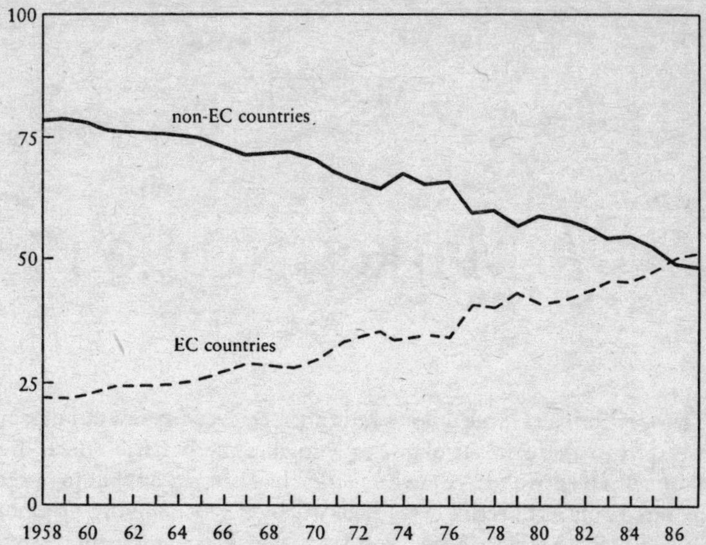

(Source PA Cambridge Economic Consultants)

or Decline?', which argued: 'It is not enough to hold on to those common policies that the community so far has.... If it is to survive, if it is to maintain and strengthen the loyalty of its member nations and their citizens, it needs to rediscover and demonstrate a sense of overriding common interests, *to regain in far more difficult circumstances the dynamism with which it began – before it is too late*' (author's emphasis). That challenge was sounded in 1983 but the search for the old dynamism has only just begun.

CHAPTER
5

A Market Solution

The way forward needed not a return to the drawing board but simply a return to the original plans 'to eliminate the barriers which divide Europe'. The drive to a common market had petered out but to restart it required only a collective exercise of will by the Community's members. British policy has since been firmly set within this context, our discretion limited by our treaty commitments. The journey on which the Community has embarked has two distinct phases: the creation of the single market by 1992 (including the ending of exchange controls and the free movement of capital between the member states by 1990) and the development of a common currency and a European Bank.

At the meeting of the European Council in Luxembourg in December 1985, the heads of government resolved to complete the internal market. The Single European Act amends the Treaty of Rome in a number of respects, drawing within one framework several separate proposals for completing the market. On the British side the by now familiar approach was evolutionary, a desire to allow events to take their course. The other Community members would have none of it. They insisted on a greater sense of urgency and at Luxembourg Britain was outvoted. We then accepted the majority view and the British Parliament ratified the Single Act in November 1986.

Eleven months before its adoption, Lord Cockfield had assumed office as one of the two British Commissioners. He was allocated responsibility for the implementation of the Act and he spent his four-year term in pursuing this objective with rare singlemindedness and effectiveness.

Arthur Cockfield had first come to prominence in the Conservative Party in the 1960s when, as a former senior official of the Inland Revenue, he was asked to advise the Shadow Cabinet on their tax strategies for when they returned to government. At the time he was the successful managing director of Boots, the drugs company, where he more than doubled their profits in six years. After the Conservatives regained office in 1979, he served as a Treasury Minister from 1979 to 1982, then entered the Cabinet as Secretary of State for Trade from 1982 to 1983.

Lord Cockfield's term as Commissioner was not renewed in 1989. If he was judged guilty of any offence, it can only have been that of obeying orders. He confronted his political masters with the consequences of their rhetoric. They asked for a single market and he set out in detail what they had to do to achieve it. This is uncharacteristic of the European Community, whose leaders find more satisfaction in uttering grandiloquent phrases than in facing facts, particularly facts which seem to threaten narrow national interest.

The Cockfield agenda shows no mercy. It is about deregulation and enhanced competition. It is a liberating crusade for capitalism. It identifies every barrier to the free movement of goods, people, services and capital. Anything that disrupts and distorts that goal is revealed and attacked. Different national practices, often evolved in the mists of history, are castigated if their vagaries might blur clear choices based on market forces.

The case for Europe must rest on the argument that we will achieve more for our people within a more competitive European market than they can hope for within a collection of purely national markets. Attempts have been made to measure those potential benefits. The most ambitious effort is the report, 'The Cost of Non-Europe', produced for the European Commission by a team led by Paolo Cecchini, who retired as Deputy Director-General of Internal Markets and Industrial Policy in 1988 after a career spent with the Commission. This report is openly propagandist. Convinced as I am of the advantages for Britain and her partners of moving towards a united Europe, I am sceptical of reports which attempt a spurious precision about events years ahead. As a businessman I did my best to look ahead in each year's budget; but every budget was changed, and changed again, as reality overtook its assumptions. As a national politician I have known even Chancellors of the Exchequer, with the infinite wisdom of the Treasury to guide them, update their forecasts within weeks of uttering them. I will therefore buy Cecchini's arguments but treat his statistics with caution.

The arguments themselves are powerful enough and easily digested in a complementary publication, 'The Economics of 1992', a study published in March 1988 by the European Commission. A single, open market will present companies with greater competition. As the market is enlarged, costs will be reduced by the removal of existing barriers: the different technical regulations, the delays and bureaucratic burdens that they cause, the lack of competition in public procurement and the immobility of labour all impose costs which have to be cut. In addition the confidence and stability of closer economic and monetary policy are essential to give the enlarged market the psychological boost from which real and lasting benefits will flow.

In 1985, the base year for the Cecchini calculations, the total gross domestic product of the Community was 3,300 billion ecu. The report is properly cautious about the unreliability of the figures but gives an outline of the magnitude of potential gains from the creation of a true European market:

A. The removal of direct frontier and associated costs: 1.8 per cent of goods internally traded, or 9 billion ecu.

B. Savings in industrial costs arising from such items as the abolition of conflicting technical standards: 2 per cent of industrial costs, or 40 billion ecu.

C. Enhanced market penetration and intensified competition in public procurement: 10 to 20 per cent of contract value, say 40 billion ecu.

D. The rationalization of industry to create more large-scale competitive companies (a large market can sustain more large companies in each sector and thus intensify competition): reductions of 1 to 7 per cent of costs, say 60 billion ecu.

E. The intensification of competition generally as companies respond to a more open market, the new investment generated to service that market, and deregulation which encourages the growth of small company activity: 140 billion ecu.

However cautious an approach we properly adopt, even a modest fraction of Cecchini's forecast would justify the effort. The European market is 40 per cent of the world market, so even a small improvement would benefit not only Europe but the world at large.

The Commission's study analyses two scenarios: first, the prospective gains from a mechanistic response to the proposed measures; and second, the additional gains that might flow from the momentum that a psychological enhancement can provide. The greater Europe's economic cohesion and the determination of its governments to pursue rigorous anti-inflation policies Community-wide, the better the prospect of higher growth levels gathering pace as the success of the policy creates confidence.

A number of general but fundamental conclusions emerge, notably that the real benefits of the enhanced market are more in the growing interplay of competitive economic forces – the genuine market – than in the technical adjustments of standards or removal of constraints. A sense of excitement generates its own added momentum.

So, what did Lord Cockfield set out to do? His proposals are grouped in the White Paper of June 1985 under three headings: physical, technical and fiscal barriers. His analysis examined what might need to be done to eliminate each barrier. Can it simply be moved? If not, can it be made less obstructive? How can this be achieved? How do different barriers interact? Will the removal of one barrier create another or inhibit other moves towards liberalization? From this scrutiny, the Cockfield plan set an agenda consisting initially of some 300 legislative proposals, later reduced to 279.

This is fine in theory but the political problems seem daunting. The plan requires the removal of all border controls by 1992 so that police and customs checks reflect the new unity of the market. Present controls cannot be removed overnight but the Cockfield plan proposes wherever possible to speed up procedures and to remove inconsistencies. Once improved arrangements affecting movement by road, rail, air and sea are in place, the customs controls within the market can go.

An original intention of the Treaty of Rome was to introduce a common tax base throughout the Community so that different national tax systems did not result in price distortions for the customer, nor in internal border delays. Moves to approximate taxes now present each Community country with peculiar problems. The British government has committed itself not to impose VAT on children's clothes and on food, and would risk unpopularity if it were to impose it on books and periodicals. Moreover, high taxes on tobacco and alcohol are supported by an unexpected coalition between a British Treasury interested in tax revenue and a society increasingly concerned with public health. Of course, if harmonization can be disguised in a counter-inflationary cloak, the Treasury can kill two birds with one stone, while few notice the irony.

France has different problems: with a more complex system and higher rates than in the UK, VAT produces 19 per cent of the French government's resources. Approximation downward of VAT means increases in other French taxes. What French politician is going to advocate that?

Things so often seem impossible before they are attempted. Ten years from now, few people are likely to remember what the arguments were about. Until then compromises will be found, with two-tier VAT levels offering one route to convergence and national derogations the last line of defence for the more reluctant nations.

Few politicians see any advantage in calling for tax increases which their governments decline to make. But if supporters of the British government have to defend increases in VAT there are arguments that will fortify them: they can point to compensating decreases in other taxes and stress the compensating adjustments of the index-linked tax and social security systems.

If VAT rates are approximated and applied across Europe, then customs and excise officials at internal frontiers need no longer be engaged in tax collection. There would be a loss of revenue collected at Europe's internal frontiers but business people would more speedily come to regard their market as an entity. Unless we can get the tax collectors off their backs, too many will still find exporting too much of a hassle.

This issue must not be confused with the battle against crime. There can be no let up here, but nothing in any existing proposals prevents the police from exercising their powers to stop and search suspects. There is no logic in the continued existence of red or green customs channels. Scrutinizing citizens at frontier posts, and random examination of a tiny fraction of vehicles and passengers, has not stopped the flow of drugs into Britain nor prevented the IRA from being able to move large supplies of weapons and explosives around the Community.

What is needed is more effective intelligence, more effective counter-terrorist forces, more specialist drug forces: in fact, a battle against international crime on a scale as yet not attempted. Saving the cost of the empty gesture of customs scrutiny would allow spending on new security measures which offer a greater hope of success. Closer co-operation with the security forces of Europe is a necessary part of that.

There are powerful and particular arguments for British participation in specialist counter-terrorist and anti-drug forces on a European scale. The Trevi group of Community ministers continually examines the ways and means of tackling these issues, and new arrangements will certainly be needed to deal with the documentation and physical checks on goods, animals and plants; but the Channel Tunnel will bring them about in any case. We shall need to be robust in assuring ourselves that our partners have adequate and enforceable arrangements for the admission of passengers and goods into the Community, and we can, of course, allow them to scrutinize ours. Drugs and arms, once inside Europe, are only a yacht trip away from Britain. By all means build random or spot checks into any continuing system – at frontiers or wherever seems appropriate – but to argue that the present arrangements are an essential or effective protection does not fit with the evidence.

With the removal of technical barriers, the Cockfield plan envisages a common approach to standards without at first attempting to harmonize every component of a product. All public procurement tenders must be open to competition from any companies within the Community and all services such as transport or insurance will be open to cross-frontier competition. The movement of labour is to be eased by the mutual recognition of qualifications; the free movement of capital across the national boundaries of most countries will be possible by 1990; and a European legal framework for companies will be created and will include a common approach to intellectual property rights, taxation and competition policy.

The discomfort which approximation of taxes promises for politicians looks slight beside the agonies of frustration that lie ahead for the businessmen. Companies which operate in a number of European countries must operate within different laws; fill in different forms, in different languages; submit to different standards; observe different public holidays; employ nationals with different qualifications; and adapt their methods to different social routines. Together these differences may require a host of extra employees to advise on and comply with local practice. This is the burden and the cost that larger companies must carry. There is also the hidden cost to the Community in deterring medium and smaller companies who turn their backs and give up.

Politicians and officials have been unravelling these complexities since the target of 1992 was set, and with no little success: half of the items on the Cockfield agenda were resolved by the spring of 1989. Professional qualifications are to be mutually recognizable, so that an appropriate national professional qualification will soon enable its holder to practise anywhere in the Community. The complication of initiating new general qualifications has been avoided but the result will be the same: professional institutes and societies will be induced by the pressures of the larger market place to harmonize the requirements of each national qualification. It is then but a short step to issue a common European qualification.

If the EC had been imposed by military conquest, a single legal and commercial framework might have been part of a conqueror's legacy. The builders of Europe are having to fit together a job lot of unmatched components, of differing ages and worth. Community companies need a certain and simple set of rules to live and work by – a single modern corporate structure that spans the market place. The idea is simple, the case for it unanswerable; and yet the practical difficulties at present seem insurmountable.

Worker participation raises particularly difficult problems, with high-profile politics well to the fore. The range of European practices, each imposing costs on companies and distorting competition, is vast. While British practice in this field is much improved, further progress is certainly urgently needed. The times have passed in Britain when a northern shipowner consulted his workforce every Monday morning on the quayside at 7.30. 'Isn't that a rather cold and inhospitable environment?' he was asked. 'Aye,' he replied, 'the meetings don't last long.' Those days have gone but British shipbuilding has gone too, for much the same reason.

The Conservative Party can take pride that some of the most important early legislation to improve working conditions was enacted in the 1840s at the instigation of Lord Shaftesbury, in the face of bitter opposition. This tradition has continued in the Party's history, in the social legislation of Neville Chamberlain in the 1920s and again in the health and safety legislation devised in the early 1970s.

This is not to argue for the structure of worker participation currently found in the Federal Republic or for the costs incurred by Dutch or French companies. We have travelled along different paths. But it is strange to hear established continental practices equated by some British observers with socialist centralism. The Germans have a flourishing capitalist system with a rather better record of industrial relations and productivity than Britain. I have yet to hear Unilever, Royal Dutch Shell or Philips dismissed as loony lefties by the Dutch or by anyone else. Other European societies have developed other forms of capitalism, different from the British, and the adjustments which will have to be made are practical, not ideological. The worst of all worlds would be achieved if the industrial relations of Europe were to be fought out in an atmosphere of trench warfare. There are no absolutely right ways to enthuse and motivate employees but there is certainly an absolutely wrong way and that is to ignore them. A highly skilled and educated workforce has a profound and continuing day-to-day contribution to make in the search for improved techniques and productivity. Each in their own way, European industries must harness the commitment of their workers and it should not take Japanese management to come here and show us how to do it.

There is, as it happens, a highly practical way forward. The Commission can devise a model European company, the objectives and constitution of which would be enshrined within the equivalent of what in Britain is called the Memorandum and Articles of Association. The model could have two tiers. Into the first and essential tier would go the items that relate to the purposes, powers, composition and structure of the company. Into the second would go the optional extras, one of which would deal with employment policies. A European company would have to follow European law for Schedule I items but would be bound only by national law for Schedule II items. Companies would be free to move items into Schedule I if they chose and thus bring themselves under European law.

The market would then exert its influence and management would locate their plants where the efficiencies of production attracted them, with consequent pressure on those parts of the European market which were found to impose unacceptable costs on their companies. German companies might find this a convenient tool with which to prise out some of their more expensive practices.

But it seems to me that here is an area in which Britain has missed a trick. We have focused on what we find unacceptable: we are clear about the things we are against. In our resistance to a rigid pattern of worker participation we are right, but we earn little credit for that because our overall attitude is seen as negative. It does not need to be. Britain has achieved a major advance as a share-owning democracy in the 1980s – an advance which owed much to the privatization of state industries. In 1974 there were 2.2 million shareholders in the UK; by

1988 this had increased dramatically to nine million. Within the Community we are among the leaders in the proportion of the population owning shares. But we would do well to study the effect of France's *Loi Monory*, introduced in 1978, which allows a taxpayer to set against tax a proportion of the cost of share purchases. This scheme – widely copied on the continent – is of much wider effect than Britain's Personal Equity Plan.

The initiative Britain should take in the context of European company law is to set out proposals, not to shift the responsibilities of management on to employees but to widen their opportunities to own shares. At the same time, and with the same intention of focusing minds of both managers and managed on the long-term health of the company, we should propose initiatives for a more direct relationship between companies, their pension funds and their pensioners. Combining the German option, whereby companies may invest the pension funds in the business, with the best British practice (for example in ICI, Unilever, Shell and BP) of electing representatives of pensioners to the fund managements boards, would offer exciting potential for Britain to lead Europe towards the capital-owning society in which we believe. Investing pension funds partly in the companies that make the wealth in the first place seems to me to have advantages over the centralized, institutionalized practices which prevail in Britain today. As the pension funds receive tax concessions on their investment income to the value of £4.4 billion, the opportunities to switch these incentives to the corporate sector are dramatic.

The creation of the single market may present problems for us in Europe but we have the advantage of being on the inside. What of those outside and suspicious? If we are hell-bent on creating a single market, for whom are we doing it and at whose expense? The language, the exhortations, belong to the battlefield. We are to be strong; to win in the world; to look the most powerful nations in the eye; to protect our destiny. It sounds – and is designed to sound – great on the hustings of Hanover or Hastings. But the reverberations seem ominous in Washington and Tokyo. With mutual suspicion growing ever more intense around the world, and each trader ready to hit back at the first sign of protectionism, real or imagined, the free-trade forces had hoped for the opposite signal from the General Agreement on Tariffs and Trade (GATT) negotiations in Montreal in 1988. The Prime Minister of Canada, Brian Mulroney, voiced his concern that the world would '... slip backwards towards more insidious forms of protectionism'. The talks failed to progress and a slip backwards may well be in prospect. The anxieties are everywhere to be seen.

In much of the world, particularly in the booming export-led economies of East Asia, there is growing concern that the Americans and Europeans could be tempted to form defensive regional blocs. Japan suspects that the European Community's single market after 1992 could become a 'Fortress Europe'. In November 1988 Karl-Heinz Narjes, a vice-president of the European Commission, suggested that Japan pay retroactive compensation to European exporters for having kept them out of its markets for years. Although his comments were disowned by Brussels, there was an outcry from a jittery Japan.

Other signals have come from France, whose Defence Minister, Jean-Pierre Chevenement, recently attacked the idea of a free-trading Europe wide-open to its commercial partners and called for new customs duties – already under consideration in Brussels – on the import of military equipment. France is at the moment fighting to restrict imports of Japanese cars made in Britain.

Japan entered the big league of exporters, her success founded on a high economic growth rate and a rapid enlargement of a protected domestic market, her efforts orchestrated by a highly supportive government. A deliberately planned, rapid penetration by Japanese products of the United States and European markets, and of the newly industrialized markets of the Pacific, has caused many in the West – and particularly in the US – to question the existing liberal framework for world trade. The questioning is made more anxious by the high penetration increasingly achieved by a number of other developing countries such as Taiwan, Korea and Hong Kong.

The activities of multinational companies have added to the unease as they set up manufacturing capacity in developing countries with relatively cheap labour. Manufactured goods from these low-cost countries, imported 'back home', are presented as job destroying and an irritant to balance of payment difficulties.

The Japanese and the Europeans are concerned about the trade practices of the United States and particularly the Omnibus Trade and Competitiveness Act passed in August 1988, which provides for tougher action against nations indulging in 'unfair' trading practices.

The Act leaves 'a wide-open door for protectionist legislation', as Martin S. Feldstein, a former chairman of the President's Council of

Economic Advisers, said recently. The share of total US imports subject to quotas or official restraint has climbed from 10 to 25 per cent. The President has been granted sweeping powers to impose barriers against nations found to be guilty of unfair trading practices. 'It creates a new kind of political pressure on the President to do something,' said Mark Anderson, an economist with the AFL-CIO. It emphasizes 'fair' not 'free' trade. In October 1988, the US Treasury issued the first reports required under the revised law and promptly raised charges against Taiwan and South Korea for manipulating their currencies to gain an unfair trade advantage.

The Omnibus Trade Act reflects Washington's increasing impatience with its Asian and European trading partners and is a highly visible sign of its toughening attitude as the administration comes under increased pressure to trim the trade deficit. President Bush is expected to maintain policies of 'selective' protectionism. 'Anything is possible,' said Claude Barfield, an economist with the American Enterprise Institute. 'If the administration needs the support of some Senator from an industrialized state who is under pressure to produce some results on trade, there might be some arrangement.' In matters of free trade everyone sins, while all proclaim their virtue.

Yet free trade remains the key to world prosperity. The gradual move towards freer commerce this century has contributed dramatically to the wealth of nations. The trade wars of the 1930s led only to slump and depression. The establishment of GATT in 1947 was a breakthrough. Twenty-three countries committed themselves to lowering tariffs and to opposing import restrictions, state subsidies and practices which might frustrate tariff agreements. But today GATT is increasingly seen as an ineffective and slow-moving forum, where everything must be agreed and nothing can be imposed. Although world trade has exploded since it was first set up, new circumstances are replacing the old.

Nigel Lawson in his Chatham House speech in January 1989 set out the British position very clearly: 'We have consistently fought to break down barriers, to reduce protection, to free up trade. Not just within Europe.... Just as it makes no sense for Britain to isolate herself from what is happening in Europe, so it makes no sense for Europe to isolate herself from the rest of the world.'

As long as the United States and Western Europe led the world in industrial development, they had an obvious interest in keeping other markets open. Now that other countries, led by Japan, are rapidly gaining ground, it is the Europeans and Americans who are on the defensive. European business leaders have warned that increased competition in the European Community will heighten demands from European companies for external protection at the EC frontiers, on the grounds that they cannot be expected to compete with Japan and their European rivals simultaneously.

The Europeans insist that their trade relations will be determined by the principle of 'reciprocity' and that this will make free trade easier, not impede it; but the Community's trading partners fear that it will lead to a 'tit-for-tat' approach that will squeeze them out of Europe. They were given some grounds for such fears in December 1988, when a trade war threatened to break out between Europe and America over the EC ban on £150 million worth of American hormone-fed meat imports.

That crisis was a warning that the only sensible trade wars are those fought to make trade freer. Every quota, subsidy or tariff is a tax on some consumer. It should not need Mr Gorbachev's desperate attempts at reform to remind us that the most efficient economies are consumer-led, not producer-protected. Europe's 320 million or so consumers have a shared interest in their own trading bloc – the world's largest – being the most competitive and least obstructive to business. America, with its growing interest in exports and overseas investment, should be urged to see the 1988 free-trade agreement with Canada as the right precedent for dialogue with Europe.

Europe will increasingly identify its own legitimate trading and consumer interests. To fight for these interests should be a stated aim of European policy, not seen as an act of doubtful political purpose. Europe must pursue these trading interests with coherence and confidence. After many years of practising neither virtue, the Community – spurred on by the prospect of 1992 – is rapidly acquiring both. A united and harder-hitting European Community in its battles for freer markets, particularly with the Japanese – over everything from financial services to building contracts – will find an ally in America.

Britain should not forget the advantages of empire in claiming particular virtue as an upholder of free trade. We ruled much of the world's surface and that gave us a head start. It is as well for us to remember, indeed, that we abandoned imperial preference only when the United States made it a condition of her post-war financial aid. (It was this that caused the veteran imperialist, Leo Amery, to persuade Churchill that the imperial markets would have to be replaced with those of Europe.)

None of this reduces our need to ensure that the Community is not hijacked by specific, and nationalistic, protectionist lobbies. We must advocate domestic competition and its international equivalent of freer trade; and we must encourage a measured response where the forces against us are seriously protectionist and not simply more competitive. Europe will need to choose firm ground and appropriate weapons to fight for its legitimate interests: we want no repetition of the hormone beef fiasco. The selfish interest of each nation complicates the dismantling of fresh barriers. In the end, like all negotiations, it is a matter of will and of muscle. Britain, committed now to be one of the major players, must use – and enjoy the use of – Europe's collective strength. The real problem facing the Western world is not addressed by throwing paper darts at the half-open doors of Fortress Europe while failing to explain how we assault the granite-like structure of Fortress Japan. While we can admire the competitive vigour of their domestic market place, we have to solve the riddle of how to get into it. That will not be achieved by rhetoric alone: Japanese economic imperialism is made of sterner stuff.

The Commission in Brussels is charged with levelling the playing fields. We should not see the substitution of European for domestic regulations as anything more than a necessary part of the transition from national markets to the Europe-wide domestic market. To smooth away differences in national regulations is to promote competition, not suffocate it. From time to time the Commission will be over-zealous, sometimes even crass in its misjudgments. But not all the criticism of it is honest: sometimes governments open fire on Brussels to distract attention from compromises to which they themselves have assented but for which they fear they may be blamed.

Europe is in the business of competition and has no choice: Britain should support that and rejoice. In practice we are creating a capitalist Europe and we must get its capitalism right. There is no room for socialism and if there were, it would only increase the urgency of the argument that Britain should play a leading role in influencing the direction of the Community. In presenting this discussion as right versus left we may excite a narrow political following but only by alienating natural allies on the continent.

This leaves us with the most controversial of the substantive issues: economic and monetary union. Britain's reservations about the Delors committee, which is examining the possible role of a European central bank and the options for further monetary union, have a familiar ring. Britain was a sceptic but went along with the decision of the European Council at Hanover in June 1988 that the inquiry should be pursued and the concept of monetary union either dismissed as unrealistic or turned into flesh and bones.

The sixteen members of the committee, which includes the Governor of the Bank of England, sit under the chairmanship of Jacques Delors, acting in his personal capacity and not as President of the European Commission – an arrangement which is one of the more bizarre compromises in the Community's history. Delors was due to report in time for the Council of Ministers to discuss his findings in the summer of 1989.

Some see a central bank as compatible only with the abdication of national sovereignty and the creation of political union. Others take a more relaxed view and see the committee's objective as merely to advance a step beyond the common exchange rate mechanism – in effect, a more sophisticated degree of co-ordination between the central banks of Europe, with daily working practices entrusted to a committee composed of central bankers, acting with a certain degree of autonomy but overridden in the last resort by the intervention of national governments.

Initially there were four different camps. In one there were the minimalists, who argued that there should never be a central bank or common currency. Then there were those advocates of treaty amendments to establish monetary union but with delayed implementation; thirdly, the evolutionaries, who favoured a step-by-step approach; and finally, the 'market-firsters', arguing that implementation of the Single Act should be allowed to create a demand for new institutions before the politicians attempted to create them. The real debate was focused on the arrangements which would give some degree of union but would leave political power in national hands: a European monetary institution, for example, responsible for monitoring events and with power to make recommendations to governments but without the ability to hold reserves or issue currency.

There will not be a massive transfer of sovereignty as a result of the Delors committee report. Any such recommendation would require unanimous support in the Council of Ministers and endorsement by each national parliament; any debate on far-reaching and controversial proposals would be protracted and divisive, and would distract energy from the pursuit of more immediate goals. But the debate about economic and monetary union will be conducted in elastic terms. People can define words to mean whatever they want. Some argue that a common currency is unattainable without a central European reserve bank, independent of national politics, while others argue that it is the rapid expansion of the use of the ecu which has created the need for such a supporting structure.

Nothing will be achieved quickly but there are some principles that should guide our approach: European institutions should grow and their growth should not be forced; sovereignty, even in penny packets, should be transferred to a higher authority only where there is an overwhelming case for it; initial commitments should be voluntary and, to encourage confidence, should be retractable also. But against this must be set the responsibility of statesmen to combine such proper caution with a practical perspective of what nations can achieve when they are correctly led. The art of the possible is not necessarily the defence of the *status quo*.

The programme for the 1992 single market will increase interdependence of macro-economic policy as currencies flow freely across borders. The ability of central banks to define and attain money supply targets or set interest rates independently is already prejudiced by the flow of currencies in the world market place. National currencies have prices imposed on them. It must suit Britain as much as the rest of Europe to seek stability in the market where most of our trade is conducted.

The EMS must in any case be strengthened to cope with the increased strains imposed by free capital movement. A closer association of monetary policies will be needed if the single market itself is not to be put at risk and member nations are not to fall back behind new barriers (as the French proposal for a withholding tax on the interest on bank deposits foreshadows) as protection against currency outflows precipitated by diverging economic performance.

In any discussion there is a fixed point. No progress is negotiable that challenges the realities created by the strength of the deutschmark and the independence from political direction of the *Bundesbank*. German memories of pre-war inflation and its savage consequences, combined with their pride in the disciplined advance of their currency to its present pre-eminence, define the room for manoeuvre. But there is little here to concern us save the pain of emulation, since they are further down a road along which it is the ambition of the Conservative Party to travel.

No truly unified market can exist without a single currency. We in Europe have twelve different ones and, so long as divergent economic policies are reflected in exchange rate adjustments, a single common currency is unattainable. As we have seen, however, Europe has successfully evolved a parallel 'currency', the European Currency Unit, or ecu.

One casualty of the oil crisis in the early 1970s was the Bretton Woods system of fixed exchange rates. As part of the European quest for greater stability, and to meet the demand for a measure of value less subject to fluctuating exchange rates, the ecu was born. (Strictly, it was resurrected, for the *ecu* was originally a gold coin circulating in thirteenth-century Europe, during the reign of Louis IX of France.) Technically the modern ecu is not a currency; it is a unit of value, calculated about once every five years by reference to a basket of European currencies adjusted to reflect the strength of the different currencies in the Community. The escudo and the peseta will be included in the basket during the adjustment in the autumn of 1989. The ecu will then reflect all the Community currencies. The precise relationships of each currency to the ecu are governed by reference to objective economic criteria. A report in the *Economist* of 23 February 1989 by Christopher Johnson, chief economic advisor to Lloyds Bank in London, gave an assessment of the likely composition of the basket after the forthcoming autumn adjustment (see Table 5.1).

Within the ERM the ecu provides a means of measuring the divergent performance of individual currencies against the other members of the system. It is a unit of account with important defensive properties, linked as it is to more than one currency. It acts as a reserve currency and as a currency in banking and bond markets. Its use had by 1989 reached substantial proportions both within and without the Community. In 1987 the European Commission estimated that 3 billion ecu per day were dealt in by individuals and 10 billion by banks in foreign exchange dealings. Trade argeements between the USSR and Sweden and between Italy and France have recently been concluded in ecu.

The British government has given strong support to the increased use of this common currency and, indeed, took an important initiative when the Treasury began to issue ecu bills in the autumn of 1988 to provide underwriting for the liquidity of the market. Britain has consistently supported a higher proportion of currency reserves being held in ecu.

Table 5.1 The Ecu Basket Weights

	September 89? %
German mark	30.2
French franc	17.9
Sterling	14.1
Dutch guilder	9.5
Italian lira	9.5
Belgian franc	7.7
Danish krone	2.5
Greek drachma	1.2
Irish punt	1.1
Luxembourg franc	0.3
Spanish peseta	5.0
Portuguese escudo	1.0
	100

The economies of Europe are converging in many ways. The governors of all the national central banks are in constant contact and the committee of central bankers meets frequently. This process will become more formal; and, as the scale of capital movements increases, the ecu will develop as the European currency most frequently used by companies to finance and conduct their growing home trade. The pressure will continue to grow to fuse economic policies in order to sustain the process.

It does not matter what you call this new monetary coherence; it is clearly not a fully fledged central bank. But it will undoubtedly develop its own secretariat and it will provide advice to member countries on the key elements of their policy that may affect exchange rate parities. Governments will find it difficult to ignore the advice because the markets will certainly heed it as whispers spread.

The British government, having decided to allow the Governor of the Bank of England to take part in the Delors committee, is playing a cautious and prudent hand: present at the top table, determined to give nothing away, but seeking to influence the evolution of the conference in Britain's interests. This is a defensible negotiating position, because the situation is fluid and many national interests are at risk. But if it were to prove that the British representative was there not to negotiate but to spoil, then the most serious risks would have been taken with Britain's national interest.

I accept that the tensions involved in completing a single European market may prove too much. There are plenty of historical grounds to indicate that the warring, scrapping instincts of the Europeans might reassert themselves. The European enterprise may grind to a halt as it has before, especially if the economic weather takes a turn for the worse. But the British government is now committed by treaty to the more optimistic alternative: we have chosen to pursue a European destiny.

We have embarked upon a journey in which our eleven partners are as influential in determining the pace and direction of progress as we are. The very nature of the journey will raise the sights of our people. The industrial and commercial managers and the workforce are being asked to force the pace towards European-scale companies. On the shop floor half the packing cases are heading for Europe. Our children will have careers in European companies promoting them to Milan as well as Manchester. Changing aspirations and experiences, new working practices, enlarged market strategies – these will all create their own momentum. The politicans can influence the rate of flow of this European current; but if they try to stem it they will be swept aside.

No European nation would countenance submerging its institutions in some banking conglomeration, so there is no fear of that happening. What Europe needs and intends to have is a logical, patient, systematic evolution of arrangements which will simplify and make more efficient the process of trading in goods and services, and will create in managers the confidence to act in the context of a single market.

The best of British managers and board members will demand – as will their equivalents on the continent – that politicians work out something better than the present obstacle course. Companies enjoined by their government to embrace a European market, and to stand up to the competition of Japan and America, are not going to tolerate the inefficiencies for much longer.

But there is still the timorous view that the politicians might get too far out ahead, stumble in some exchange rate crisis, become discredited and thereby harm the cause of European unity. It is therefore better, say the faint-hearted, if the market place creates its own demand for change to which politicians can then respond with appropriate structures.

This typically British approach might present fewer difficulties if it were for Britain alone to decide – but, of course, it is not. Somewhere between this evolutionary approach, which waits upon the market place, and the politically more challenging and bolder continental approach of establishing a framework to guide the market, we will no doubt find a compromise. Britain must be wary lest the cautious approach proves unacceptable to our partners, who may then go on without us, creating organizations to suit their own financial and monetary institutions. As Sir Nicholas Goodison, a former chairman of the London Stock Exchange, has said, 'The momentum is such that economic and monetary union in Europe are now on the agenda for practical action.' He spoke there for much of British business, and he was right.

From all of this, companies will evolve on a European scale from mergers and acquisitions, and Europe's financial institutions will be forced to meet their needs. European companies must have efficient and competitive services to transfer money, finance trade and promote growth, and the consumers of Europe too will expect the same efficient service for financing their house purchases, banking, savings and insurance needs. The revolution in communications, already well advanced, will bombard people daily through television and newspapers telling them where the best services are, what the lowest prices are, what other people are enjoying. The market place will do the rest and no single government, no national interest, will be able to resist it.

There are no rights, only opportunities. The distribution of benefits will follow the market and there is no rule that says that, if one national company or sector loses, others in the same country will make compensating gains. Whole national economies or whole regions may fail to share in the general increase in wealth if their lack of enterprise or of natural endowments puts them at a disadvantage.

There is a clear warning here for Britain, though not for us alone. There are substantial gains for the taking and all of our partners hope to be beneficiaries. But none of them can count on such good fortune and no one in Britain should dare to. Government has an inescapable role of leadership, in shaping the new market and in helping to equip Britain to thrive in it. But success is not in the government's gift alone: Britain's companies and the people who work for them will determine the measure of our success.

CHAPTER
6

Our Agenda: Britain's Opportunity

Politicians seeking election know that the promise of change wins a ready response. The disgruntled and frustrated, vested interests under pressure, fat cats eager for more cream, all make receptive audiences if they are promised that things will be different. Very rarely does it occur to them that change might be uncomfortable. To argue that Britain must sell what the market wants conjures up a vision of some glossy motor car delivered gift-wrapped to the door, not the end of that cosy monopoly which the family firm has enjoyed since granddad's day. A clarion call for Britain to lead Europe is more likely to get an audience to its feet than the sombre thought that our deficit in manufacturing trade with Europe could be but a warning of worse to come.

So it is with 1992 – safety belts fastened, we are on our way and there is no turning back. Or are we? Is it all words, the easy phrases that hide the lack of adequate action? It is time for change but who is moving? Are the boardrooms deciding? Is the British government ahead of the game? What do we need to do to win?

There are many unanswered questions but they do not obscure the opportunities for Britain in a single European market, nor the uncomfortable fact that opportunities confer no rights. The new openings presented by 1992 will find many British companies ready to seize the advantages of a dramatically expanded home market of more than

320 million consumers. But for some companies, some industrial sectors, even whole regions, the change will present overwhelming problems. There will be both winners and losers.

As we weigh the challenge of 1992, we can be sure that Britain has at least two significant assets. The first is a fact of inheritance: Britain's position as an English-speaking country, with a tradition of open trading, attracts inward investment from companies outside Europe which are anxious to establish themselves within the Community. The second notable asset is no accident but something that the country has secured by its efforts during the 1980s: British companies have grown steadily more competitive after ten years of a free enterprise climate, of market discipline and deregulation, and of an expanding economy.

Since 1980 the growth of manufacturing productivity in this country – more than 5 per cent a year – has been faster than in any of our major competitors, though starting from a lower base, and manufacturing output as a whole has increased by more than 8 per cent. Trade union reform has created a new attitude of co-operation and enterprise in industry and, as a result, the number of days lost through strikes has fallen dramatically from nine million in 1978, the last full year of Labour government, to fewer than four million in the year ending October 1988. Unemployment dropped by four points between 1986 and 1988, yet the rate of increase of average earnings rose by only 1 per cent, and manufacturing unit-wage costs have actually fallen steadily from 1985. Britain's 1978/9 budget deficit of £9.2 billion (5.3 per cent of GDP) was transformed into a surplus of £13.9 billion in 1989 (2.9 per cent of GDP). Business taxation has been sharply reduced: since the 1984 budget, corporation tax has been reduced by stages from 52 to 35 per cent; the rate for small companies has been reduced to 25 per cent. There has been an average net increase in the number of VAT registered companies since 1980 of around 500 a week – a total net increase of 224,000 between 1980 and 1987. Privatization has returned major undertakings – and well over half a million jobs – to the private sector, greatly boosting efficiency.

Rightly, the government is determined to take advantage of both these assets but its success will be measured by the response of Britain's companies to its exhortations to exploit the market. No one can question that the Department of Trade and Industry, with the co-operation of the CBI, the chambers of commerce, the trade associations and numerous professional bodies, have thrown themselves wholeheartedly into the campaign for 1992. The message has been clear and well publicized. Though a late starter, Britain has now done as much as any of her partners and more than some. By the beginning of 1989 most British firms had been made aware of the significance of 1992; the DTI's campaign 'Europe – Open for business' had achieved its primary purpose. A remarkable 90 per cent of businesses, responding to a poll, claimed to be aware that something was up.

But how much had they understood and what did they mean to do to prepare? In January 1989 the CBI surveyed a sample of its members to find that 90 per cent of companies with sales over £20 million were undertaking no market research on the continent; 93 per cent were taking no initiatives to train employees in continental languages; 95 per cent had no sales agents in the rest of the EC, and only one in a hundred was opening any new manufacturing plants on the continent. The findings read more like an obituary notice for those companies than a response to the government's leadership.

From my earliest days as a salesman of advertising space, I can recall that all too familiar refrain: 'I like your new magazine. Come back to me when it's a success and I'll see what I can do.' If that is Britain's corporate response, we are in trouble. I hope that the overwhelming majority of British firms will rise above that attitude; and fear that the rest will not be around long enough to do more than temporary harm. All the same, I wait with fascination to meet the first industrialist to ask in 1993 why no one told him!

In 1988 UK Limited (now, I suppose, UK plc) turned in a visible trade deficit in excess of £20 billion and a balance of payments deficit of £14 billion. The benefits of North Sea oil are less evident, while the cushion of the proceeds of privatization is only temporary. It cannot all be the fault of the politicians! Norman Tebbit dropped a hint to the unemployed to get on their bikes. If the CBI sample is a true reflection, the 90 per cent of Britain's trading companies whose managers gave those depressing answers had better get off their bottoms.

The approach of 1992 is forcing those British companies which are determined to survive and succeed to lift their horizons and develop imaginative strategies. But what are the rest doing? Awareness that a market is to be created never sold a lollipop. It is the salesman with the product that someone wants – to an appropriate specification and at a price that makes sense – who alone can bring home the bacon.

First of all, British companies need an analysis of the likely impact of the new legislation on existing markets and customers, and then they must study the other EC markets. Do they have people who are fluent in the languages of the new markets? Is their information technology sufficient for providing that added competitive edge? Are the products adequately designed and how will they compare in the new context?

If a company decides to expand in Europe, there is a range of options – organic growth, strategic alliances, joint ventures, mergers, full acquisitions, taking minority interests and making grass-roots investments. Whichever option is chosen, further decisions follow. For example, is the distribution strategy adequate? Location poses difficult questions for decision. Some companies may decide to relocate closer to the new distribution networks – a development which threatens to exacerbate Europe's regional problems, though distribution needs alone will not determine location. Property acquisition is a major factor, and property issues are not covered directly by the single market programme. Many EC member states have a different legal basis for property and different forms of land-holding to ours; different taxes on ownership and occupation; different planning procedures and restrictions. Having threaded their way through this maze, companies must then determine the best financial arrangement and whether to buy or lease. The availability of regional aid or EC financial assistance can greatly affect net acquisition costs.

Next, they must discover what sources of funding are available and whether they can benefit most from expansion through organic growth – establishing offices in other member states – or by the acquisition of existing firms on the continent. In weighing these choices, companies will need to know how EC financial legislation will affect their business. Even this framework is not stable: many of the present compromises are designed to overcome short-term hurdles while the market smooths out the underlying differences. They must look ahead and gauge what lasting arrangements are likely to emerge. Strength and market domination will count, so current marketing strategies must be reconsidered from top to bottom in order to cope with the scale of the expanded market.

The big companies – the household names – are experienced in international markets and in many cases already have subsidiaries or associate companies in other European countries. From their own experience they will know that the European Commission's proposals and the directives so far adopted will affect a small portion of the single market; and that widespread differences of culture and taste will remain.

A recent Hill Samuel report emphasized that it is '... as crucial for companies to spend as much time studying competitor reactions as it is for them to absorb the detailed implications of EC regulations'. Will existing prices remain competitive, given that prices for similar goods and services currently differ widely throughout the Community? Hill Samuel's study argues that 'some of the most serious consequences of 1992 may be felt in existing pricing policies and profitability'. Every company therefore needs a defensive as well as an offensive strategy. You may not have worked out yet how to attack them but you can be sure that someone is out there calculating how best to attack you. American, Japanese and a host of non-EC companies are as determined to get a share of the market as other European companies are to expand theirs.

If companies feel unable to assess where they are vulnerable, there are plenty of people ready to advise them. The advice may turn out not to be worth much but absorbing it will at least clear the mind. They should put a senior person (not a committee) in charge, with direct access to the board; not someone soon to be pensioned off but someone with a career to make and who will be around to answer for what he does or does not do. On the desk of every chairman there should by now be a list of questions to which he wants answers about what 1992 holds for his company and a date by which a named person is going to provide those answers: 'Action this day'.

There is no excuse. Across my desk every week comes a flood of invitations to attend conferences, seminars and workshops in which the right questions are usually raised. Only the leadership of each company can see to it that the right answers – different in each case – are found and acted upon. In truth Britain depends upon its companies themselves to do this. Companies in industries at the top of today's growth league may stay there only briefly, while within relatively weak sectors there will be dynamic manufacturers who confound the experts.

While the first and most dramatic changes are likely to occur in the bigger companies, the growth predictions for the enlarged market rest in large part on the benefits of enhanced competition and deregulation. This, coupled with the shake-out in employment to which I have referred, will repeat in Europe what has been so conspicuously evident in Britain since the early 1980s: the stimulus to small-scale entrepreneurial businesses. It is a dynamism that Europe must embrace.

The difficulty, especially at a time of high economic activity, is to interest the smaller company in exploring export opportunities. Innovative and competitive products from small companies may be incorporated in the products of their larger brethren but somehow these small concerns must be persuaded that their future lies in serving the larger companies of all Europe, not just of Britain.

For most of our manufacturing companies the opportunities of 1992 will flow from existing experience. There will be fewer barriers and more equal competition but the ball-park won't change. The same is not true for many of our financial services companies. They are presented with an even greater challenge, since many of the 1992 changes will strip away protective regulations from their continental counterparts and open up markets previously closed to all but national businesses.

The City of London is ahead of the field in deregulation. Other financial centres in the EC have yet to advance along the same learning curve and, by the time they do, London's experience will have made it all the fitter to challenge their newly deregulated markets. In almost every area, London already operates on a larger scale than the financial centres of continental Europe. Over three-quarters of a million people in Britain, almost 4 per cent of all employees, work in banking and insurance. The City's net overseas earnings exceeded £9 billion in 1988, of which about half came from the insurance industry.

The City's success can be attributed to a number of factors – its long history as a financial centre and its inherited expertise; the availability of qualified personnel; its position in the time-zone between the US and Japan; the emergence of English as the world's dominant commercial language; and the long-established openness of London to foreign banks and financial firms.

The City of London is a centre of service industries. The Bank of England holds a loose sway, presiding over a maze of clearing and merchant banks, stockbrokers and market-makers, unit trusts, investment managers and pension funds. The influence and skill of these companies should enable Britain to extend its already powerful domestic and international base into Europe-wide success, particularly in three areas which present real opportunities: banking, insurance and the creation of a European stock exchange.

The European Commission has put forward about two dozen directives – part of the Cockfield agenda – designed to allow financial institutions, including banks and insurance companies, to trade freely within the Community. With the free movement of capital by 1990 provided for by the Single European Act, the relevant directives of this programme are designed to enable a financial firm anywhere in the Community to open a branch in any member state, subject to the supervision of the authorities in its home country. When the Second Banking Directive is implemented, a bank's authorization in the UK will act as a 'passport' giving access to a wide range of banking business in any EC state, the Bank of England's regulatory competence being recognized by all.

The British clearing banks, though household names in Britain, stand relatively low in the world league, because their economic hinterland has simply been too small and access to a large domestic market is critical. The top four European banks, ranked by asset size, are French or German. *Crédit Agricole*, *Banque Nationale de Paris*, *Deutsche Bank* and *Crédit Lyonnais* each holds larger assets than Barclays, Britain's largest bank.

But ownership of the banks tells only part of the story. London is an international financial centre. The majority of loans transacted by British banks are in foreign currencies rather than sterling. In June 1988, external loans in dollars ($488 billion) and yen ($92 billion) accounted for 28.6 per cent and 5.4 per cent respectively of the loans by banks operating in London. Moreover, by far the largest part of loan business is transacted by foreign banks, predominantly Japanese and American. Even counting their domestic lending, UK banks now have only 48 per cent of the total bank assets in the UK. American banks have 12 per cent, Japanese have 32 per cent. As long as the business flows through London, much of the profit is earned here and the jobs will stay.

From the British clearing banks' point of view, retail banking on the continent is virtually a closed book. The market is saturated with existing branches of established banks. The cost of setting up branch networks from scratch is daunting and would have to be limited to major cities. Barclays estimates that to set up a branch system comparable with its high street presence in the UK would cost £12 billion. To acquire existing bank networks on the continent would also be expensive. It is more attractive to market services through other firms, anxious to spread their existing high fixed-cost overheads, than to set up in competition.

Even mergers and acquisitions are at the moment taking place on a smaller scale in banking than in some other sectors, though a significant number of continental banks are buying 10 per cent stakes in each other.

Article 221 of the Treaty of Rome requires member states to treat other EC nationals in the same way as their own in their participation in the capital of a company. However, most governments maintain formal or informal controls on foreign ownership of banks and tensions may be expected over takeovers of major banks. British banks are more likely to be on the receiving end, in spite of the Bank of England's strong indication that clearing banks are off-limits to foreign predators, because their shares are cheap by continental standards. Pressure on profits in the early years of increased competition will make banks more vulnerable.

One way forward, however, may be through cross-border alliances which will allow firms to sell each other's products – for example, a life insurance company marketing mortgages for a foreign credit institution or a smaller commercial bank offering products on behalf of an insurer from another EC country. British banks and building societies could succeed with only marketing representation on the continent provided they concentrate on areas where they have comparative advantage, such as mortgage lending, foreign exchange dealing, investment management, private banking and life insurance. But if the United States abolishes the 'Glass-Steagall' rules, which prevent traditional banking from undertaking investment banking, the bulk of American securities business could return to Wall Street.

Britain is well placed to exploit the significant opportunities which will emerge within the insurance field. A directive giving firms the freedom to provide non-life insurance across borders was adopted in June 1988. Further directives aim to secure the same freedoms for life and motor insurance. With a population of some 320 million, compared with 220 million in the US, the Community has 22 per cent of the world's premium income against America's 50 per cent and Japan's 17 per cent. The potential for growth is therefore substantial.

The larger UK insurers – six of the largest fifteen in Europe are British – have long experience of international business, with worldwide networks of branches, subsidiaries and agents. The North American and Commonwealth markets have traditionally produced a greater volume of business for them than the Community, because a common language and traditional relationships have encouraged UK firms to concentrate their efforts there. Up to now they have neglected, or been denied, access to the tougher European markets. The removal of barriers and the strength of our industry should change all that.

The UK insurance market is already open to worldwide competition; none of the other EC markets is as free. Open competition has already required UK insurers constantly to develop and improve organizational efficiency and to serve their customers with maximum flexibility. British insurance policies offer a greater range of choice, sophistication and flexibility than those available generally in other EC markets, giving the UK insurance industry the infrastructure to compete successfully. It may take time for these benefits to flow and a necessary precondition is the free cross-border transfer of personal savings – something which not every European capital is thought likely to welcome.

Despite Britain's competitive edge, it will not be easy to break into more diverse European markets. Many customers are intensely nationalistic and prising them away from their existing relationships will be difficult. Much business on the continent is associated with family firms established over several generations. Others are publicly owned: for example, four of the largest insurance companies in France. Government-owned operations are often served only by government-owned insurance companies. These traditional practices will not immediately change, even with the new competitiveness of the single market, but early progress may be made by British insurers more easily through the development of specialist and regional markets.

The British government's support for the Commission's 1992 proposals for financial services is consistent with its record in deregulating and promoting competition within the UK financial system. One of the first acts of the incoming Conservative administration in 1979 was to abolish exchange controls. Since then the government has ended direct controls on bank lending, opened the acceptance market to foreign banks and sanctioned a range of new financial instruments.

It would be wrong to see deregulation of London's markets as a preparation for Europe alone. The change reflected a global trend towards the internationalization of financial markets and it was designed to enable the City to maintain its leading role. But it has given Britain an added competitive edge at a particularly fortunate moment, when deregulation and enhanced competition are about to sweep Europe. The changes were not painless: the replacement of the former regimes of the London Stock Exchange with those introduced by the Financial Services

Act has led to a different set of values administered by unfamiliar faces in newly created posts. The seeds of bureaucracy sprout easily and anxieties grow in their shadow. The new regulatory regimes seemed likely at one time to strangle the City with complexity and detail, and the less regulated markets on the continent – notably Luxembourg – watched in eager anticipation. Good sense has since prevailed and the bureaucrats have retreated. London showed an encouraging determination to win – a determination which loosened the grip of the Department of Trade and Industry. This escape from suffocation by intrusive domestic regulation has brought the new competitive opportunity within reach.

Spanish financial services are the most expensive on the continent; Italy, France and Belgium have costlier insurance policies than Britain's; banking services are more expensive in Germany and France. There should, therefore, be immediate benefits available for British corporate banking and commercial insurance. However, the other member countries will seek to extract concessions from Britain, as a *quid pro quo* for opening their markets to our more competitive companies. The British financial sector will want to watch with hawk-like attention their continental rivals, whose governments, while proclaiming the advantages of open competition, may in practice try to rig their home markets in their national self-interest. The British government, too, will need to be on its toes.

The Second Banking Directive and the Investment Services Directive specifically raise the issue of reciprocity. They provide for powers to deny to non-EC firms the freedom to conduct business in the community if European companies do not enjoy the same freedoms in return. The Europeans intend collectively to negotiate better access to the Tokyo markets in exchange for the access the Japanese want to enjoy in Europe – and already enjoy in London. Essential British interests demand that, in the confrontations ahead, the foreign companies already here are not forced out. We have already allowed in non-European firms and we want more to come rather than any to leave.

This is good old-fashioned politics, although it is at times dressed up in the romanticism of 'free trade' versus 'Fortress Europe'. I have always been curious about how free-traders expect to penetrate the real fortresses – Japan, for example – if they deny themselves the only battering ram available. Deep down the British know well enough that free trade, before it can be peacefully enjoyed, must sometimes be fought for tooth and nail. That is why we included reciprocity clauses in the Financial Services Act of 1986. The Bank of England also has powers under the Banking Act of 1987 to promote reciprocity. But are they never to be used and have they no deterrent effect? Applications from Japanese dealers for licenses to operate in London might make greater progress if more British brokers were admitted more readily to the Tokyo Stock Exchange. Whatever you do, you want to be sure that you have the clout. Europe in concert has all the clout it needs. What we need to ensure is that careful political control is exercised over the use of such powers. We want no regulation-happy bureaucrats running amok. The early draft directive seemed too anxious to let them loose.

In 1986 the London Stock Exchange renamed itself the International Stock Exchange. In doing so it displayed exactly the confidence which the expanding opportunities of the new Europe should implant in every British business. According to figures prepared by Deloitte Haskins & Sells in 1987, Britain dominates the EC stock markets, with 3,062 companies having a market capitalization value of nearly 568 billion ecu; while West Germany has 574 companies with a market capitalization of 168 billion ecu; and France has 1,467, with a value of 138.5 billion ecu.

The environment of the Exchange is one where the doors are open to all but with membership conditional upon high standards being attained and kept. Whether a respected accountant was justified in describing some companies quoted on one of the smaller continental exchanges as 'pure bandits' is not for me to judge but what cannot be seriously questioned is that, in the prime task of establishing investor confidence, London has made much of its reputation for probity and the maintenance of standards, though – as the Barlow Clowes depositors will remind us – there are no absolute guarantees. If the City is to exploit its position to the full, not only in the International Stock Exchange but in all its dealings, it will need to be increasingly vigilant that the high standards, once second nature within a largely British-owned and dominated trading community, are scrupulously maintained. Any failure here will either drive business away or provoke intervention by governments or both.

Although Britain has established a pre-eminence in European financial markets, the skies are not entirely clear. There is a half-heard rumble of approaching thunder, in that our success has been in providing services while continental Europeans have preferred to channel their savings into their industries, with less reliance on the quoted company.

They have concentrated rather on *making* things while we have developed the service sector. This pattern is even truer of Japan, where the world's most powerful banking sector has been built on the back of its booming manufacturing. In 1970 six of the ten largest banks in the world were American; by 1987 nine of the ten were Japanese. Our trade imbalance reflects a different emphasis.

We cannot, however, ignore the fact that European nations are about to compete openly in the very service sectors in which we have been pre-eminent. Hitherto their instinct has too often been protectionist but we should not complacently assume that once their energies are released and focused afresh they will not prove formidable rivals. But even if we do not hold our share of the enlarged market, a somewhat reduced share of a rapidly growing market would still leave us much better off than today.

For Britain to win permanently, to gain a full share of the expanding market, all our companies have to enter the fray. The government has spelled out the urgency. But more needs to be done to equip Britain to use all her energies and resources to the full. In this chapter I shall cover only some of the oustanding items on the agenda.

There is much important preparatory work which the public and private sectors are already doing together; and more still that they should do. For example, much of the substantial increase in expenditure by the Department of Employment on training has found its way through the chambers of commerce into training agencies and companies. This has given a new confidence to Britain's previously patchy chamber of commerce movement, which is ripe for a resurgence as Britain prepares for the new Europe.

If only a part of the anticipated decision-taking within the completed market finds its way to Brussels, the focus of attention will follow and Britain's industrial and commercial leaders – at local as well as national level – will seek representation and influence there. The task of fighting for British industry and the regions could in theory be left to central government (although local government would want its own voice heard), but this would be a grave mistake. The private sector must know that it will have to fight for fair treatment. To win that treatment, for which businesses in the regions may have good claim, the fighting will require every available armament. To leave matters to even the most resourceful of politicians or bureaucrats would inevitably let large parts of their case go by default.

The representative system of British industry and commerce is not well enough organized and their leaders should do something about it. At national and regional level the CBI is the leading voice, a task it performs with polish, outdistancing and out-influencing the Association of British Chambers of Commerce (ABCC). But in the trenches, where the industrial foot-soldiers fight their daily battles, the CBI is often nowhere to be seen. Instead, in varying degrees, local chambers – especially the stronger ones – have it all their own way.

In part, it is true, they perform different roles. Traditionally, the CBI is more deeply involved in the political debate, arguing over merger policy and debating strategic national issues; the ABCC is involved more in giving routine advice and help to its members. But this distinction becomes less clearly defined as the ABCC increasingly raises its profile at national level, while many of the CBI's leaders privately recognize the inadequacy of their local follow-through.

In 1971 the two organizations considered merging and a report by a joint committee chaired by Lord Devlin recommended it. The initiative floundered but if it were to be revived there would be much to be gained. There may be political difficulties, and possibly even problems over personalities, but if two companies considering an amicable merger first sort out the names of the new chairman and chief executive, and put the two in charge of the restructuring committee, then the job is half done. I believe that the leaders of the two organizations should agree in principle, dust off Lord Devlin's report and have a go.

An employers' organization, effective nationally and locally, could take over many services now provided by government on behalf of the private sector. Most advice about markets, exports and trade, standards and specifications, would be better given locally, closer to those who would use the service and by people in daily touch with their clients. A civil servant in London or in a government regional office can answer questions about exports to Japan if anyone asks; but an effective chamber of commerce might persuade its members to ask the questions in the first place and then to act on the answers. It could even introduce them to someone who exports to Japan already. A visit from a private sector employee of a local chamber, invited to talk about marketing strategy to a medium-sized, rather old-fashioned engineering company, will be heard with more trust than the man from Whitehall, who probably knows as much and is as anxious to help but who may be suspected of being an undercover agent of the Customs and Excise.

The biggest prize of all would be to privatize or delegate the training programmes completely. This is the logical step from our present position. The government's admirable White Paper 'Training for Employment', which Norman Fowler, Secretary of State for Employment, laid before Parliament in February 1988, stresses the need to get the programmes close to the local employers. After all, they are the ones with the available jobs.

The White Paper says: 'The programme will be locally planned and locally delivered. There will be national guidance on priorities but the local training plans will need to draw on all available sources of information, guidance and expertise and, in particular, there will need to be a major involvement by employers – individual companies, Local Employer Networks, Chambers of Commerce and many other organizations.' My proposals would hand responsibility for daily administration to employers. It would be evolutionary not revolutionary, since present arrangements already make significant use of local chambers where they are up to the job. I do not suggest that all transfers to all chambers would have to take place on the same day: the laggards would be required to catch up before they could enjoy the added responsibility. These proposals are compatible with the government's announcement in March 1989 of their initiative to establish Training and Enterprise Councils (TECs), local business-led agencies, to run the £3 billion national training programme. Such TECs would simply be built around the local chambers but with a less dominant role for central government.

The circle would be complete if training was financed by a direct charge on employers rather than from the public purse. No net cost need be involved. If corporation tax was reduced and a hypothecated charge substituted, to be collected by the local chamber of commerce as a percentage of company profits (or as a smaller percentage of an organization's turnover), an effective act of privatization would have taken place. British employers would have been given the influence and public status enjoyed by many of their continental counterparts. An effective British presence in Brussels might then be established by the private sector, who remain too willing to let the government set the pace. Government, in its growing and necessary quest for support from the private sector in so many fields, would have an effective local body to back it and to help find and train the people whose help it needs. At the same time, the less reasonable demands of government could be more effectively resisted: a strengthened employers' organization could employ specialists of sufficient calibre to stand up to the officials of central and local government who every day crowd them with exhortation and demand. They would, however, be able to complement with professional back-up the essential part-time and voluntary contribution of public-spirited but increasingly hard-pressed managers.

In post-1992 Europe the potential for an organization which combines the talents and skills of the CBI and of the chambers of commerce will be enormous. Its scope could even encompass some of the functions that are currently undertaken by the commercial departments of the Foreign Office and the Department of Trade and Industry, and provide a valuable new service to British industry in its struggles to seek out and exploit new markets.

There is one question upon which a more authoritative voice, speaking for all of British industry and commerce, could usefully be raised in Brussels even now – the crucial matter of harmonization of technical regulations and standards under Community law as set out in Council Directive 83/189/EEC. The consequences of this directive need careful watching. Our partners have been steadily working to influence the deliberations of the Commission's standard-setting authorities. French and German firms are campaigning hard to guide EC technical harmonization in their direction and to motivate armies of trade representatives and officials to conduct running battles over Europe's industrial standards. Every national advantage is being pressed as each side tries to secure as the common standard that which suits its domestic industry. Germany is pushing her standards hard (the DIN system) and, rather than blaming them, we must get ahead of them. It is essential that each British company finds out the state of the game for its own products before it is too late. No officials will fight unless our companies are alongside them. It is a classic example of where the divided efforts of public and private sectors are weak but, if combined, could be highly effective. The more thoroughly the leaders of British enterprise understand what is going on and pitch into the campaign, the better the prospects for British interests. As it is, there is a real danger that they will go by default.

I began by talking of change, and nowhere will the signs of change be more frequently manifest or more politically controversial than in the world of mergers and acquisitions, where activity is bound to be intensified by the enlarged scale of the new home market. Mergers and acquisitions are the natural companions of stiffening competition. They are also the natural and perennial concern of governments. In every country in Europe, governments – directly or indirectly – protect or subsidize their industries but they are more involved even than that. Public procurement is used extensively to encourage the development of technological advance, since government provides much of the support for the research and development programmes of private industry. The tax system can be used to encourage industry and to facilitate or impede its access to the savings for which it has to compete. Governments try to achieve the more effective employment of unemployed people, a question which will be discussed in a later chapter. The plans for 1992 are designed to change much of this by reducing and eventually eliminating all those different forms of government support which, if maintained within a single market, prevent its equitable operation.

Meanwhile there are risks for Britain. The work of drawing up rules of fair play in the new Europe is itself a highly competitive business, in which the contestants – though loosely confined by treaty – are bound by no code of fairness at all. No level playing-fields have been provided. National self-interest remains the watchword. There will be give and take, and hard-line opening positions will blur into compromise – usually late at night when the next day's papers are already printing. We are in a game of snakes and ladders – or, rather, in hundreds of simultaneous games – in which our competitors' rules allow them (but not us) to climb up the snakes, while we (but not they) find that the ladders mostly lead downwards.

This is nowhere truer than in the arena of takeovers and mergers, where the habits of investors have left British companies riper for plucking than any others in Europe. Our European colleagues do not have a history of takeover battles fought by distant shareholders; they tend to talk through the advantages, take a longer-term view and negotiate in the interests of the company. They see the British advocacy of the unfettered market as focused on the short term, exploiting today at the expense of tomorrow. This is a view shared by capitalist Japan; while in America, although their attitudes are closer to ours and their companies more freely available, the sheer scale of their larger companies effectively precludes most hostile bids, while vigilance in the Pentagon and Congress keeps a protective shield around their high technology industries.

Most quoted companies in Britain are vulnerable to takeover. Their owners have few effective forums within which to gather when under threat and to reach a collective judgment; and the advisers to individual shareholders are often in a position of fiduciary trust where anything but acceptance of an enticing offer leaves them vulnerable to legal remedy. I do not intend here to analyse the damage these factors have done to the longer-term interests of British industry. The Department of Trade and Industry has carried out the work effectively for me (see Appendix E to the DTI's publication 'Mergers Policy', published in 1988). Suffice it so say that Britain is the predator's natural hunting ground. Not only is virtually everything for sale but there are few centres where specialist skills in the management of disposals and acquisitions are so highly developed as in London.

Two questions arise. First, what rules should govern the activities of takeover and merger in the European market place? Second, how should Britain act to safeguard the future of her companies, which will be seen both within the Community and outside as easy pickings for those who wish to build up their European strength for 1992.

The logic of a single market must be that any considerations of monopoly and public interest are made first in the context of all Europe, not in that of a single national sector. If we are to bring together the resources of all twelve economies, it makes no sense to start by defining a British company's market share with reference to Britain alone. A proposed merger which combined, say, 50 per cent of the UK market, might command no more than 5 per cent of the European market. The former might be against the public interest by tending to monopoly; the latter hardly so. National governments cannot administer such policies, since each would take the most self-interested view. Imagine a French takeover bid for a British company where it fell to the French to determine whether it was in Europe's interest or not, or *vice versa*!

There is a balance to be struck: mergers below a certain scale should remain in national hands and those above should be considered by the European Commission. The draft EC regulation on merger control would proscribe any merger involving a combined value of assets of 5 billion ecu until the end of 1992 and 2 billion ecu thereafter, which would be likely to create a dominant position in the EC as a whole or in a substantial part of it. A market share below 33 per cent will be presumed to be compatible with the treaty. We are then justified in retaining national control in parallel with the EC regime, because we must be able to control mergers affecting the UK market. Monopolies could be created in regions of the United Kingdom well below a capitalization of 1 billion ecu. There must be powers to prevent or to break up such moves.

At the moment Britain is taking too innocent a view of the takeover climate. As the DTI survey so effectively demonstrates, it is not serving our economy well. Sometimes a takeover provides a corrective remedy, achieves necessary rationalization or serves as a discipline to otherwise lax management. But it carries with it dangers that decisions turn on short-term maximization of profit at the expense of the expenditure on research, training or investment on which long-term health and the greatest rewards depend.

If British companies are more available for acquisition than others, it is they that will be converted into branch offices of overseas companies. Some take the view that this does not matter, indeed that further investment will then follow. In the production line and assembly sectors of industry this may be true; but a company owned in Britain will almost certainly have its head office there, and head offices not only have control but also attract a range of service industries around them. British-owned companies will locate their research facilities close to British universities and colleges whenever possible. The spin-off is usually seen locally: innovation grows close to the innovator. When rationalization comes, in recession or under competition, it is the distant factory or branch office which tends to be first in the firing line. No one should expect companies to take unwise commercial decisions in the name of patriotism but nor should anyone assume that company directors are detached from a sense of national obligation. Nor are our fellow Europeans, or other countries anxious to see their companies move into Europe, under any obligation to play by British rules. When only one soldier in a squad is out of step, he is wise to assume that he is the one who is wrong. There is need for a new sophistication in Britian's approach to the ownership of her industrial assets if they are not to be acquired in growing numbers by our rivals as pieces in the game of restructuring European industry.

We have seen in an earlier chapter the significance that governments attach to their national research and development programmes and the impact these have on industrial success. We have seen, too, the partnership of national self-interest that links the government programmes of each country with that country's national companies and the lengths to which governments will go to protect the consequent benefits. Britain needs a policy that supports British companies, as close to the leading edge of research and its applications as we can afford. How do we stand when it comes to the scale of our research programmes?

At first glance Britain's spending does not compare too unfavourably. In relative proportions of GDP we spend 2.46 per cent compared with 2.38 per cent spent by France, 2.7 per cent by Germany and 2.89 per cent by the USA. But these figures miss the point: in absolute cash terms Britain, with its smaller economy, is way behind. Fig. 6.1 shows the position in 1983, and the gap has been steadily widening ever since. We have now been overtaken by France.

As a proportion of public expenditure, total R&D spending in Britain is larger than in Japan (4.4 per cent compared with 3.6 per cent), and much the same as in Germany. The difference is that the bulk of UK government R&D expenditure goes on defence. The French government's higher percentage is also due to greater defence R&D. The fact that British defence exports are now second only to the USA in the West would indicate cause and effect, particularly when linked with the more rigorous climate of competition in defence procurement, and points to the need for more commitment by government to R&D outside the defence world rather than a reduction in defence expenditure itself. The stark consequence of recent trends is that over the past twenty years Britain's share of European patenting in the USA has fallen by 40 per cent, with the Germans having overtaken us significantly.

The downward trend in R&D expenditure in Britain since 1981 is particularly disturbing (see Fig. 6.2) and is accounted for by a steep reduction in the government's share of civil R&D funding (from 30 per cent in 1981 to 23 per cent in 1986, with a further fall in real terms of 3 per cent between 1986 and 1987). The shortfall has not been made up by industry: the latest DTI figures show a 1 per cent drop in real terms in spending on R&D by British industry between 1981 and 1985. British business spends £250 per year per worker, compared with £300 in France and £400 in Germany. Of the top ten nations, the UK comes ninth in terms of R&D expenditure by industry. If rate of growth is taken into account, then we come last.

Between 1967 and 1983 in the UK, R&D expenditure actually fell as a share of industrial output – by 0.6 per cent. In Japan the share rose by nearly 3.5 per cent, in France by nearly 3 per cent and in the USA by over 1.5 per cent. The relatively slow rate of growth of profits in UK industry accounts in part for this gloomy picture but no company is going to invest heavily if the long-term return is ignored by the short-

Fig. 6.1 Gross R & D Expenditure, 1983

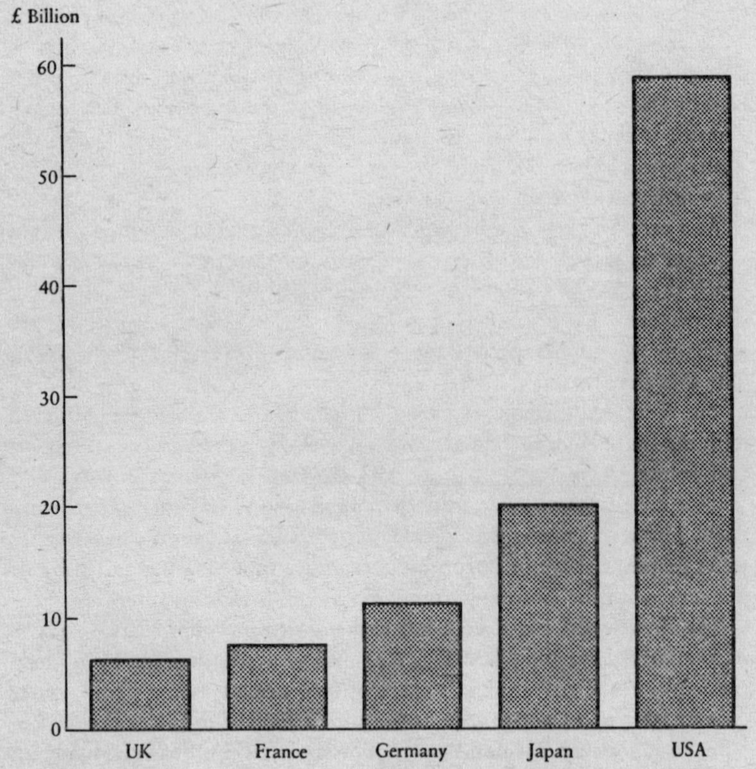

(Source: OECD 1986)

term horizons prevailing in the financial markets of the City; and when times are tough British industry has responded by making early cuts in R&D, as well as in training. A marked investment gap will inhibit our industrial performance and Britain's economic prospects will remain poor unless we close that gap.

We are now cutting military without increasing civilian R&D expenditure. I lived through the debate that led to this decision. No analysis existed to demonstrate that civil R&D offered higher returns than those

Fig. 6.2 Gross Expenditure on R & D (GERD) as a Percentage of Gross Domestic Product (GDP)

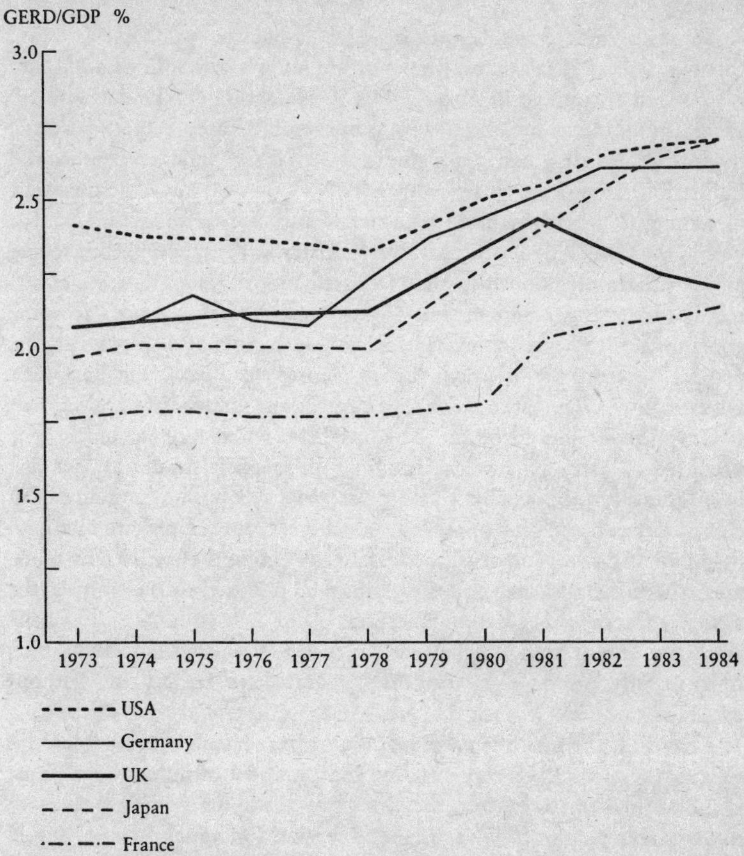

(Source: PA Technology 1987)

available from the development of military hardware. It was much simpler than that. The Treasury joined forces with the civil departments in a short-lived and unholy marriage of convenience, within which the former kept to their public expenditure ceilings and the latter shared between them the benefits from the cuts they had imposed on the

Ministry of Defence. That is politics but such manoeuvres must never be allowed to masquerade as an objective appraisal of industrial requirements.

These downward trends must be reversed but not with some cavalier, throw-money-at-it abandon. Expenditure must be disciplined and there is no set of absolute criteria by which its allocation can be determined. Human judgments are often wrong but sophisticated economies have to do the best they can, with ministers, civil servants, academics and industrialists working closely together. With that caveat, my experience in setting up the Rothschild Customer-Contractor Requirement Boards within the Department of Trade and Industry in 1973, and in sponsoring major programmes both in that Department and later in the Departments of the Environment and Defence, showed that there are some general rules to be observed. These include costing and setting targets, project by project, with clear 'break clauses' to allow cancellation or adjustment if circumstances change or progress is unsatisfactory.

Government should be more sympathetic where private industry is prepared to carry part of the funding, although it should always ask keen questions about why a viable project needs public funding at all. (It will often be helpful to recruit 'poachers' from the private sector to help monitor government-supported programmes; they will know when and where their former colleagues may be tempted to try to milk the system.) On the other hand, government will have to fund much of the seed-corn exploration which alone can lead to breakthroughs but which is too costly or too risky for the private sector to pay for without assistance.

Above all, there is one cardinal rule for intelligent, responsible politicians: they should stop pretending that this sort of industrial support is a doctrinal intrusion into the workings of the market place. It is an unavoidable part of today's competitive world in which Britain should be determined to excel.

Only governments can divide such funds as are available between public programmes (administered by Whitehall departments) and the academic world on the one hand, and the private sector on the other, though each of the prospective recipients should be expected to justify a bid by reference to the same criteria of cost, time and benefit. An element of competition in obtaining the best results would do no harm.

In setting out my belief in the need for an aggressive strategy to advance Britain's scientific and technological capability, I am saying nothing that all governments do not recognize. But there are complications. The British economy cannot of itself sustain advanced programmes in all fields and increasingly the national economy of Britain will be dominated by companies which are not British. The big players will be multinationals and although it is to be hoped that some will be British, these will probably be a minority. As the programmes grow in cost every year, the British government will be forced to make increasingly difficult choices about where to put its money (remember those civil servants who cannot spot winners?) – while international companies will make many of the most important choices for us, without reference to the British or any other government.

So Britain's need for partners, at both government and company level, will continue to grow. There are few rules limiting our choice, which must at least in part be opportunistic. But Europe offers more opportunities for negotiating partnership arrangements on fair terms because most of our fellow EC members face similar constraints and, in the real world, the protectionism of Japan and the vigilance of the US Congress limit the quality of the partnerships that are on offer there. Although there are no convenient definitions to which there are not glaring exceptions, the nations of Europe have begun to identify a common interest in sharing their programmes, both to eliminate the waste of duplication and triplication and to support each other in keeping up to date. The 1990s will be the decade of the collaborative project and the faster the process of merger and acquisition can create truly European companies, the more trivial will national rivalries become.

Examination of progress so far shows that we would not have had a European space launcher but for France, nor retained in Europe any major civil airframe manufacturing without their leadership. It was France which proposed the EUREKA project – the Europe-wide programme of civil research which was launched in 1985 as a response to the threat posed by SDI funding to Europe's technological competitiveness. There are now 213 agreed projects with a total value of at least £2.5 billion and British involvement in 74 programmes with a total value of £1.2 billion.

The European Space Agency (ESA) was established in 1973 out of a fusion of the European Launcher Development Organization and the European Scientific Research Organization, following an initiative I took on behalf of the British government when I was Minister for Aerospace. At the Agency's creation, Britain rejoined the Ariane launcher programme, entered the post-Apollo programme and secured a European lead in communication satellites. It seemed to me a better use of our national resources than trying to subsidize our national industry – as the official advice to me had originally suggested – in the hope of outdoing the French and Germans. In contrast, Britain was later to baulk at an extra contribution of £1 million a year to ESA and reduced its annual subscription from £90 million to £82 million between 1988 and 1989. Since 80 per cent of our contribution in any case finds its way back into British industry, this created resentment among British scientists as well as frustration in the rest of the Community.

If we had doubts about the Agency's efficiency, we should have insisted on a close control of its arrangements over the years; if we had seen its policies evolving in the wrong direction, we should have led them elsewhere. Sullen obduracy and negative criticism simply open doors for the competitors of Britain's aerospace companies.

In the early 1980s the Commission initiated an R&D programme in pre-competitive research, in imitation of American and Japanese examples. It was called the Forecasting and Assessment in Science and Technology unit (FAST) and it identified information technology, biotechnology, communications and food processing as the crucial areas for collaborative research work within the EC.

Based on these findings, three major collaborative schemes sprang up: first, ESPRIT (European Strategic Programme for Information Technology), which ran from 1984 to 1988 and financed up to 50 per cent of the pre-competition research and development projects undertaken by at least two member states in partnership with companies; second, RACE (Research and Development in Communications Technologies for Europe), whose principal object was to develop the technology needed for wide-band fibre-optic networks; and third, BRITE (Basic Research in Industrial Technologies for Europe), a four-year programme to run from 1985, which was organized to encourage the spread of new technologies in the manufacturing processes of the traditional industrial sector. There was also a five-year biology research programme ending in 1989.

All my commercial life I have lived within the disciplines of the capitalist system. They are tough and relentless. In a competitive system there are few corners in which to hide. Responsible government has a duty, not only to define the conditions which enable benefits to be gained from this, but also to recognize the international circumstances which make a mockery of open competition. British companies both at home and abroad face competition not only from free-standing, self-financing capitalist enterprise but from other companies that are partners, and sometimes almost agents, of capitalist governments. We live in a world not of rival toffee shops competing from either end of the same street but, in certain key industrial sectors, of giant taxpayer-financed, government-backed enterprises, all out to triumph over us. No country exploits its small business sector more efficiently than the Japanese, but this is done from within a protected economy dominated by huge companies, controlled by sympathetic shareholders, financed long-term by banks and supported by the benign influence of MITI.

However difficult the concept may be for the doctrinal purist, no government can avoid making strategic judgments about technologically advanced programmes. To do nothing is a judgment in itself. It may be no more than a judgment of indifference as to whether Britain is involved in such activities or not, or that British companies are already playing an adequate part, or that there is no commercial pay-off in a particular field. These are judgments which the market could in theory be left to make; but no other country allows that and Britain cannot simply ignore what her competitors are doing.

It is in the interests of all of us that British companies win their share. They cannot do it alone and we have no need to apologize for a national commitment to their success. Nor should we regard government support as something exceptional which is to be regretted. On the contrary, we should be proud of what government has achieved by backing British industries, as a few examples will testify.

The Tornado military aircraft programme is a government-backed collaborative venture in which Italy, Germany and the United Kingdom are jointly engaged; the European Fighter Aircraft will build on its success, welcoming Spain into the partnership; the European Space Agency enabled a British commerical leadership to develop in satellites; the Airbus participation is a triumph for the foresight of Sir Arnold Hall of Hawker Siddeley, who put his company's money into the project when a Labour government pulled out in the late 1960s. Without his boldness subsequent British governments would have been denied the opportunity to participate in the only non-American manufacture of large passenger aircraft in the West. The evidence is abundant that Britain *can* win – but not from the touchline.

* * *

The rest of this chapter may seem out of place in a book about Britain's opportunities in Europe. Its theme is a secondary but vitally important one: that these opportunities must be available to all of the United Kingdom and that only government can see that they are. To persuade the British people of the advantages of Europe will stretch the political skills of those committed to the venture. The arguments presenting the negative case, highlighting the excesses and dramatizing the mistakes, will be readily exploited not only by those in opposition, willing to seize any stick with which to beat the government of the day, but also by those who are in heart and mind fighting again the case for Britain's membership. All such negative rhetoric, as we enter the 1990s, amounts to defeatism and must itself be defeated. Above all, the advantages of Europe must attract not just one region in the South of England but the United Kingdom as a whole, not just the prosperous majority but the less secure minority. In fighting what will be a relentless battle for industrial and commercial supremacy, every community in our nation must be enrolled and every national resource must be committed to the full.

We must develop transport systems that will make the market of Europe as relevant to the North as the South, to Scotland and Wales as to Kent and Surrey. Issues of regional balance are fundamental to the winning of support across the nation. Improved transportation, high-technology communications and the rapid flow of information all make it easier today than ever before to run major companies from the provinces. But the Department of Transport will be making decisions about infrastructure that will critically affect the ability of the nothern and western regions of the United Kingdom to compete in the enlarged market, while the future quality of life in the crowded South-East will be affected just as much by those decisions as it will be by the planners in the Department of the Environment.

Changes in Europe's transport infrastructure over the next decade, such as the completion of the Channel Tunnel and the Rhine-Danube canal, will require a radical reappraisal of commercial distribution policies. It is no purpose of this book to make detailed recommendations on future transport policy but I confess to an unease.

Britain's transport system is close to breaking point. London traffic is often at a standstill, motorways are choked, the air polluted, commuter trains packed. And the statistics move relentlessy upwards. In 1981 there were fifteen million cars; by 1987 nineteen million. Does that mean twenty-five million by the year 2000? According to their annual reports, British Rail now meets a demand for 20.5 billion passenger miles a year (compared to 18.4 billion in 1984/5) and freight has risen from 7.5 billion tonne/miles in 1984/5 to nearly 11 billion in 1987/8. The number of air passengers in the UK has increased from 46 million in 1980 to 87.5 million in 1987. This increased activity is nowhere near evenly spread. The South-East already takes most of the strain and the Channel Tunnel, due to open in 1993, will add extra pressure to an already overcrowded system. The case for massive infrastructure expenditure is irresistible, and much of it is already committed.

If the tunnel is the route to tomorrow's opportunities, and if all of Britain is to throw itself into Europe with the commitment that the opportunity warrants, then communications within the whole of Britain as well as to the continent will be critical. And time is of the essence in taking these strategic decisions. British manufacturers will need to be persuaded that their goods will reach continental destinations as easily from Cheadle as they will from Chatham, otherwise Kent will simply become one gigantic industrial estate. Whatever the decisions, there is work for the construction industry: the issue is where that work should be carried out. There is a choice: investment in better roads and railways, to give all Britain's industry access to Europe's markets, or infrastructure investment in the South and South-East on a scale that must cause unacceptable damage to the environment. Five or ten years from now we shall either have provided an adequate system to take all of Britain into Europe or there will be unacceptable contrasts between the South-East, which may suffer from rather than enjoy more economic prosperity, and other parts of the country. Remote from the capital, they will watch resentfully the growing wealth of the new Europe as far out of their reach as ever.

Of course, we must be cautious about assuming too readily that the trends of the past will continue. Ministers can get their fingers burnt by statistics. I remember sitting in Marsham Street in my earliest experience of government, as Parliamentary Under Secretary of State for the Department of the Environment, plotting the development of a new town on Severnside: 'Essential, Minister, to cope with the exploding population.' No one had told the Department's statisticians that straight-line extrapolations need to be checked against the most up-to-date evidence of breeding habits. The babies never came! I remember too the heady days in 1972 of economic expansion and the commitment to a massive increase in steel-producing capacity. That was just before the oil crisis destroyed the market but left intact, needless to say, the determination of the new Labour government to spend the money. Things often go awry as the future turns into the present; and ministers are rarely still around to account for their decisions. But excessive caution can be as expensive and damaging as reckless investment. Politicians have to find the balance.

We had better get this right. The ports on the east coast, for example, if free, like Felixstowe, from the crippling handicaps of the dock labour scheme, could take some of the traffic away from the South but they will need the necessary roads. And the law will have to be changed to end the dock labour scheme.* Inland container depots, where the long-distance trains bound for the continent can be assembled, must be planned and built; better air services from the regional airports to lighten the load on the (by then) three London airports are needed. These are only part of the integrated approach which is vital.

It will be expensive. The private sector should wherever possible be enlisted but not allowed only to pursue projects designed to achieve an assured profit on the basis of an over-cautious projection of demand, with the result that essential related infrastructure is skimped. The M25 has proved an expensive lesson that excessive caution can lead to extra cost but, if we have learned the lesson, we may yet profit from that misjudgment. There must also be room for planning and design. Have we not the imagination to conceive of a land bridge from Liverpool to the Channel Tunnel which an effective rail link would create, so that the Mersey can compete with Rotterdam for lucrative Atlantic trade?

As the British Secretary of State for Transport, Paul Channon has the chance – literally – to pave the way for our entry to the continental markets. He can produce one of the most important and exciting White Papers in a long time, and one which may determine the level of Britain's success in Europe profoundly and irrevocably.

Two further items demanded inclusion in any government agenda to meet the challenge of the European market place: first, the waste of resources represented by the number of people unemployed who are paid to do nothing, an overhead which the working population has to cover; and, second, the regional imbalances which, even when the overall economy is buoyant, still leave large parts of our capacity under-used.

* On 6 April 1989, Norman Fowler, Secretary of State for Employment, announced the Government's intention to abolish the dock labour scheme.

The twilight worlds of the black economy, the poverty trap and the virtual absence of incentives to return to work are now deeply ingrained in much of our society. Parts of prosperous Britain, which twenty years ago could sustain employment levels of 97 per cent or more today, record figures of only 90 per cent. That says something not only about lost jobs but also about people's willingness and fitness to accept jobs – about the lack of training and educational standards that they need to enable them to cope. On practical grounds alone – well understood by everyone who has ever drawn up or read a balance sheet – the cost of this wasteful consumption of our national resources is appalling. To pay people to do nothing is about as useless a way of spending a nation's wealth as one could conceive.

The market is not going to provide jobs on the scale the present crisis demands, though it will find some. The number of people seeking work will decline but even in ten years' time levels of unemployment are expected to be about 1.5 million and the distribution of the out-of-work will remain as uneven as it is today, both geographically and in its bias against inner urban minorities.

There is little scope for sharing existing jobs, which is attractive in theory, but hard to apply in practice. The demand for shorter and more flexible working hours will grow. People will change jobs more frequently and will require more mid-life training to enable them to do so and, while the better off may retire earlier, others will be encouraged to work longer. Yet the heart of the problem will remain: are we to continue to operate on the present basis that cash is available to the unemployed without any commitment from the recipient, other than a fortnightly visit to the local employment office?

We need to challenge the assumption that you can expect to draw unemployment benefit without giving some of your time in return. The best use of an unemployed person's time may well be some form of retraining, because the key objective must be to help people to get and keep proper jobs; but there is much else to be done as well, and we live in a climate in which to take a job or stay on the dole often makes only a marginal financial difference. We must establish a relationship between the provision of support for those out of work and the concept of community service in exchange. Finally, we need a policy to address the imbalance between the regions and enable the more distant parts of the United Kingdom to compete more equally on even terms.

The location of private industry is not the only concern. A quarter of a million people directly employed by the government as civil servants live in the most crowded part of the country. In the armed services, we are recruiting disproportionately large numbers of young people in the North to station them in the South: 60 per cent of service personnel are stationed there. Many of them could be relocated, thus reducing the need to provide all of those one million extra houses that we are told will otherwise have to be built in the South-East by the end of the century.

Too many civil and military research laboratories and facilities are crowded into the South-East. There is an urgent need to give the whole of our country a fair share of their wealth-creating potential. Land released in the South would not only help to finance the relocation but would ease the pressure for more greenfield sites, while the new facilities and employment elsewhere would be the most constructive regional policy possible.

Tim Sainsbury, the junior Defence Minister responsible for procurement, set out the position clearly on 9 March 1989 when he announced the transfer of 1,500 jobs from London to Teesside. He told the British Parliament that the decision represented 'the most cost-effective solution for the headquarters and laboratories of the Directorate General of Defence Quality Assurance now at Woolwich and Bromley. The move would concentrate the headquarters functions and main laboratories of the Directorate on a single site with fully modern facilities, while at the same time releasing the Woolwich and Bromley sites for disposal and redevelopment.'

In some respects government can help best by refraining from doing harm. I have written elsewhere* of the almost wanton weakening of regional economies by some aspects of the British tax regime. High capital taxes on death can force independent companies on to the market place, where remote, publicly quoted companies compete for their purchase with tax-deferred shares against more local entrepreneurs offering cash, the acceptance of which attracts up to 40 per cent capital gains tax liability there and then. Mortgage interest relief to the home-buying public has done much to promote a central Conservative objective, the creation of a property-owning democracy. This has given a stake in society to millions of British families and helped to foster responsibility and local commitment. But life assurance companies,

* See Heseltine, M., *Where There's a Will* (Hutchison, London, 1987).

which provide much of the cover for mortgages, have been indirect beneficiaries of Exchequer support for the home buyer. Of the twelve biggest life companies, half are in London and through them billions of pounds annually are drawn from the provinces to be invested through the City where the return is highest – in property, in government funds or overseas. Tax subsidies to the pensions industry, running at some £4.4 billion a year, similarly help to draw savings from all over Britain towards the London investment markets. More than a quarter of their investments are in foreign governments or companies. If the expression 'fiscal drag' had not already been coined to mean something quite different, it could well describe this extra burden – gratuitously imposed by the fiscal authorities upon the regions of the United Kingdom but a heavy handicap for the whole national economy in the race towards 1992.

The new Europe offers Britain unparalleled opportunities and, if we miss them, no little danger. In our relations with our European neighbours since 1945 we have, as I have discussed, been blind too often and missed those opportunities. As for danger, it has often been observed that our national habit is to arouse ourselves, as in 1939, only when a threat is so strong and close that we can no longer ignore it.

This streak in our temperament puzzles us as much as it intrigues our foreign friends and rivals. Is it idleness, or bravery, or just lack of imagination? Are we even a little pleased with ourselves for tending – in the modern idiom – to be 'laid back'? Our past political leaders have responded in various ways. Some have adopted and embodied this quirk of cheerful casualness that sometimes overcomes us; some have grown resigned to it – one recalls Disraeli saying that the English were 'a very hard people to move', and a few, when the need was pressing, have managed to rouse us.

But no government and no leader alone can do the British people's work for them. In the approaching test within Europe, we can choose relative decline or accept it unwittingly. Preferably we will do no such thing but will stir ourselves to the efforts of which leadership is made. The government can do much to facilitate the choice, to ensure that it is available. Only the people can make it. Our future hangs on hundreds of thousands of decisions, to be made in the next months and years in factories and foundries, offices and laboratories across Britain; and on the actions which follow them.

CHAPTER
7

Education: Raising Our Sights

Not long before his death twenty years ago, Jean Monnet, the man generally seen as the founding father of the European Community, declared: 'If I could do it all again, I would start with education.' His was an idealistic vision of more self-consciously European generations being nurtured in the schools. Yet the Community's impact on education has been extremely small. To the pupils, parents and teachers of schools in Bordeaux, Bradford or even Brussels it has been irrelevant.

When the Community was established, however, there was recognition of the part education might play in its economic development. The Treaty of Rome stressed the promotion of 'basic and advanced vocational training' (Article 118). It is the duty of the Council to 'lay down general principles for implementing a common vocational training policy' (Article 128). But not until 1971, two years before Britain joined the Community, did EEC Ministers of Education meet to seek common ground for a possible European education policy. The Council of Ministers adopted a formal resolution on education in June 1974; its objectives were sensible but modest – naturally enough, since this is an area of some sensitivity. How far should a central bureaucracy as remote as the Commission be involved with something as directly personal as education and something regarded as of such central importance by most states, as well as by powerful interests such as the churches?

Indeed, the United Kingdom has followed different paths of educational development from those of the major continental countries. The two Napoleons provided France with a more centrally directed state education system than in Germany but in both countries the belief was established in the nineteenth century that the promotion of learning and especially science was a duty of government because from it sprang national power and influence. The classics remained a far stronger force in English education, together with a belief in self-help which often put learning on-the-job before academic studies. There has, however, been common ground on the essential right of the family to invest in private, independent education.

The British have traditionally allowed the subject matter and methods of instruction to rest in the hands of the professionals – the teachers and head teachers in the schools. The state in Britain has tended to intrude only to determine the institutional structure. The Labour governments of the 1960s and 1970s were preoccupied with the effort to convert secondary education into a comprehensive pattern and it is symptomatic of the devolved nature of our education system that Labour's Secretary of State for Education, Anthony Crosland, set out in Circular 10/66 no less than six possible comprehensive structures which local government could choose to implement. So strong was the commitment to teacher autonomy in the classroom – reinforced by the close relationship between the Labour Party and the teaching unions – that the curriculum and teaching methods were deemed not to be matters for the involvement of central government at all. The change came when James Callaghan, as Prime Minister, in his speech at Ruskin College in 1976 raised the need to reassess the balance, relevance and quality of what was being taught. It is an irony that more interventionist socialist governments on the continent have preferred to maintain selective and elitist systems.

It is important to recognize the radical nature of the changes which the 1988 Education Reform Act is bringing about in the schools of England and Wales. National not local responsibility was firmly established and extended into determining nationally a core curriculum common to all secondary schools. But the Act also puts Britain ahead of the field in devolving responsibility further down the system, to rest in the schools themselves. Local financial management will provide head teachers and school governors with control of the school budget and free the operation of the school from interference by local government. The result should be more efficient use of resources, greater self-reliance and the achievement of higher standards. Other European countries look set to follow Britain in devolving independence within a clearly defined national policy.

Only a tiny fraction of the Community's budget (which is itself a mere 1 per cent of the combined GDP of the twelve constituent member states) is devoted to education. Britain's annual contribution to the Community's spending on education is currently no more than £20 million, which is about £1 in every £1,000 of the total public expenditure we spend on education in the UK. It is less than a tenth of what we spend ourselves on in-service teacher training.

Yet there are two very sensible considerations for the Community collectively to address and these are reflected in the deliberations of the Council of Education Ministers and the Education Resolution of June 1974. That resolution was careful to stipulate that 'educational co-operation must make allowance for the traditions of each country and the diversity of their respective educational policies and system'. But it also recognized that vocational education and training would be the mainspring of future success. It saw too that opportunity starts first with education and that those who fail to seize early educational opportunities, or have been denied them, need another chance in adult life both to improve themselves and to retrain. However, the 1974 resolution stipulated that 'on no account must education be regarded merely as a component of economic life'. The initial focus of the Commission's approach – and one very relevant to Britain – has been to help promote the ethos of the European Community. Significantly, the school reforms proposed by the second Mitterrand government set 'international co-operation and the building of Europe' as a goal.

The Commission's first step on this road has been the provision of better facilities for the education and training of nationals who have to live or work outside their own countries within the Community. Secondly, they have sought greater co-operation between institutions of higher education, above all to achieve the mutual recognition of qualifications. They want to promote the movement of teachers, students and research workers, and to facilitate this by improving foreign language teaching in member countries.

In this context, just outside my Henley constituency at Culham in Oxfordshire, near the site of a large EC research project on nuclear fusion named JET, is one of nine European schools funded by the Community and its member states. It is intended mainly for the children of EC employees. It has just celebrated its tenth anniversary and shows what can be done if the will is there to develop on a broader and larger scale. It offers the attraction of an international baccalaureat. The 800 boys and girls are taught for nearly half the time in at least one language other than their own, right through to university level. Many emerge virtually trilingual.

British disdain for foreign languages is deeply rooted in geography and history. Since the Second World War it has been reinforced by the rapid growth of English (under American influence) as the most widely spoken language in the world apart from Chinese. To their credit, a few British universities (and the British Foreign Office) have ensured that a tiny number of men and women continue to learn the 'hard' foreign languages such as Arabic and Chinese. But, at least until recently, the British businessman travelling in Western – or Eastern – Europe has seen no reason to learn more than a smattering of his hosts' languages. He has expected and usually found that they will be able to discuss with him in English almost anything from the European Cup to the price of his product. A recent survey by the Confederation of British Industry showed that only one British company in seven with a turnover of more than £10 million provided any language training for its staff. Many must have regretted this as they witnessed contracts going to their German competitors. It is one thing to buy in English, quite another to sell.

The enormous growth of British holiday-making in Western Europe has not been accompanied by any equally large yearning to increase the knowledge and use of other languages. The tourist in Marbella or on the Côte d'Azur, encouraged by the ability of shopkeepers and restaurateurs to speak at least a smattering of English, has rarely bothered to pick up much Spanish or French. Even school parties abroad often find it all too easy to speak only English with their continental contemporaries who are eager to improve their knowledge of it.

The universities, with their domination of the examining bodies and still, in too many cases, the emphasis in their undergraduate courses on the literature rather than the spoken languages of other countries, must take some of the blame. But the root of the problem is in the schools. The Department of Education and Science's experiment with Nuffield French in more than 100 primary schools in the 1960s and 1970s petered out not so much through lack of competent language teachers but rather because both parents and local authorities saw it as an esoteric sideshow and because secondary schools were not prepared to follow it up. Indeed, at a time when employers, ministers and others have preached the need for more scientists and engineers, most secondary schools have given little priority to modern language teaching. As a result, the numbers of British pupils taking GCE 'O' and 'A' levels in French, traditionally the first foreign language in British schools, have fallen in the last decade; German 'A' level classes are in danger of collapse in many schools; and there has been no countervailing growth in Spanish (the language of most of Central and South America and, increasingly, of California). In consequence, foreign language places in higher education remain unfilled.

The situation is very different in other Community countries. English has long been the first foreign language in the Netherlands, Denmark and much of West Germany. In recent years in France, it has become the first choice of nearly 90 per cent of secondary school pupils. For many of those who stay at school beyond sixteen – a much larger proportion than in Britain – a second foreign language is commonplace even where it is not compulsory. The much less obviously anglophone Mediterranean countries are following the trend.

Le Figaro of 23 November 1988 described a remarkable development in Noisy-le-Roi on the western outskirts of Paris near Versailles, where for seventeen years *all* the 1,000 children in the town's nursery and primary schools have, in small groups, learned English for a quarter of an hour each day. The emphasis is on the spoken word, so that by the age of eleven the children can cope in English with the everyday conversation of the playground. Much of the teaching is in the hands of what we would call unqualified part-time teachers – French people with a qualification in English, as well as American and British residents in the area.

As one of the initiators of a similar programme in another Paris suburb put it: 'Einstein could not have taught mathematics to five-year-olds. The level of formal qualification is not important: our teachers must know how to be actors.' In reflecting on this example, Britain might do well to consider 're-cycling', as it were, retired professional people – particularly those who have taken early retirement – to assist part-time in schools in those subject areas (maths as well as languages) where acute teacher shortages have arisen or are threatened.

More than 80,000 French children in nursery and primary schools are learning to speak a foreign language, most of them English but some German and a few Spanish. The inspiration for this has come from teachers and parents at the grass roots, not from the French Ministry of Education, which has been content to follow the developments with a benign eye and see that the best practice is spread more widely.

In October 1988 the Community's Economic and Social Committee argued that there was 'a case for introducing compulsory tuition in some Community languages' and that member states should be urged to introduce 'the compulsory or at least optional teaching of a Community language in primary schools'. Britain has a long way to go to begin to match this. But the national curriculum, at the heart of the 1988 Education Reform Act, presents the opportunity. It prescribes that at least one foreign language should be taught to all pupils throughout the compulsory period of secondary education. (The European Parliament in 1988 rather over-ambitiously proposed that all pupils between five and sixteen should receive instruction in at least *two* foreign languages.) What is needed to achieve this is a well-qualified and motivated teaching force but also a willingness by local authorities, schools and teachers to accept heterodox qualifications and teaching methods.

It may be an ambitious goal but we should aim to give at least a rudimentary working knowledge of a European language to all children, especially for daily conversation, leaving study in depth in one or more languages to the interested minority. There is some good practice in English schools, however. At Cranford Community School near Heathrow, for example, fourth-year students, by conducting job interviews in French with IBM French personnel, having first studied IBM spreadsheets and put their CVs on word-processors, acquire a wide variety of skills in one go. Since Community funds are to be made available in the language area, we must be ready to seize the opportunities – perhaps greater in this country than in any other except Ireland – to extract the biggest possible benefit from them.

The over-arching desire of the Commission and Parliament is to design programmes to help forge a new generation of young Europeans who could be more receptive to each other than past generations, conscious of their future as citizens not only of their own countries but of the Community as a whole. Apart from the initiatives on the language front, co-operative programmes in higher education began in 1976 and since then two specific projects of importance have been launched – COMETT and ERASMUS.

COMETT (Community in Education and Training for Technology) was approved at the end of 1985, initially for four years, and its extension on a larger scale for a further five-year period was approved early in

1989. The objective is to help more than 10,000 computer science and technology students to gain six months' experience within industry in another Community country. There are also places for 350 academic staff and 350 business graduates. The budget is more than £40 million for the first four years; both national governments and the Community contribute. The ultimate aim is to establish a European network of university/industry training partnerships which will facilitate technology transfer. Britain and France, some of whose universities and polytechnics were early on the scene, have been particular beneficiaries of this programme.

ERASMUS (European Community Action Scheme for the Mobility of University Students) is concerned with all disciplines. It was approved in May 1987 for an initial three-year period at a cost of about £60 million. It is intended to encourage a period of study of three to twelve months in another member state. The ultimate aim is that some 10 per cent of the student population of the Community should spend part of their course in another country's university. And there are 3,000 institutions in twelve states to choose from. It provides also for the development of a system of credit transfer and mutual recognition of academic qualification by institutions within the Community and for an increase in the exchange of academic staff. Here again British universities and polytechnics, a number of which had developed before 1987 exchange arrangements with other European institutions, especially in France and Germany, have been well placed to take part in (and gain financial support from) ERASMUS. By 1992, of course, educational barriers as well as trade frontiers will be abolished.

It has to be said, however, that here again the British way has not been the general way. The transfer of academic credit has been an appallingly neglected area of British education policy-making. The sheer conservatism of so much of British higher education, and a student grant system which militates against doing 'extra' years, have delayed this essential step. Only in 1983 did the government throw its weight behind an Open University initiative by funding a three-year development programme for a computer data base called ECCTIS (Educational Counselling and Credit Transfer Information Service). This will ultimately provide details on the qualifications needed for entry to or transfer between degree courses, including the alternatives to 'A' levels which are available for mature students and an essential credit-rating for each course. In August 1985 the then Secretary of State for Education, Sir

Keith Joseph, announced the government's commitment to extend the scheme nationally, yet in 1989 it was still not fully operational. Adult learning could leap forward from this whole data base being brought directly to the home through TELETEXT.

In March 1986 the Council for National Academic Awards (CNAA) launched a 'Credit Accumulation and Transfer Scheme' (CATS) covering courses in those institutions of higher education under CNAA auspices. Its credit ratings are to be fed into ECCTIS so that work done in different institutions, which in the past would not have been taken into account, can be treated as 'credit blocks' which together lead to a degree. The objective is to create greater flexibility while maintaining quality.

If better guidance leads to more effective use of resources and to instruction more appropriately suited to an individual's requirements, then it will be money well spent. We might also find that, if we lift the ceilings on student admissions and give the appropriate financial incentives, credit transfer could attract into the shorter, more intensive British courses substantial numbers of continental students.

Over the years since 1974 it has been the Commission in Brussels, rather than the member states, which has sought to extend the range of the Community's educational activities. Both the slow progress to date and the need to prepare for the single European market in 1992 have recently inspired the Commission to press for greater urgency. In May 1988 Manuel Marin, the Spanish Commissioner whose portfolio then included education, set out the Commission's preliminary ideas on education for the period 1989–92 (COM(88) 280 final), in what we would call a Green Paper.

In his introduction, he wrote: 'Without investment in the present and future workforce, and their skills, versatility and entrepreneurial capacity, Europe's ability to innovate, to compete [with the USA, Japan and the newly developed countries of Asia] will be impaired. In this sense, education and training lie at the heart of the process of European development.' He defined three central objectives – the identification and application of the contribution of education and training to the creation and exploitation of the internal market; the closer integration of education and industry; and the need for education policies which would contribute to the reduction of regional disparities within the Community and increase its 'social cohesion'.

In some detail he spelt out the measures the Commission would wish to see taken in pursuance of these objectives. The lack of people competent in at least two Community languages, he called 'the EC's Achilles heel'. His other priorities were an improvement in the quality of basic compulsory education and the promotion of Community-wide vocational training for those leaving school at sixteen.

Marin believed in 'encouraging more active partnership between schools and parents', which is the principle at the heart of the great increase in parental representation on school governing bodies established by the British Education Act of 1986 (which took effect in 1988) and of the much greater powers given to parents by the 1988 Education Reform Act. He called for 'school-level review of the appropriateness of provision for the weakest pupils, with a view to adapting courses, teaching methods and practices so as to enhance motivation and achievement'. Again, these are precisely the considerations which led British ministers, initially against strong opposition from teacher and local authority opinion but with strong support from parents, to devise a legislative framework for national testing in English and Welsh schools at the ages of seven, eleven, fourteen and sixteen.

He also called for 'increasing provision for regular teacher in-service training, including co-operation with teachers in other types of school and work experience in industry'. Here too he was speaking to the converted in Britain: since the 1986 Act, the Department of Education and Science has funded through specific grants to local authorities (who over the years had failed to recognize the inadequacy of much of the initial training of teachers in the 1960s and 1970s) a major expansion of in-service training. In 1989–90 grants will be paid on over £300 million of expenditure.

The United Kingdom has already, then, anticipated many of Commissioner Marin's proposals. But we still have much to learn from the longer experience of a coherent curriculum and supporting services enjoyed by some other Community countries, especially perhaps France and West Germany.

West Germany shows how, if the will is there, progress can be made – even in a federal country where the role of the *Länder* in education is entrenched in the constitution. In Britain the 1988 Act is clear evidence of the government's willingness to take new powers over local authorities in order to ensure that the national interest prevails. In our own interest, as well as those of the Community, British educators have to do a lot better: in school standards, in training and in improving the flow of top-quality graduates into industry.

The Commission has particularly emphasized the need for more co-operation between schools and firms on training and retraining, stressing the need for the 'creation of closer links between the world of education and the world of work.' The British government has sought for over a decade to link schools more to the world of work but progress has been slow. The most significant move in this direction has been the Technical and Vocational Education Initiative (TVEI), introduced by the Conservative government in 1981. It was viewed with such suspicion by Labour education authorities as some sort of Conservative attempt to warp education that it took seven years to be extended to every local education authority. It is designed only for fourteen- to eighteen-year-olds, providing work experience and courses which place particular emphasis on practical problem-solving skills, technological competence and personal effectiveness. The hope is that TVEI, which is seen as a sustained programme of educational change, will alter school attitudes and help to promote 'active learning' across the board.

As part of Industry Year, 1986, many companies launched work 'shadowing' for sixth formers to observe the role of managers in industry and commerce. The DTI has since pulled out of this initiative but it has real potential and needs to be extended on a significant scale to embrace teachers. Additionally, all pupils should undertake work experience or job sampling of some kind during their final year at school.

The CBI has led a number of initiatives, establishing (with the Chambers of Commerce) Local Employer Networks to help develop more responsive vocational education and producing a stimulating report in 1988 from its Business/Education Task Force. This highlighted the need: half the respondents to a company questionnaire had no regular links with a local secondary school and fewer than one school in three had good enough links with businesses to meet the new government target for providing work experience for pupils and teachers.

There has been much teacher opposition to all of this 'vocationalism'. But I do not regard the widening of horizons to the world of work – provided it is effectively done – as a narrowing of education, the charge levelled so often by the more traditional forces in the education world. Teachers should obviously have regard for character development but education should not be something abstract, disconnected from the world, and relating it more to the world of work can do a great deal to motivate the learner. This split between the intellectual and practical lies deeply embedded in British culture. There has been a century-long struggle to attune our schools and higher education more to the application of knowledge, and to the needs of industry, as we have looked anxiously at the more technical approach of the French and even more of the Germans.

This concern is not recent. It was strongly evident in the latter part of the nineteenth century and a constant refrain throughout the first seventy years of this century. In British education there was a deplorable neglect of science. The Clarendon Royal Commission on the Public Schools reported in 1864 that 'natural science ... is practically excluded from the Education of higher classes in England.'

Between the Great Exhibition in London in 1851 and the Paris International Exhibition in 1878, Britain lost headway in industrial Europe. The new German empire in particular was threatening British industrial supremacy. As people examined the trends, increasingly their attention focused on education. A House of Commons Select Committee in 1868 commented on the 'extraordinarily rapid progress of Continental nations in manufactures' and pointed out that one reason was 'that the facilities for acquiring a knowledge of theoretical and applied science are incomparably greater on the Continent than in this country'. A Royal Commission in 1884 warned in bleak terms that 'the one point in which Germany is overwhelmingly superior to England is in schools ... in evening science teaching ... and in the multiplication of polytechnics'. By 1900 the fear of Germany's growing industrial strength was at last bringing demands for 'national efficiency' and reform in education. G. M. Trevelyan was later to observe that Britain had possessed 'the worst industrial peasantry in the West of Europe'. In 1900 Britain had seven universities, Germany twenty-two.

Eventually British ministers stirred themselves – no doubt prompted by the series of articles run by *The Times* in 1900 on 'The Crisis of British Industry'. The 1902 Education Act, put through by Lord Salisbury's Conservative government, saw a massive expansion of secondary schooling and the National Physical Laboratory was opened the same year. In 1907 the new Liberal government founded the Imperial College of Science and Technology.

The First World War highlighted British neglect of science and technology. In May 1916, scientists began calling for the creation of a National Chemical Advisory Committee and a government White Paper of July that year responded with a permanent organization for the 'promotion of industrial and scientific research'. This began as a Committee of the Privy Council but from December 1916 became a separate government department with a ministerial head in the shape of the Lord President of the Council. This new Department of Scientific and Industrial Research took over control of the National Physical Laboratory.

The war was also the major stimulus for the Medical Research Committee, which gained permanence as the Medical Research Council. Yet, despite the lessons of war, the Fisher Education Act of 1918, which called for local authorities to produce schemes for education to a minimum leaving age of fourteen and abolished all fees in elementary schools, made no direct provision for industrial training. Between the wars no more than 20 per cent of fourteen to sixteen-year-olds were in full-time education. There were some moves in the 1930s towards a more scientific and technological orientation for British industry but the demands of the Second World War again demonstrated the country's shortcomings. A Board of Education memorandum of May 1942 pointed out that, whereas in a range of industries there was 100 per cent vocational training in Germany, there was only 10 per cent in the United Kingdom. The Ministry of Aircraft Production never stopped despairing. Britain in 1939 lacked a comprehensive training strategy. Fifty years later, in 1989, the deficiency remains.

The Spens Report of 1939 deplored our failure to establish 'quasi-vocational' schools but the proposal to try to match the technical tradition in France and Germany was lost after the war when at last we created a coherent system of schools following the Butler Education Act of 1944. The idea was to have a 'tripartite' system of secondary education: grammar schools, modern schools and technical schools. Alas, very few of the latter were built. As a result secondary education concentrated on the intellect and restricted more practical and vocational studies to the less able.

At least further efforts were made on the research side, though British inventiveness was not applied commercially with the success it deserved. The Development of Inventions Act of 1948 led to the establishment in 1949 of the National Research Development Corporation, one of whose major tasks was to promote the development of computers, an area in which we were able to establish a commanding lead over the West European countries, though we lost it in the 1960s. It remains to be seen whether our lead in the 1970s in the life sciences, microbiology, molecular biology and immunology will be similarly eroded.

What is also extraordinary is that over 100 years, while there has been a clear perception of the inter-relationship of educational and economic success, no person and no government in Britain has apparently been able to establish the relationship effectively. The underlying problem is one of attitudes – an ethos in society, reflected in the schools, which is critical to science and technology and which remained strongly evident a decade after Sir Monty Finniston's Royal Commission Report ('Engineering: Our Future') in 1980.

One of many Royal Commissions launched by Labour governments as a substitute for action, the Finniston report addressed itself to the 'national undervaluation of engineering'. The report had a long pedigree as the latest but far from last of the weighty official inquiries with similar remits: the Royal Commission on Technical Education, 1867; the Select Committee on Scientific Instruction, 1868; the Devonshire Royal Commission on Scientific Instruction and the Advancement of Science, 1872–5; the Samuelson Royal Commission on Technical Instruction, 1884; the Balfour Report in 1929; and the 1968 Dainton inquiry into 'The Flow of Candidates in Science and Technology into Higher Education'. The reports showed good intention sacrificed to the classical tradition, a cult of amateurism and sheer inertia. And Finniston has fared little better in awakening policy-makers. How could the British have debated so intelligently for more than a century the dangers of their growing technical backwardness and have done so little about it?

Though standards in maths and science have been rising in recent years, they have fallen further behind the Germans and Japanese. According to research on seventeen countries published in 1988 by the International Association for the Evaluation of Educational Achievement, England was one of the poorest performers in science up to age fourteen, though the minority of pupils staying on to eighteen performed as well as the best. There is a particularly alarming weakness in mathematics among British thirteen- to sixteen-year-olds: the lower half of the ability range is about two years behind their German equivalents. In common tests set for school leavers in 1987, fifteen-year-old Germans did far better in maths than sixteen-year-old British pupils, and the average Japanese twelve-year-old was roughly at the same academic level as our average fifteen-year-old.

Nor is much done to redress this failure once British pupils have left school. On vocational training for school leavers, Britain's record is lamentable compared with continental practice, especially at the intermediate and lower levels of skill. The traditional apprenticeships, which in any case declined sharply in the recession of the early 1980s and seem unlikely to recover, were dominated by the unions and produced only narrowly competent plumbers, bricklayers and others whose training gave them little capacity for changing to other more modern or more flexible skilled employment. Part-time day release of young employees for further education has always been optional. Rab Butler's intentions in the 1944 Education Act for compulsory attendance at 'county colleges' were never implemented because of the priority given to raising the school-leaving age to fifteen and then sixteen. As a result, part-time education and training have been patchy, achieving most penetration in the predominantly women's occupations of clerical work, hairdressing and the like.

The Manpower Services Commission, now renamed the Training Commission, was created by a Conservative government in 1973 primarily to co-ordinate the work of the Industrial Training Boards, to determine manpower needs and to plan more effectively the making good of skill shortages. Almost at once its purpose was subverted by the succeeding Labour government's concern over mounting youth unemployment. Effort and resources were diverted from the long-delayed priority of training into the Job Creation Programme (often creating non-jobs, as it happened). Characteristic of this and several other programmes at that time, apart from TOPS (Training Opportunities Programme), was the paucity of the training actually provided.

Political considerations understandably encourage governments to act to combat unemployment. That is very proper and the provision of training and work experience has to rank at the top of any list of methods for doing this. But it is important not to lose sight of the whole picture. Anti-unemployment programmes by definition aim at the unemployed and those who find it harder to get work. In large measure these will be the least qualified or educated entrants to the job market; and the higher the proportion of the training benefit used to counter unemployment, the higher the proportion of limited resources that is spent on the less skilled or adept members of society. The corollary is true: a correspondingly lower proportion of available funds is spent on those who, as a consequence of their abilities, might benefit the most. The market in the end rewards excellence but this balance of policy neither helps the pursuit of excellence nor reinforces success; it does the reverse. The statistics of training programmes do not by themselves show the effect of this under-provision in Britain of training where it would have the most benefit.

The Youth Training Scheme, which eventually succeeded Job Creation and its successor, the Youth Opportunities Programme, has been extended into a two-year programme, including a six month training element. But it needs to be even more directly geared to job competence and less to mere work experience. It is not yet an adequate building block in a coherent training and retraining structure which would stand comparison with the provision made in Germany or France.

Other initiatives in British education taken by the Conservatives in the 1980s include: the Certificate of Pre-Vocational Education, the secondment of teachers into industry, the encouragement of industrialists to help in the running of schools as school governors and the development of school 'compacts' – partnerships between schools and local employers. The 'compact' employers guarantee jobs with training to those young people leaving full-time education (whether at sixteen, seventeen or eighteen) who have met attendance and attainment targets agreed between them, the school and the employer.

Only in Britain do a majority of sixteen-year-olds head immediately for the job market. The proportion is dramatically less elsewhere. The Japanese take the long-term view and have a clear national perspective which results in 94 per cent of the relevant population staying on at school for the three-year upper secondary programme and 37 per cent going on to higher education. As in Germany, education in Japan does not abruptly cease upon entry to work. National policy stresses 'lifetime education' and a self-development within the firm. Workers' attendance at courses in their own time is a feature of life in Japan, as it is in the United States.

In West Germany the number of young people remaining in school full time after age fifteen has increased immensely. Some 80 per cent of those not aiming at higher education enter full-time vocational schools or various pre-vocational courses or are provided by employers with training and day release. It has long been accepted by employers and the educational world alike that *all* school-leavers should receive vocational training. And it must be of good quality: it is allowed only in state-recognized training occupations, with courses that are statutorily prescribed and usually last three years. Training courses are recognized only when they ensure a nationwide, uniform, inter-sectoral vocational qualification, which guarantees the occupational mobility and flexibility of the trainees. Indeed, the content of the training is geared to this. In the first year the course comprises a complete vocational area (e.g. metal-working); in the second and third there is specialization leading to qualification as a skilled worker.

The greater part of vocational training, three or four days a week, is provided by employers at the place of work, with one or two days at a part-time vocational school. Small firms, unable to provide from their own resources the staff and equipment for the range of vocational training required by law, send their trainees to inter-firm training centres or to other firms. This 'dual system', as it is called, is designed to ensure that most of the training takes place with staffing and with equipment (both of which must satisfy government regulations) that reflect the current state of the art.

No employer is obliged to provide vocational training and no young person to undertake it. But because of the shared conviction that it is economically profitable for firms and a means of reducing the risk of unemployment for the trainees, almost all employers provide vocational training and almost all sixteen- or seventeen-year-old school leavers embark on it. From 1970 to 1984 the number of places increased by a third to reach more than 1.7 million.

The basic structure of vocational training set out in the Federal Vocational Training Act, 1969, is the responsibility of the Federal Ministry of Education, assisted by representatives of the *Länder*, the employers and trade unions. At the *Land* level there is a similar pattern; and below that the vocational training committees of the chambers of commerce, including educational and union representatives, are responsible for the content of training courses, the recognition of employers' arrangements and the establishment of examining boards. Finally, at works level, joint employer-employee councils determine the character of the on-the-job component of the training and the recruitment of instructors.

The vocational training schools themselves and their staff are provided by the *Länder* and the municipal authorities; and the Federal and *Länder* governments provide financial assistance to young trainees who need it, for in-firm training centres for smaller firms and for special schemes for the educationally disadvantaged. But much the greater part of the annual cost, nearly £10 billion gross (i.e. without allowing for the value of goods and services produced by the trainees) or more than 1 per cent of GDP, is met by the employers themselves, without financial assistance from public funds. Employers regard this as a necessary part of their operating costs – an investment which yields returns in the most skilled and adaptable workforce in the Community and a major source of West Germany's economic success.

The Germans themselves would not claim that this system is always as successful in execution as in design. And it would not be possible to translate it as it stands into the very different governmental and industrial framework of Britain. But a better combined expenditure on industrial training by the Department of Employment (formerly by the Manpower Services Commission), the Department of Education and Science, local authorities and employers, if properly harnessed, would take us some way towards a similarly effective system of vocational training in place of the present patchwork of good and bad, duplicated and non-existent.

The third significant area of neglect is that of training in industry. British employers have not yet noticed the writing which has for so long been emblazened on their walls. Unlike their counterparts and competitors in West Germany, they do not value investment in training as highly as investment in plant and equipment. Tom King put his finger on it when, as Secretary of State for Employment, he said: 'It is ironic that every company report and accounts include the most meticulously accurate calculations of depreciation of building and plant and their replacement cost, yet no such assessment is made of the knowledge and skills of those who will utilize these resources. Would anyone suggest that the latter depreciate any bit less quickly than any fixed assets? It is time that investors and the Stock Exchange took an interest in what provision companies are making to maintain and enhance the level of skills and competence in their workforce.' The government will have to accept that it cannot leave vocational training, any more than basic school education, entirely to market forces.

Training is yet another area where Britain faces 1992 with one hand tied behind its back. The key role must be performed by private industry but who will take the lead? In order to encourage private firms to expand their committment to training, the government can choose exhortation, the stick, the carrot or a combination of these.

There has been no shortage of exhortation. Many ministerial speeches have emphasized that corporate training leads to improved corporate profits. According to the Training Commission's figures, British employers on average spend some £800 per employee but a typical German firm is spending over £1,000. Moreover, the Labour Force Survey for 1984 highlighted significant disparities of training provision across the country. Training – so far as it is done – has tended to be concentrated on the younger end of the workforce, on the workers who are already skilled and chiefly in those southern parts of the country dominated by the service and high-tech industries. The survey found that relatively little *retraining* was available in the older industrial areas. Even the high-tech sector has stayed extraordinarily complacent: a third of respondents to a survey had no formal training provision and simply poached staff from other companies.

Europe should note the scale of the Japanese effort. The Nippon Telegraph and Telephone Company enrolled 240,000 workers out of a total of 312,000 in company training courses in 1985. The giant electronics firm, Hitachi, estimated in 1988 that its annual company training budget had reached £70 million, or about two-thirds of its advertising expenditure. In the 1990s we in Britain must aim for a vocationally qualified workforce which can match Japanese and West German levels of skills, competence and flexibility. The Germans have for almost two decades made a priority of vocational education, linked intimately with employers. The French training system for young people is also now expanding and improving at a much faster rate than in Britain.

There is no sign yet in Britain of the scale of retraining which the falling number of school-leavers will necessitate. The problem of skill shortages will become acute over the next decade, because of the so-called demographic 'time bomb'. The French do not face the same crisis (Fig. 7.1). The demographic trend in Britain will reduce the supply of young people entering our labour market in the early 1990s by 30 per cent. This will be the case in Germany too. Employers in both countries will have to rely increasingly on older workers acquiring new skills and there is no doubt about which country is doing most to prepare.

According to a National Institute Economic Review at the end of 1988, France produces three times as many mechanical and electrical craftsmen as Britain, and Germany is further ahead still. All the indications are that France has in recent years made a concerted effort at seeking a better deployment of skills. As a result, French manufacturing employers are much better placed than British to take advantage of new technology by introducing more flexible working practices, multi-skilling and team working. The result has been that output from France's engineering industry increased by 36 per cent between 1970 and 1987 whereas in Britain output in 1987 was much the same as in 1970.

Fig. 7.1 Estimate and Projections, 15–19–year-olds, 1950–2025

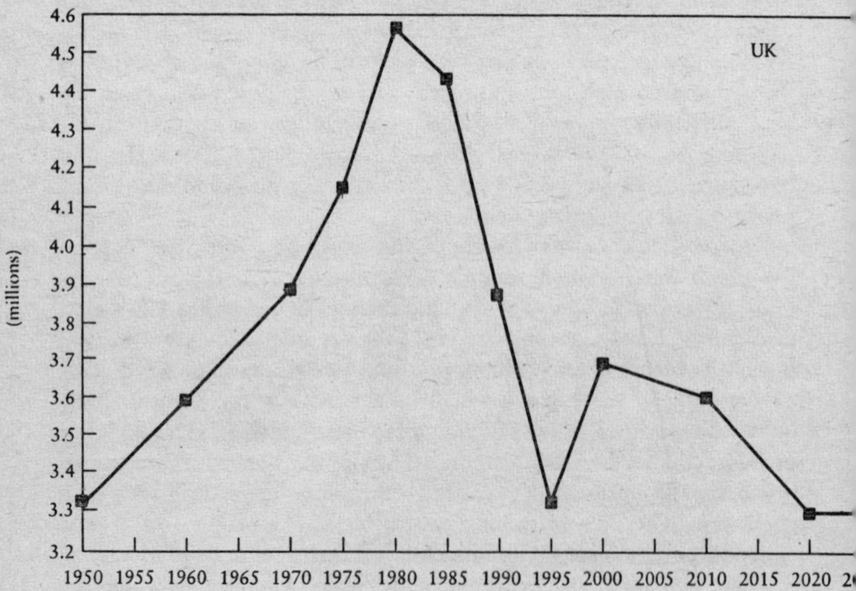

Of course there are pitfalls here for the government. No sensible government wants to underwrite the full training costs of industry, if businesses can be persuaded or cajoled to underwrite these costs themselves. Britain needs a comprehensive new Skill Improvement Programme to provide direct encouragement for training and retraining. The latter is a vital component, both because of the legacy of inadequate schooling and because the demographic bulge of the 1970s – under-educated and poorly trained – will, as the thirty-five to forty age group, be the single largest sector of the population as the single market takes shape.

Over the last few years the government has cut the taxation on jobs by reducing National Insurance contributions. It should now devise changes in the taxation system which positively encourage training. Alternatively – and at least worth consideration as an option within the package – employers could be provided with grants to cover a proportion of replacement labour while those capable of training to higher levels

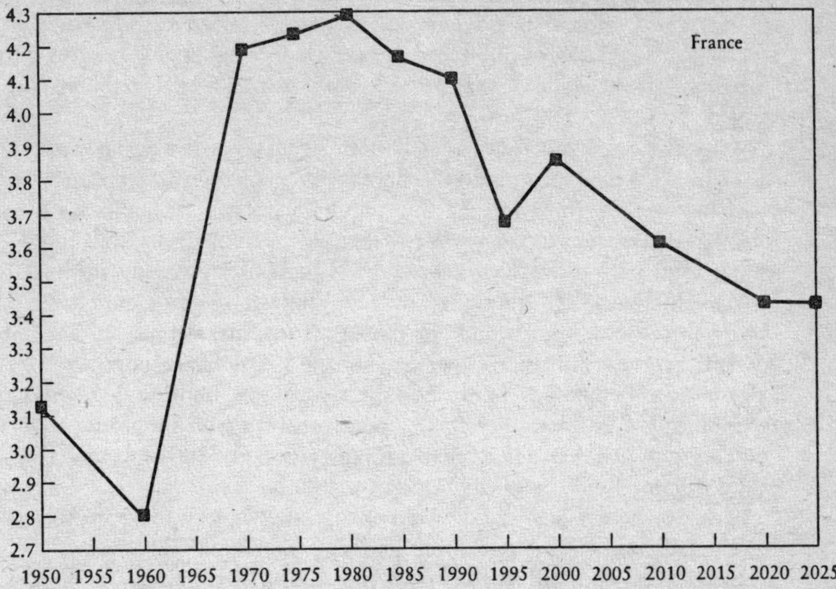

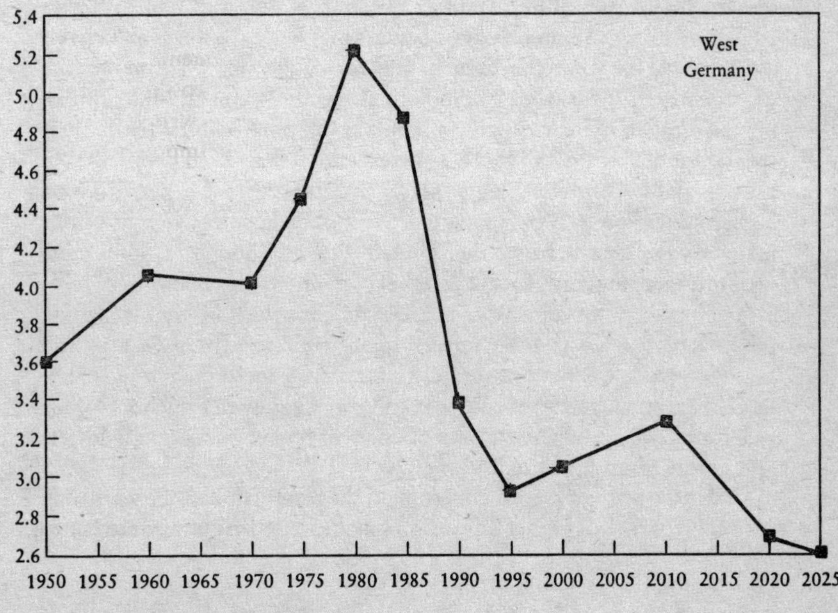

Source: UN World Demographic Estimates and Projections)

undertake intensive retraining. By helping to upgrade the quality of the workforce, the government would be improving the supply side of the economy at a critical stage when skilled labour is scarce, and saving a considerable outlay of public funds because moving people progressively up the jobs ladder makes room for others to climb on to the first rung.

Many employers are already encountering shortages of workers with the right skills, and information technology is intensifying the problem by changing the nature and the skill requirements of vast numbers of jobs. For this reason, successive West German governments have all laid strong emphasis on this sector. Britain has particular problems in this area, as the House of Commons Trade and Industry Select Committee report on Information Technology (1988) made clear, estimating that, currently, there is at least a 10 per cent shortfall. The final report of the Information Technology Skill Shortage Committee implied that one solution might be assistance for training consortia run by groups of companies. In America the Reagan administration provided substantial pump-priming funds for such projects.

The government has to carry the chief responsibility for both the basic education of the workforce and the training of the scientists and engineers who will in turn train the scientists, technologists and researchers of the future. The key question is how can British higher education produce enough world-beaters in science, business and engineering. That is what the French *grandes écoles* and in America the Massachusetts Institute of Technology successfully aim at. Many British universities and, increasingly, a number of polytechnics (with their special emphasis on sandwich courses) more than hold their own in Europe and beyond. In the first place, Britain's current expenditure on higher education as a percentage of GDP is higher than in any of our main rivals, apart from the United States, though a quite disproportionate amount is spent on student maintenance grants (see Table 7.1). Thanks to a rigorous system of student selection, ample staffing (about one teacher to ten students against one to fifty in France) and grants to students that are several times more generous than in France or Germany, a first degree course is still usually only of three years (four years in Scotland, where the age of entry of higher education is lower) and graduates of high quality emerge.

Under the present British government the proportion of the age group *entering* courses of higher education has increased from 13 per cent to

Table 7.1 Current Public Expenditure on Higher Education as a Percentage of GNP

		All Expenditure	*Excluding Student Support & Welfare*
USA	1982	2.5	2.3
UK*	1983	1.1	0.8
France	1982	0.7	0.6
West Germany	1983	0.6	0.5
Italy	1983	0.5	0.5
Japan	1982	0.4	0.4

*Excluding expenditure on nursing and paramedical courses at DHSS establishments.
(Source: DES Statistical Bulletin 4/87)

over 15 per cent (see Table 7.2) and is planned to reach over 20 per cent. The enrolment figure looks low on superficial comparison with British competitors but Table 7.3 tells a different story, when we consider the numbers *completing* their qualifications.

Very low wastage rates from full-time courses – only one in ten in universities compared with up to one in two in France – and the important contribution made by part-time courses leading to degrees, diplomas or professional qualifications have meant that Britain's output of qualified scientists and engineers has in recent years been greater than in France or West Germany. Germany's main advantage lies not in the numbers graduating at degree level but in those at the level just below the top. The National Institute of Economic and Social Research estimates the comparisons as outlined in Table 7.4.

The overall figures for Britain hide acute shortages in critical areas of engineering in particular, despite the demand for highly trained experts increasing year by year. Between 1985 and 1987 applications to study electronics fell by 21 per cent; physics by 13 per cent; mathematics by 12 per cent; and all engineering and technology courses were down by 11 per cent. But if this latter figure is broken down, the real crisis emerges: whereas applications for university places in 1989 in civil engineering rose by 21 per cent over the previous year, mechanical engineering attracted 4 per cent *fewer* students, electronic engineering 7 per cent fewer and combined technology departments attracted 12 per

Table 7.2 Enrolments on Higher Education Courses 1984 (per 100 of 18–24 population)

USA	44
Netherlands	22
Japan	21
Germany	20
France	19
Italy	18
UK	15

Table 7.3 Numbers Completing Higher Education Courses

	Year Obtained	*Total Number of Qualifications Awarded (000s)*
USA	1983	1811
Japan	1984	576
UK	1984	284
France	1982	270
Germany	1983	217
Italy	1984	91
Netherlands	1982	56

(Source: DES International Statistical Comparisons 1987)

Table 7.4 Engineering Comparisons (Units '000s)

	UK	*France*	*W. Germany*	*Japan*	*US*
Bachelor Degrees	14	15	21	30*	19*
Technicians	29	35	44	27*	17*
Craftsmen	35	92	120	44*	n/a

*reduced in proportion to UK population
(Source: *Independent*, 28 February 1989)

cent fewer. Computer studies drew a miserable 3 per cent increase in applications and the universities expect to see by 1990 a shortfall of a quarter in their planned number of students in this critical discipline.

If the report on the output of qualified students is 'all right but could do better', Britain's record in research leaves a lot to be desired. Research and development are often confused. For many companies their ideal is to do the development work 'in house'. To them, the role of the university is to provide them with talented manpower and bright ideas in basic research.

One of the most depressing aspects of the British industrial scene is the slide in R&D. As Table 7.5 shows, apart from Italy the smallest share

Table 7.5 Higher Education R&D 1981–5 as a Percentage of GDP

	1981	*1985*
USA	0.35	0.37
Japan	0.56	0.57
West Germany	0.40	0.40
France	0.33	0.34 (1984)
UK	0.32	0.32
Italy	0.18	0.26

(Source: OECD 1988)

of Gross Domestic Product spent on higher-education-based R&D is the UK's. The emphasis has not increased for many years. Although the government has increased science funding in 1989/90 by 16 per cent in real terms, this only serves to highlight the inadequacy of our inheritance and the difficulty of redressing a long-deteriorating situation. The 1974–9 Labour government did not increase the science vote at all and between 1979 and 1987 there was only a 1.5 per cent average annual increase.

The sheer scale of funding needed has forced even the Americans to embrace government-sponsored programmes to provide incentives for pure research. In 1986 the United States Tax Reform Act established a new incentive called the Basic Research Credit. This was similar to an earlier tax credit established in 1981 which had been allowed to lapse in 1985. The Basic Research Credit can be claimed at a fixed rate of 20 per cent. (The earlier tax credit was 25 per cent, but could only be claimed for *increases* in R&D spending.) The new credit is paid on all amounts above a certain minimum level of R&D expenditure. This is to enable each company to obtain credit on each year's payment as long as that payment exceeds the fixed guaranteed amount throughout a multi-year contract. The credit applies to a company's contribution or contract for basic research conducted at a qualifying institution. It is geared to encourage company support of basic research in science, engineering and mathematics. Congress's aim was to speed the process by which new ideas are discovered through innovative research and translated into company products and processes. A similar scheme would be well worth trying in Britain over, say, a three-year initial period.

From the Robbins Report of 1962 onwards, British governments have fought shy, rightly in my view, of any detailed planning of higher education on the basis of manpower forecasts. But the Treasury never sleeps: realizing that numbers in higher education will have to rise if the efforts of Britain's competitors are to be matched, it has launched a Whitehall study on how public funds could be limited to specific manpower areas. What is needed instead is a broad assessment, in which major employers must be involved, of the probable technological changes over the next decade or so which will alter the balance of skills required. With a free – or freer – movement of people within the Community from 1992, this study should also take account of the extent to which Britain (now that English is the first foreign language of so many in Western Europe) will attract talent from other countries.

A key difficulty in producing a comprehensive account of relations in Britain between the universities and industry is that there are so many departments with differing responsibilities for policy in this area. There has been a flow of initiatives from these departments over the last few years, matched by initiatives from industry, some from individual firms and others from representative bodies such as the CBI and the Council for Industry and Higher Education. The truth is that whereas in 1967 21 per cent of all graduates entered industry, by 1980 the proportion had fallen to 13 per cent and by 1987 it had only managed to climb back to 17 per cent.

A number of government initiatives have been introduced to promote links between higher education and industry. Specific measures include:

the Enterprise in Higher Education Initiative, which was launched by the Secretaries of State for Employment and Education and Science in December 1987; the appointment of people with experience of industry and commerce to such academic bodies as the Council for National Academic Awards, the new Universities Funding Council and the Polytechnics and Colleges Funding Council; and the launch of research programmes which involve various research councils with the Department of Trade and Industry.

Notable examples of initiatives jointly supported by government and industry include the Engineering and Technology Programme and the Manufacturing Systems Engineering Programme, which are designed to provide an additional 6,500 graduate and postgraduate places in engineering and technology disciplines by the end of the decade. Employers participate by providing equipment on loan or as gifts and giving access to leading-edge technology which educational institutions do not always possess; sponsoring students on relevant technician, undergraduate and postgraduate courses; and providing opportunities for students to obtain industrial and commercial experience within academic programmes.

A highly successful means of promoting active partnerships between universities and polytechnics and industry in recent years has been the Teaching Company Scheme, sponsored jointly by the DTI and the Science and Engineering Research Council. Under this scheme young graduates undertake key projects in companies under the joint supervision of academic and company staff. The scheme has proved a valuable means of developing the technological and managerial capabilities of young graduates. It is proposed to increase its size substantially by 1992 and to base an increasing proportion of programmes on smaller and medium-sized firms. It should possibly be more targeted on to crucial sectors, such as information technology.

There has been little attempt to quantify the success of all these initiatives. The most helpful review was one drawn up by economic development consultants for the MSC. The report focused on the effects of skill supply on industrial development.

The report finds that university/industry links are extremely diverse in the UK and their success or failure depends on a complex set of social and economic factors, including the enthusiastic support of the local community, its bankers, planners and entrepreneurs, and the availability of public money.

There is no single public body with overall responsibility for the role in national innovation policy of university-based research and development, and the absence of such a body impedes necessary progress. As long as several government departments have partial responsibility for this area, they will all have an imperfect grasp of the whole subject. The USA has long had a 'round table' forum on academic-industry relations where government, university and industry discuss the issues as players of equal standing. In 1987 the British government established the Advisory Committee on Science and Technology to fulfil a similar role.

Though links with industry and commerce will be central to the long-term future of universities, science parks should not become a substitute for, but should be seen as a useful stimulus to establishing close relationships with companies in particular communities. Nor must generating income become a short-term goal that conflicts with the imperative of excellence in research.

After more than thirty years of an egalitarian education policy, a massive building programme and the emission of millions of words on education, overall standards in British schools are still too low. Employers with depressing frequency deny the ability of school-leavers to fill skilled jobs. But think of it another way: should we not accept that there will always be underlying inadequacies, that thousands of pupils will never learn as much as they could or have the motive or stimulus to do so? British education has begun to improve, certainly by comparison with past performance. The challenge is how to stay with or move ahead of the competition in the European Community and beyond. So should we not look questioningly at policies which make school-level education the main priority and concern ourselves rather more with how to make opportunities available after school and throughout life?

The existing pattern of financial support for students overwhelmingly favours the traditional full-time student entering higher education straight from school, at the expense of mature students and those studying part-time. Britain needs a comprehensive system involving both grants and loans, a system which would encourage individuals, employers and taxpayers to share the burden of an extended training programme to provide the country with a flexible and mobile labour force with up-to-date and adaptable skills. By reducing the extent to which grants are available to the traditional full-time student, resources could be freed to provide help for those to whom no incentive is given to take part-time or retraining courses.

A recent comparison of student aid showed that British undergraduates bear a significantly smaller proportion of total costs than their German, French and Swedish counterparts, but that we also provide much less financial aid for non-traditional students, including adults.

Employers themselves are loath to act in this area because of the disruption and cost of releasing experienced workers for training and the fact that the life-time benefit from their investment is less than from an equal investment in their new entrants. The sacrifice of earnings is also a disincentive for the individual. In France and Sweden, employers and employees contribute to a training tax to fund a comprehensive system. The NEDO report, 'Competence and Competition', showed that British employers invest only a fraction of what the United States, Japan and West Germany spend on training and upgrading the adult workforce. The UK workforce as a whole receives about fourteen hours off-the-job training a year, compared with the thirty or forty hours which in Germany is considered good practice.

Many sections of British industry are quite unaware of the range of educational services which is available to them. Better information, both to excite interest and to help people to find the right opportunity to develop their particular talents, is essential. A plethora of sources now produce pamphlets and leaflets on adult educational opportunities of all types. A range of information booklets, explaining in simple terms what is available both to employers and to potential learners, is now available in Job Centres. Libraries are also increasingly used. Some local authorities publish free newspapers on the provision of adult education.

Promotional material can be misleading, so there is still a great need for accurate, comprehensive and efficiently co-ordinated information. People sometimes need guidance in deciding whether they need 'education' or 'training', which course might suit them best and where it is available. Many potential adult students have little time and there is an important missing link if there is no one with whom they can discuss such things.

Counselling services will be essential in a society in which the majority of people may change their career several times in a working life. The need is even more acute when they are also unemployed. But how can we ensure that the recurrent opportunities on offer are relevant? Unless they are clearly so, there will be no interest on the part of the company or of the student who is looking for a course germane to the demands of his or her job. Again it requires closer links with business and commerce.

Britain has recently made major advances in many areas of educational provision, at least by the standard of past performance; but in scale and standards our competitors' efforts put them well ahead. The double challenge is to remain one of the world's leaders in science and technology and to derive the fullest commercial advantage from that leadership.

This demands both high standards and the resources to reach them. Wide availability of appropriate high-quality education, excellence in research and a systematic approach to skill training are all essential if the engine of economic growth is to run smoothly and if Britain is to maintain her proper place in the Europe of the 1990s.

Above all, if Britain is serious about competing in a better educated and technologically sophisticated world, we must break out from over a century's acceptance of second best in education and training. We need to understand where the public programmes of the nations, with which we must compete, will take their coming generations, and set targets that will get our children there as well. The ability to afford this should be one of the proudest claims for our revitalized economy.

CHAPTER
8

Environment: a World Without Frontiers

I must declare an interest in the environment. When I was seven, a master at my prep school thrust a packet of Virginia stock seeds into my hand and pointed to a square yard of heavy mud – I was away. Within weeks I was the triumphant owner of a blaze of colour and scent. Today I am planting an arboretum. There are still earlier memories in South Wales. With my grandfather I watched the elvers – frenetic wriggling hyphen marks – chase each other up the streams of Clyne Valley. With my father I collected cowries on Langland beach, where Swansea then gave way to the beauties of the Gower Peninsula.

Every moment that I could tear away from my Virginia stocks in that early summer was devoted to watching, breeding, ringing and rearing birds. Later I would cycle for miles to discuss the finer points of the crested canary. Jackdaws and magpies put themselves – well, found themselves – under my protection, hopping on and off my fingers. I remember feeling very responsible when my two budgerigars, in a gratifyingly short span, became forty. I still recall my stumbling for words of explanation when the headmaster of Shrewsbury School, the late Lord Wolfenden, caught me wheeling some Heath Robinson contraption full of greenfinches across the school site.

Nor was the competitive zeal missing. In 1942, or thereabouts, I became the junior angling champion of Brynmill Park, Swansea. It is no mean feat to hook and land thirty-nine fish in two hours, even if the triumph fades away when it is revealed that the whole lot of them only weighed 11¾ ounces. Still, 7 shillings and 6 pence the richer (although about seventy maggots the poorer) I had something to show for my pains.

The fourteen-year-old who lay still for hour after hour, waiting to pull the string on luckless blackbirds inveigled into home-made traps, so that they would for ever wear the ring of the Royal Society for the Protection of Birds, found himself thirty years later in 1979 at lunch in the Athenaeum with Ian Prestt the Society's director. We were discussing the proposals for the further protection of birds in the forthcoming Wildlife and Countryside Bill: 'Is there anything more I can do to help?' I was able to ask him. 'Nothing' was the gratifying answer. The Bill, which extended the law protecting wild birds (among its many other provisions), gave him all he needed; what mattered now was enforcement. I was privileged to be Secretary of State for the Environment at that time.

To my life-long love of the natural environment was added, as time went by, a growing interest in Britain's and Europe's cultural heritage. So the Department was to me a spiritual home. I was the political custodian of the natural world in England and the richest patron of its heritage.

The Wildlife and Countryside Bill in 1981 was inevitably the product of compromise – an attempt to make those who live and work in the countryside familiar with those whose main interest is to enjoy it. Habitats were protected, nest robbers denied and the first comprehensive statute for wildlife protection enacted. It is a major credit to the government's record of environmental achievement. The Act created maritime nature reserves. Fishing interests were suspicious but I have spent too much time with mask or aqualung to have any doubts about the degree of damage that is being done. Lifeless lochs and reefs, the accumulation of toxins and refuse, were a terrible warning of what happens when man's worst excesses go unchecked.

In much of the Department of the Environment's work we recognized the European dimension. Tom King, as Minister of State, first persuaded the rest of Europe to back his initiative to save the whale, then, with their support, was able to move world opinion. It was a British initiative but without full European support it would not have been so persuasive nor so effective.

The weakness of isolated national effort in the environmental field becomes ever plainer. What is the point of campaigning to save a few sea creatures when the waters around Europe are daily polluted on an alarming scale? And Britain is among the worst offenders. What worthwhile protection can be offered to migrant birds nesting in Britain if they continue to be slaughtered by our European neighbours on their autumnal flights south? What can we say about Britain's contribution to conservation in 'Plant a Tree' year, when acid rain is destroying abroad more trees than we plant at home?

If Venice sinks or rots, is not all Europe's heritage the poorer? The buildings we list, protect and restore in Britain, whether the product of Greek or Roman, or of purely domestic inspiration, are preserved also for the peoples of all other lands to share. Europeans cannot take the view that whatever they do, or fail to do, is up to them; far less can they imagine they are at liberty to confine their environmental efforts and concern to their own country.

Our museums are filled with treasures which British scholars or public servants, some more distinguished than others, removed from the threat of thieves and vandals or acquired in competition with other European collectors. Is it not right to pay in part for what the British people have accumulated from abroad, by displaying a practical concern for sites and monuments elsewhere in Europe which have not been plundered or destroyed?

The environment of the twelve countries which make up today's European Community is rich in its variety. Its diversity encompasses the moorlands of the Scottish Highlands and the near-deserts of Southern Spain and Greece, the sub-sea-level lowlands of Holland and the high mountain ranges of the Alps and the Pyrenees. The Community's shoreline borders seven seas and an ocean. Its climate is as varied as its topography.

The varied geography of the 2.25 million square kilometres which make up the land area of the twelve provides habitats for a large number of species. As well as some 320 million human beings, the Community is home to 6,000 species of plant, 600 species of bird and about 130 species of mammal. Bear, wolf and lynx still run free in some wilder parts of this vast land mass.

It is a territory that has been dramatically shaped by the hand of man. From the earliest times, Europeans transformed their environment for agricultural purposes. The great forest that covered much of the Northern European plain was cleared early. Later, the grasslands were ploughed and the wetlands drained. In more recent times, the intensive agriculture fostered by the Common Agricultural Policy has accelerated many of these transforming forces, adding new factors, such as fertilizer and pesticide use, and encouraged the vast fields favoured by modern agricultural machinery.

These forces have created, modified and destroyed habitats. They have eliminated some species, encouraged others and altered the course of natural succession. They have caused soil erosion and sedimentation in streams, lakes and reservoirs. Some two-thirds of the land area of the European Community is used for agriculture. The landscapes we see around us, whether here in Britain or in any other member state of the Community, are the outcome of generation after generation of farming and forestry.

But for most of Europe's citizens, the daily environment is that of the city or town. They not only work there, but shop, eat, travel and sleep there. More than 60 per cent of the Community's population live in towns of more than 20,000 people. For them the quality of daily life depends on the state of the urban environment – its noise, fumes, dust, smells, crowds and buildings. The towns are also the most visible repositories of Europe's history and culture, containing in their buildings the most tangible expression of Europe's values and aspirations.

Europe's towns and cities are highly concentrated along the corridor of industrial activity that runs in a broad swathe from the North-West of England through London to Belgium and Northern France, and then along the Rhine and its tributaries into Northern Italy. It is here that the bulk of the European Community's heavy industry is found. From here come the eleven million cars a year produced in the Community – more than the total number of cars produced in the United States and the Soviet Union combined. From here too come the chemicals, pharmaceuticals, machine tools, consumer durables, electronics, plastics and ten thousand or so other varieties of product upon which Europe's wealth depends.

Not surprisingly, it is here too that we find the concentration of Europe's industrial pollution – the emissions of sulphur and nitrogen oxides, the heavy metal-contaminated soils and the chemically polluted waterways. These pollutants not only affect the immediate environment and the health of our city dwellers, they are also carried in large quantities by our rivers and the wind to the rest of the Community and to the other countries of Europe.

The sheer quantities are staggering. More than four million tonnes a year of sulphur dioxide and another two million tonnes of nitrogen oxides come from Britain alone. To these must be added the millions of tonnes of hydrocarbons from vehicle exhausts, oil refineries and industrial solvent releases, hundreds of thousands of tonnes of the chlorofluorocarbons (CFCs) that damage the ozone layer, and thousands of tonnes of lead and other heavy metal waste. The consequences of this air pollution are all too visible. In some parts of Germany three quarters of the forests are dead or dying. In Switzerland, avalanche dangers have increased as air pollution from the factories and power plants of Northern Italy damages the trees that act as natural protection. Even in Britain, it is now becoming clear that as much as half of the forests are beginning to show signs of damage. The same air pollution has badly damaged antiquities, statues, stained glass windows, cathedral masonry and other elements of our cultural heritage from Athens to Aberdeen.

A similar story could be told of the pollution in Europe's rivers and estuaries, and there have been increasing signs of ecological stress in parts of the seas surrounding Europe's coastline. In the summer of 1988 there was a widely reported death of seals in the North and Baltic Seas, at the same time as there were algal blooms in both those seas and the Adriatic. There has also been considerable damage to many of our plant and animal species and the habitats on which they depend. Marshes and wetlands have been transformed, hedgerows cut down, moorlands afforested and coastal ecosystems overdeveloped throughout the European Community. Almost a third of Europe's vertebrate species – the higher animals such as mammals, birds, fishes and amphibians – are officially regarded as under threat of extinction.

However, it is not all gloom and doom. It is now clear that we have passed the peak of emissions for many, if not most, air pollutants. The record on water pollution, however, is mixed. Some of Europe's rivers and streams are at last beginning to recover. The River Thames is one of the most notable signs of this change. It was almost devoid of life in the sixties but by the middle of the eighties more than 100 species of fish had returned to its much cleaner waters. But after years of progress the situation is now worsening again and Britain's rivers are being increasingly poisoned by waste. Sewage and industrial and farm discharges are higher than ever along a growing proportion of rivers. The capital investment programme on sewage disposal was cut by more than half between 1974 and 1979, one of the many victims of the Labour government's axe.

I recognize the conflict of interest within a department that acts as both regulator of standards and sponsor of industry. The Department of the Environment has carried such a responsibility for the water and sewerage disposal industries. It does not enjoy unfettered discretion. The Treasury, properly concerned with the overall level of public expenditure, restrains the public investment programmes which are essential to achieve higher standards. The present proposals are to privatize these industries and create a National Rivers Authority, under the chairmanship of Lord Crickhowell, formerly Nicholas Edwards, Secretary of State for Wales 1979–87, with tough powers to set standards and targets for the control of pollution while enabling the water industry to raise the long-overdue investment free of public expenditure constraints. Improving the environment will not come cheap.

It has become clear that, for all its diversity, Europe's environment is a fragile and vulnerable unity. No other event could have brought this fact home to the people of the Community as forcibly as the accident to the nuclear power station at Chernobyl in the Soviet Union. The cloud of radioactive debris from the destroyed reactor spread across the whole of Europe with no regard for national boundaries. The acid rain that damages trees in Scandinavia originates in Britain and Germany. The chemical pollution that prevented German, French and Dutch water authorities taking drinking water from the Rhine was caused by an accident in Switzerland.

The CFCs that are reducing the ozone layer do so over every country in Europe indiscriminately. The tourists whose increasing numbers are causing severe damage to the slopes of the Alps and to the Mediterranean coastline come from each of the twelve member states as well as from the rest of the world. British bird lovers are reduced to impotent fury by the inability of the French government to prevent French hunters slaughtering 'our' songbirds as they make their perilous migratory way across France.

We may not yet live in one Europe politically but we certainly do so ecologically. We Europeans are bound together by a web of environmental relationships that link us via our rivers and seas, our flora and fauna, and the air that we breathe. We are also bound together by our common concern for the fate of that environment.

This concern manifests itself in opinion polls which show that, throughout the Community, almost three-quarters of Europeans are concerned or very concerned about pollution and that nearly as many worry about the destruction of forests and the extinction of plants and animals. It also manifests itself in the rapid growth in membership of Europe's environmental organizations. The European Environmental Bureau is a coalition of 120 of the major organizations from the twelve countries. The total membership of its organization exceeds twenty million people. In Britain, perhaps as many as four million people belong to environmental organizations; in Denmark there are said to be more members of environmental bodies than there are members of the population, since so many people belong to more than one organization.

This shared concern manifests itself too in the growing strength of the Green Parties in Europe. Although they remain marginal everywhere other than in Germany, their presence in many parliaments indicates the strength of public feeling about the environment, particularly among the young. And it sends a clear signal to the mainstream parties about public expectations.

The unity of Europe's environment is reflected in this collective concern for its protection; and the concern is shown in the success and vitality of environmental policy-making within the Community. The creation of a common policy on the environment has been one of the Community's great triumphs, though it has gone largely unrecognized. It is customary to complain of the slowness of Community institutions in arriving at decisions on politically awkward matters and to fret at the need to compromise in order to achieve agreements. I have made such complaints myself and they are often justified. No one looking at the body of European environmental legislation now in place and at the growing pressure on member states to comply with its requirements – often, as Britain has discovered, at great cost – could imagine that such a comprehensive set of measures would ever have been adopted in so many countries if national governments had been left to their own devices.

The European Community is unique in its ability to draft and enforce supranational law. Nowhere else have nation states yet agreed to surrender an element of national sovereignty for the common good; nowhere else in the world is there a comparable set of binding policies to protect the environment across national boundaries. We should not underestimate the importance of the experience that has been gained in the European Community. As we approach a more complex and critical future, in which all who live on our planet will have to co-ordinate their policies closely if we are not to undermine the very conditions that make life possible, then the experience gained during the fifteen years it has taken to put this policy in place will be invaluable.

The European Community is the only laboratory the world presently has in which to develop the full range of political tools that will be needed for planetary management. No other international forum combines environmental policy making and economic policy making within the same institution. As has been recognized by political leaders on many occasions, the economy and the environment are interdependent.

This unique role presents us as Europeans with a challenge, an opportunity and a responsibility. The challenge is to our imagination and our determination to find new approaches and put them into operation. The opportunity is to offer a better environment and a better quality of life for our children and their successors. The responsibility is not to let short-term frustrations and small-mindedness prevent us facing the challenge and taking the opportunity, so that we may offer the rest of the world a practical model for solving our common environmental problems.

Given the importance now attached to environmental policy it is something of a surprise to discover that the environment was not even mentioned in the Treaty of Rome. No provision was made in that founding document for the development of a common environmental policy. It was not until 1971, during the run up to the United Nations Conference on the Human Environment, that the Commission first proposed such a policy. The following year, in the wake of the Stockholm Conference, the leaders of the Community met in Paris and adopted an environmental resolution.

Until the Single European Act came into force on 1 July 1987, this resolution was the sole resource of legal authority for the whole body of environmental policy. Before 1973, only ten items of environmental legislation had reached the European statute book; since then over 200 further items of legislation have been adopted by the Community. The absence of a clear provision for the environment in the treaties incorporating the Community meant that the legal base on which the policy stood remained shaky. Thus most environmental provisions were technically described as efforts at harmonization in order to remove obstacles to trade.

The Single European Act added a new title, headed 'Environment', which provided a firm legal base for Community actions on the environment. There is now a specific article (Article 130R[2]) which stipulates that 'environmental protection requirements shall be a component of the Community's other policies'. This clearer legal base will give the Commission a freer hand to propose measures that will integrate environmental concerns more closely into the formation of other common policies such as agriculture, transport or energy.

In practice, the absence of a proper legal foundation has had little effect on the development of the Community's environment policy. This has taken the form of a series of action programmes of which there have so far been four. The action programmes serve two purposes: they are the launch platform for specific legislative proposals and they provide an occasion to discuss the broad ideas of environmental policy and suggest directions for the future. The action programmes establish a policy framework which indicates the general thrust and priorities for action but each individual proposal has to be meticulously debated in detail before it becomes law.

The First Action Programme ran from 1973 until 1977. Coming hard on the heels of the Stockholm Conference and the first great flush of public concern over large-scale pollution, the Programme was very much concerned with cleaning up acute pollution problems. It dealt with air, water, wastes, noise, chemicals and wildlife. It also established the basic principles on which the Community's policy would be built, including the 'polluter pays' principle, a commitment to prevention being better than cure and to the idea that proposals should be science-based.

The First Action Programme contained far more proposals than could possibly be taken up in four years and for that reason the Second Action Programme, which ran from 1977 until 1983, was little more than an elaboration of its predecessor. By the time the Third Action Programme was adopted in 1983, however, the emphasis had shifted. It had been recognized that simply curing the obvious abuses did not go far enough and that it was important to anticipate new and emerging problems. Thus was born the belief in integration – the idea that environmental considerations should be built into the earliest stages of policy making in other areas. The European Community was the first body anywhere to adopt and try to give practical effect to what is a fundamental principle.

In 1987 a Fourth Action Programme was adopted, which developed the concept of integration and placed strong emphasis on implementation and enforcement of Community legislation. It is easy to point to a thick statute book and assume that it is making a great difference to the state of the environment; in fact, too often environmental laws are honoured more closely in the breach than in the observance. This is not only bad for the environment, it is also very unfair on those countries and industries which comply conscientiously and fully with the legislation. The Fourth Action Programme has stimulated a vigorous round of actions in the European Court as the Commission has tried to insist that countries do what they have agreed to do.

The action programmes thus serve as platforms for ideas and priorities, and they set the agenda for Community action on the environment. The formal renewal of this cycle of activity every four or five years maintains the momentum and allows everyone – member states, industrialists, environmentalists, local authorities, scientists and all the other people concerned with the environment – to judge what progress is being made and how they can best adapt to the requirements of a better environment. This is one idea that Britain might usefully copy from Europe. We have tended to make environment policy in recent times by leaflet, pamphlet and glossy brochure; and such documents, though they may be useful for spreading information, do not establish the clear policy framework that is necessary if we are to get the best response from industry and commerce.

Politicians in all the member states, not least in Britain, are often to be heard complaining about the burdens imposed by Brussels. This is somewhat disingenuous. The specific legislative proposals that are derived from the action programmes are each negotiated line by line by all the member states. All the environmental legislation agreed before the Single Act required unanimity for adoption. All that the Commission in Brussels is able to do is to require that member states stand by their word. In this field, as in many others, it has proved much easier to make promises than to keep them.

With one notable exception, Britain's record on the environment is as good as any in Europe and better than most. We have by far the most comprehensive and sophisticated system of planning control within the

Community. We also have a far more developed network of protected areas in our National Parks, Areas of Outstanding Natural Beauty, National Nature Reserves, Sites of Special Scientific Interest, Heritage Coasts and the rest. There are few European equivalents of our national Nature Conservancy Council or Countryside Commissions with their special status as statutory advisors to government. Many of our rivers are improving in quality, although some too slowly and others have standards that are quite unacceptable. We have made significant progress in reclaiming land left derelict by industry. Our system for hazardous waste disposal has been roundly criticized by the chief inspector of the Hazardous Waste Inspectorate, and clearly improvements are urgent, but we do not have the acute toxic waste dumping problems experienced by some of our neighbours. As far as nuclear waste is concerned, the accidents at the Sellafield reprocessing plant have focused our minds sharply on nuclear safety and how best to handle nuclear waste disposal.

None of this is meant to suggest that everything is perfect in Britain's attitude to and protection of the environment. Far from it. But the positive side of the story is considerable. If we in Britain have excelled at the protection of much of our natural environment, protected wetlands, scheduled the vital sites, surely the appropriate British response should be to take a lead and influence events from our successful experience, rather than resist as though we neither care nor wish to contribute?

It is also a striking enough record to prompt the question: 'Why, then, has Britain acquired such an unsavoury reputation throughout the European Community?' In part this reputation derives from one major failure – our failure to respond positively to international efforts to control acid rain. Britain is by far and away the largest producer in Western Europe of the sulphur oxides that contribute to the formation of acid rain. Because of the 'tall stack' policy instigated after the smogs of the 1950s, much of the sulphur dioxide pollution we produce no longer falls in the UK but is exported to other countries. Britain's reluctance to admit that this was causing serious problems, and her unwillingness to agree to measures designed to solve them, alienated both public and political opinion throughout Europe, especially in those countries that were suffering very dramatic and visible tree death. Even now that we have finally agreed to European legislation (the Large Plant Emissions Directive, 1988) which will require us to reduce our emissions by 60 per cent by 2003, we will still remain the largest air polluter within the European Community.

But there is another – in some ways more serious – reason for our poor image. We have far too frequently been reluctant partners in joint efforts to protect the environment, often bringing up the rear in reaching agreements. This reluctance has stemmed in part from that deep mistrust of becoming too involved in things European that has characterized our wider approach to membership of the Community. It has also stemmed from more than a touch of arrogance. We have had a tendency to feel that we know rather more about these matters than our neighbours; that we began dealing with environmental problems before anyone else and have very little to learn. Immediately we joined the Community we became embroiled in a doctrinal dispute over water pollution theory which held up agreement on important issues for many years. Eventually, in 1987, at the ministerial conference on the North Sea, we changed our position and fell into line with the rest of Europe.

Similarly, we resisted adoption of an environmental impact assessment procedure for major developments (Environmental Impact Directive, 1985) for several years on the basis that our development planning system already covered much of the ground. In doing so, we wholly failed to recognize the obvious point that we would therefore have to adapt our procedures rather less than would other countries and that a small effort on our part could produce major environmental gains in countries whose systems of environmental management were less developed than our own. It is not surprising that our colleagues found us frustrating, to say the least of it.

We are short-sighted to react so defensively to Community initiatives on the environment. Too often we have been caught saying 'no' to the proposals of others. Sometimes we have acted with good cause, but all too often without proposing any positive ideas of our own. On the few occasions when we have made our own proposals – banning the import of whale products into the Community or inserting provisions to allow for the designation of environmentally sensitive areas which permit farmers to receive CAP funds for conservation measures – they have been swiftly successful.

Unnecessarily, we make ourselves a target for criticism from others with inferior records on the environment. Far better, then, that we take our expertise in dealing with the environment and put it to work effectively throughout Europe. Britain's environmental record is something to build on. Among our scientists, policy makers, voluntary bodies and industrialists are many of the world's experts in solving environmental problems. This is an asset for Britain and should be exploited within the Community. And it is an asset that, used properly, will not only help to improve the quality of our environment but also do much to maintain Britain's economic strength. If the British government adopts a little-by-little approach, that is the approach that British business will follow. Thankfully, the atmosphere has begun to change, thanks in large measure to the concern and effort displayed by William Waldegrave as Minister of State for the Environment in 1986/7.

The year 1992, when the single European market is to become a reality, will also be the twentieth anniversary of the famous Stockholm Conference which first focused world attention on the planet's environment. This happy coincidence should concentrate our attention on the twin challenges of the coming decade: the economy and the environment. They are interdependent. The creation of the single market can enrich Europe's citizens. Indeed, the thrust of the inner city strategy that the government developed in the 1980s was precisely to restore the ability of such areas to compete for new owner-occupied housing schemes and industrial investment by improving the environment in them. But a single market that does not deliver a better quality environment will not long retain the support even of those who benefit the most. This was recognized at the Rhodes meeting of the Community heads of government in December 1988, when they declared: 'The industrial and competitive future of Europe on the world market partly depends on the application of [a] high level of environmental protection....'

Many environmentalists fear the single market. They see it only as an opportunity for industry, imposing pressure to lower environmental standards. They see a trade-off between vigorous economic growth and the quality of life, with the one able to improve only at the expense of the other. This misses the point. It is not an accident that the worst environmental degradation is to be found in the countries with the weakest economies. Similarly, within each country, including Britain, it is in the economically weak inner cities and centres of older, uncompetitive industry that the environment is at its worst.

But the fears are not wholly unfounded. We must now recognize that not all development is sustainable, that we can no longer afford growth at any price. Nevertheless the report of the World Commission on the Environment and Development, the Brundtland report, has shown that it is possible to reconcile economic with ecological imperatives. It has also shown that a world without growth would be intolerable, ecologically as well as morally. What matters is the kind of growth we have.

The Brundtland report called it 'sustainable growth', others have used the term green growth. The arrival of the single market in Europe affords an exciting opportunity not just to secure Europe's competitive position in world markets, but to do so in a way that is sustainable, to create not just a single market but a green market.

Too much of the environmental debate has concentrated on the problems rather than on the opportunities. Too much effort has been placed on constraining the bad rather than encouraging the better. It is time to shift the focus of the environmental debate from the negative to the positive. The creation of the single market presents us with just such a chance. We in Britain have a unique role to play for it was in this country that the green consumer was first recognized.

Public concern about the environment has been steadily rising for many years, as shown both in public opinion polls and in the growing membership of environmental organizations. Recently there has been fresh evidence that the public wants to translate its concerns into choices in the market place when they are available. The response of British consumers to the news that Prince Charles had asked his wife not to use hair sprays propelled by the chemicals that destroy the ozone layer was dramatic. Within weeks many of the major suppliers of personal products which used CFCs announced that they were phasing out their use. All major retailers in Britain now offer non-CFC alternatives on their shelves.

At least two studies by leading British market research companies have begun to chart the emergence of the green consumer. They have found that if product performance and price are roughly comparable, most consumers, especially women, prefer to buy a 'greener' product. These findings were supported by the success of Green Consumer Week in September 1988 and the rise of the *Green Consumer Guide* to the top of the best-seller list in the same month. Since then there has been a spate of articles and conferences on the green consumer written for and attended by leading industrialists. Many commentators have seen this trend as an extension of the trend towards healthy eating that has transformed consumer preferences during the 1980s. The decision of the Tesco grocery chain and Sainsburys to launch green consumer campaigns in January 1989 reinforced this perception.

It also reinforced another perception. When major retailers begin to compete to improve their environmental performance, the competitive forces of the market place are being turned to the advantage of the environment. And, since the green consumer has emerged, Britain has a head start on her partners before the advent of the single market. Here we have a positive idea that reconciles economic and social goals which we can market successfully to the rest of the Community.

The stakes for industry and commerce in getting environmental matters right grow greater by the year. The British car industry, for example, has lost export orders because of its inability to meet more demanding anti-pollution emission standards (Air Pollution from Motor Vehicles Directive, 1988). Other industries have done better. Rolls Royce were able to penetrate lucrative American markets for their RB211-535 series engines because they were significantly quieter than rival engines. British Aerospace broke into the commuter jet market in the US with their HP146 'Whisper Jet' largely because it offered advantages to operators working from noise-sensitive urban airports.

It is not only access to markets that is at stake. Under more stringent environmental requirements, our German, Swiss and Scandinavian competitors are already developing and deploying the technologies which will be essential to an environmentally more sensitive world. These technologies also frequently produce significant cost savings and so improve competitiveness. It can – and must – be done here in Britain. Glaxo's largest UK factory recovers solvents for re-use, thus preventing pollution and saving itself £25 million a year. Solvent recovery systems often pay for their installation within one year or less.

Clearly it is desirable in itself, but environmental protection can pay. Environmental regulations can be seen as government imposing burdens on industry, but the environmental entrepreneurs will see them as helping to expand industry's markets and improve its productivity.

The OECD estimates that its members spend £50 billion a year on pollution control. That is a large market by any standards. In Britain, in 1985, there were 336 firms in the pollution control industry. Between them they turned over £2.2 billion. That makes it an industry about the same size as the pharmaceutical industry, one of Britain's economic success stories. Even so, it is winning less than 5 per cent of the available market – hardly an aggressively competitive performance.

The single market will give us an opportunity to do better; but only if we improve our performance, since it will give the same opportunity to our competitors. To do better we must recognize that industry alone cannot act effectively. Those companies that invest so as to achieve higher standards see their less concerned competitors undercutting the higher prices which their investment in quality requires them to charge. Some governments are worried about regulating too strongly for fear that many marginal firms will be driven to the wall. But other governments, acting in close consultation with their industries, will set the higher standards and then deny by law the opportunity for others to undercut them with environmentally damaging products. Eventually Community law will enforce those standards and those member countries which have had lax regimes will find their industries less well placed. This is not a game for the ideologue obsessed with quaint theories about the distancing of government from industry. It is a sophisticated process in which government and industry work closely together to secure the highest standards at home which will enable industry to exploit quality in export markets. These standards will often have to be European or international, so we must ensure that the British voice in their formulation and enforcement is clearly heard. The single market will provide an hospitable habitat for the environmental entrepreneur: we must make sure that the species has a chance to thrive in Britain.

There is also a need to develop a wholly new species, the green capitalist. The management of capital is one of the great British success stories, and the skills and experience of the City institutions are one of the cornerstones of our economy. But the City has been slow to respond to the environment and there are few signs that it recognizes that the investments necessary for the pursuit of environmental excellence require a longer-term view than the quarterly or half-yearly return might permit. Little of the City's formidable inventiveness has yet been put to work to help protect our environment.

Some ideas are beginning to emerge. The idea of swapping third-world debt for conservation could contribute, if tight conditions were negotiated, to solving environmental problems. The first unit trust specifically dedicated to investing in environmentally benign enterprises, the Merlin Ecology Fund, was launched in London recently. It has subsequently been a consistently leading performer economically. But these are just the earliest beginnings.

Why, for example, are our banks not offering saving schemes for children, the funds from which would be invested specifically with the aim of ensuring that the quality of the environment into which they grow up is enhanced? Could there not be tax efficient loan schemes designed to encourage people to invest in energy-efficiency improvements? Could there not be a legal advisory service for those who contemplate making a will, so that, having enjoyed a healthy environment in their lifetimes, they may be helped to leave something to ensure that it is conserved for their descendants? As those of the baby-boom generation reach their middle years throughout Europe, they will be looking for financial services and products which reflect their concern for the environment. Britain should be taking a lead in developing those products. The greening of the City of London's more energetic and imaginative people would be one of the most significant of all contributions we could make to the creation of a green market in Europe.

Getting the environment right is not only crucial to getting our economy right; it is also becoming an increasingly important part of maintaining our security. For long something of a political backwater, the province of enthusiasts and experts, the environment has recently been catapulted to the top of the political agenda.

The environment has also been high on President Bush's agenda. During his election campaign he pulled off a notable *coup de théâtre* by highlighting the pollution of Boston harbour in Governor Dukakis's home territory. He also made a pledge to call a global summit on the environment early in his administration and took pains to meet the leaders of America's environmental groups shortly after his election.

By a trick of the time zones, Margaret Thatcher and the Soviet Foreign Minister, Eduard Shevardnadze, both made speeches on 27 September 1988. Both speeches came as surprises to their audiences. Mrs Thatcher's was widely reported for the contribution it made to the public debate about the environment. In it she established four themes as setting a global agenda – global warming, acid deposition, ozone depletion and the achievement of sustainable development. She has subsequently returned to these themes on a number of occasions and swiftly followed words with actions by calling a ministerial conference on 'Saving the Ozone Layer' which was held in London in March 1989 and proved most successful.

Mr Shevardnadze's speech was delivered to the UN General Assembly. Unlike Mrs Thatcher's speech on the same day, it has remained largely unreported in the British press. But it has profound implications for the West. He made some forceful proposals. The first was to turn the United

Nations Environment Programme into a global 'environment council'. This institution was to have the job of taking 'effective decisions to ensure ecological security'. The second proposal was for a series of emergency meetings intended to 'co-ordinate efforts in the fields of ecological security'. A three-part cycle of meetings was proposed, beginning with a meeting of experts in 1989, to be followed by a mini global summit in 1990 with the leaders of fifteen to twenty states, and then by a second United Nations International Conference on the Environment in 1992.

These proposals are an invitation to vigorous action. They will appeal to the swelling ranks of green voters throughout Western Europe. They will also appeal to the far wider general public whose concern about the health of our planet continues to grow. Mr Shevardnadze's speech also adds a new phrase to our vocabulary – 'ecological security'. It is clearly intended to join Mrs Thatcher's 'sustainable development' as one of the signposts towards a healthier planet. 'Sustainable development' is no doubt to be the achievement of 'ecological security'.

But what is 'ecological security?' Mr Shevardnadze is not very forthcoming. Fortunately his deputy, Mr V. F. Petrovsky, is more explicit. In a statement he issued on 11 October 1988 we find that '... in the face of the global ecological threat ... the paradigms of national security based on egotism and military, above all nuclear, deterrence require urgent revision'. It is not hard to imagine what is coming. 'The problem of environmental pollution has been exacerbated as a result of squandering the planet's resources that are not by any means limitless. The arms race, above all nuclear, constitutes a most dangerous worsening of the natural balance.' Thence to the punch line: 'We believe that the renunciation of certain military programmes, whether planned or undergoing, could be made use of to channel the released resources to establish an international regime for environmental security.'

'Ecological security', then, is a rather straightforward idea. We should stop spending money on arms and spend it on protecting the environment instead. This does not mean, of course, that Gorbachev, Shevardnadze and Petrovsky are not genuinely concerned about the state of the planet's environment. They have more reason than most to care. Their hopelessly inefficient economies do more to squander scarce resources and their outmoded technologies pollute more than most.

Their record speaks for itself. Chernobyl left 33 dead, at least 2,000 more to die and 150,000 evacuated. The town of Chernobyl is to be demolished and the rest of Europe was left to clean up as best it could. In the rice fields near Rostov, excessive pesticide use had led to a 27 per cent increase in cancer in just five years and a rise in birth defects by 55 to 60 per cent. Water quality is deteriorating nearly everywhere. The river Ob and its tributary, the Irtysh, in West Siberia, have twenty times the permitted level of oil products. The concentration of phenol in the Caspian Sea is nine times the permitted level and in the Baltic four times. Most dramatically of all, the Aral Sea is drying up. It has lost 60 per cent of its water. Its shoreline has retreated sixty-five kilometres in some places, dropping water levels thirteen metres and creating an ecological catastrophe.

The Soviet Union has huge environmental problems of its own making. Mr Gorbachev may genuinely want to solve these problems. Indeed, since many of the people responsible for these environmental disasters are the same people who have wrecked the Soviet economy, it may suit him domestically to make much of the issue. But we should not let these thoughts blind us to the fact that what we are also seeing is a well thought out attempt to hijack the environmental agenda, partly for ulterior purposes. You do not have to be a cold warrior to recognize that a new arena has been opened up in which to fight some of the old battles.

Gorbachev has spotted that the West's environmental record leaves it with a long and vulnerable flank exposed. The message of the rise of the Green parties in Western Europe is clear. The environmental record of governments on both sides of the Atlantic, even when seen through the eyes of their own supporters, no longer matches the expectations of their democracies. Western leadership is now under threat for its perceived failure to respond early enough or adequately to the developing ecological crisis.

In this campaign as in others, Mr Gorbachev has one advantage in a battle for hearts and minds: he does not live in a free society. He has no vigorous environmental groups rousing public opinion and applying pressure to improve performance. He has no free media to uncover the real scope of environmental damage. He can deploy resounding language without fear that anyone will be able openly to point out the gap between his rhetoric and Soviet reality. This climate is changing, but it is not yet comparable to that in the West.

We face the prospect of a difficult round of weapons modernization within the Atlantic alliance. We have complex negotiations to pursue on conventional force reductions and on the next round of strategic nuclear arms limitations. The linking of the environment and security offers many opportunities for mischief-making with Western public opinion.

To take the most obvious example: the Montebello decision of the NATO alliance was to modernize our short-range nuclear capability. As the British Secretary of State who signed that declaration, I profoundly agree with it, as I do with the coincidental decision to reduce dramatically the number of such weapons available to the alliance by the destruction of older weapons systems. There is every argument to reduce nuclear weapons and to rely on smaller numbers of more effective weapons. There is no argument worth the name to rely on any weapons system that is out of date and thus ineffective in its deterrent role.

Gorbachev would dearly love to prevent this modernization. He can analyse the significance of green voters in the Federal Republic of Germany where the issue of short-range weapons is most acute. His new 'green peace' is tailor-made for the West German electorate. (I owe the device of separating the 'green' from 'peace' to Shevardnadze who first used it in his General Assembly speech.) We must not close our eyes to these realities simply because we agree with the Russian premise, namely that the planet faces unprecedented environmental threats. Indeed, if we are too gullible in our response to Soviet ecological initiatives, we run the great risk that progress on protecting the environment will be slowed as the question becomes confused by the tangles of super-power struggles.

It is not difficult to imagine that many genuine environmentalists may be swept up in a wave of enthusiasm for the superficial attractions of 'ecological security'. Nor is it difficult to imagine further how the Soviets might develop this line: siren calls may be heard for resource and technology transfer, not to help an ailing economy recover from the self-inflicted wounds of an overstretched defence capability, but simply to help the Soviets play their part in the global effort to protect the environment. Mr Petrovsky's speech is quite explicit: in his call for United Nations action 'to adopt binding principles and rules of behaviour', he suggested the definition of main areas of international co-operation in the ecological field including 'mutual access to advanced technologies'.

It is easy to paraphrase what the Soviet arguments will be: 'We in the Soviet Union wish to reduce our defence spending, but all our proposals for doing so are frustrated by a refusal of the West to give up the most dangerous of its capabilities in the nuclear field. When we have signed an intermediate-range treaty getting rid of your Cruise and Pershing missiles and our SS 20s and are urgently pursuing strategic reductions of up to 50 per cent, you in the West are putting this process at risk by introducing new short-range weapons into Europe. And worse, we wish to reduce defence expenditure and use the cash to modernize our industry, a principal benefit of which will be higher environmental standards for us all. Not only are you forcing us to spend more on defence than we wish, denying us the chance to modernize our industry and improve the environment for all mankind, but you will not share with us the advanced technologies we need to secure such environmental improvements.' The straightforward equivalence is stressed in the Shevardnadze speech: 'For the first time we have seen the stark reality of the threat to our environment – a second front fast approaching and gaining an urgency equal to that of the nuclear-and-space threat.'

Thus the Soviet case will run. Thus Green Peace will be proclaimed. The prudent Western leader will not fall for it. Transferring technology to the Russians to clean up their industrial legacy is as attractive to the Russians as transferring technology for directly military purposes. They will be quite relaxed about the motives of those who transfer the technology – as long as the technology arrives. They will then decide how much of it is to be used for environmental purposes, how much for military purposes and how much to help an inefficient economy to catch up.

In truth much environmental technology is close to military technology. To explore the parameters of environmental damage from space, to model global climate patterns or to build the necessary data bases to co-ordinate scientific knowledge of the environment, you need the most sophisticated information technologies, including the largest computers. Already the Soviet Union has sought from both the French and the Germans access to more modern and safer nuclear power technologies. No one should doubt in the wake of Chernobyl the difficulty of denying them technology that is as crucial to our safety as it is to theirs. New material technologies based on carbon or silicon are replacing metal-based technologies with their higher environmental impact. But these newer, lighter and stronger technologies are also critical to future advances in sophisticated weapons.

The West will not underestimate the seductive power of this latest appeal to hearts and minds. As for its practical importance, it is enough to remember that it was the NATO decision to deploy Cruise and Pershing missiles in 1979 that brought the West German Green Party to prominence. But pointing out the suspect motives for the greening of Gorbachev will not on its own carry the day. His presentation will owe more to the skills of Madison Avenue than anything that Brezhnev, Andropov or Chernenko could have dreamt up.

The later 1980s have seen an unprecedented set of international meetings on the environment, over and above those called for by Shevardnadze, and the programme of political activity stretches far ahead. As well as Mrs Thatcher's ozone conference in March 1989 and the Dutch/French/Norwegian prime ministerial gathering in the same month, 1988 saw another Dutch conference at ministerial level on climate change. The environment was also discussed at the G7 meeting in Paris in July of that year. A ministerial workshop for European Community environment ministers is due to be held in Copenhagen in November 1989; and in 1990 a major gathering of ministers in Bergen to follow up progress since the Brundtland report is to be followed by a meeting of OECD environment ministers. There will be a World Health Organization Conference on the environment and health in Sweden in 1991 and the UN will be holding a conference in 1992 to mark the twentieth anniversary of the Stockholm Conference. Somewhere in this crowded agenda President Bush has to insert his pledged global summit.

We must recognize that the Soviet Union has signalled its intention to make these meetings into ideological battlegrounds. We must measure our response accordingly. We are witnessing the emergence of green geopolitics but we must not allow our attention to be distracted from the host of environmental questions. With or without the Soviets, we have a fight on our hands. Again, the British have to fight now for their place in Europe in order to fight more effectively on Europe's behalf and, in this instance, on the world's behalf.

Entirely due to human causes the climate is warming, the deserts are advancing, the forests are in retreat and the seas grow ever more polluted. What if every human being on earth were to consume natural resources at the pace at which they have been consumed by the Europeans and North Americans? Suppose we agreed to freeze our living standards – or in the last resort, reduce them – would those so far behind agree to remain for ever impoverished, denied what we have taken for granted? Of course not.

There is no point in casting blame on others. Let us confront the truth. In environmental terms no nation is an island and environmental pollution knows nothing of national sovereignty. The sins of emission of our neighbours are bestowed upon us and likewise our sins upon them.

What programmes are we to pursue? What research is necessary? By whom? When? At whose cost? These are the questions which must be addressed: an essential priority, but the answers will not be cheap. We can mobilize the resources of Europe to a position of world influence. The growing success of the green consumer, and the emergence of the green entrepreneur and the green capitalist will be among our most powerful allies. And their success on first a national, then a European scale, will improve both our environment and our commercial prospects.

CHAPTER
9

Defence: the First Responsibility

On my first day in the Ministry of Defence in January 1983 I was briefed about 'the threat'. It is a time-honoured practice and ministers the world over, when first charged with responsibility for their country's defence, have a similar induction. The gist of the message did not surprise me. We had after all lived through four decades of menace from the Soviet Union's overwhelming superiority in conventional weapons and the preponderance of her increasingly sophisticated chemical and nuclear weapons. Since the 1940s a score of my predecessors have been shown the same constantly menacing features of Soviet power ranged against Western Europe, in a stance as immobile as it was hostile.

Suddenly, in 1988, that immobility was gone and the hostility appeared to diminish. The presence of Ronald Reagan at a summit in Moscow was a powerful symbol. Less conspicuous, I too was there – one of 8,000 world commentators and journalists – each a living embodiment of *glasnost*. That summit meeting illuminated for many an extraordinary phase in the evolution of East-West relations. It came within days of ratification by the United States Congress of the INF Treaty – a marked contrast to the last super-power treaty, SALT II, which limped through the Senate before being torpedoed by the Soviet invasion of Afghanistan. The prize that we were told was impossible had been attained: a treaty to *reduce* nuclear weapons, not simply to regulate the continual growth in their numbers.

The withdrawal of Soviet troops from Afghanistan was completed in February 1989, shortly before the date pledged by Mikhail Gorbachev. The loss of world prestige the USSR suffered by the invasion was compounded by years of failure to subdue the rebels. Mr Gorbachev has taken a bold step in damage limitation but the risks are high. To pull armies out of the field in such circumstances, and to change the disposition of military forces, is to invite confrontation with the military hierarchy. Many will welcome it but there will be some, if tensions develop in other parts of the empire, only too willing to point to the precedent that encouraged them. The withdrawal from Afghanistan has precedents in recent history which the Soviet leaders must think ominous: Vietnam soured a whole American generation; France was deeply divided by the withdrawal from Algeria.

There will be those in the Red Army, and not only the young bloods, who may view the retreat from Kabul as political weakness – a refusal by the Kremlin to let them finish the job. Like professional soldiers elsewhere, they are likely to see little merit in diverting defence expenditure to civil purposes. It may be important to Gorbachev that history does not provide his generals with too many opportunities to proclaim the Russian equivalent of 'I told you so'.

Gorbachev's domestic changes would seem to weaken rather than strengthen the cohesion of the Soviet Union in the short-term. *Perestroika* confronts the power groupings that have made Russia what she is. The justification can only be a switch of resources from defence to industrial investment. But *perestroika* and *glasnost* have provoked not only debate but in some quarters dissent on the part of narrow or resentful elements whom Gorbachev has set out to dispossess. Until a popular support, based upon improvement in living standards, emerges to counter the discontent, his position must remain exposed. The elections in March 1989 demonstrated the strong desire of the Soviet people for change. Whether that change can come fast enough and in an orderly enough manner to justify the new enthusiasm is at the heart of the question, and the recent riots in Georgia give grounds for doubt.

As Defence Secretary, I served in a government determined to deploy sufficient military strength and economic and political effort to make sure that there would be no risk-free opportunities for the Soviet Union to exploit. Within the Ministry of Defence I asked to be briefed as though through Soviet eyes, in order that we might assess Soviet power realistically and recognize the problems the Soviet government faced. The value of such an exercise was not always recognized in the days of frozen rhetoric and of the easy denunciation of the Soviet military build-up, as well as the Soviet government's failure to implement the Helsinki agreement on human rights. But to attempt a fuller understanding of a potential opponent is not to be irresolute. Western resolve remained firm during the 1980s and Gorbachev's appreciation of it, and his recognition of the problems facing the Soviet economy, provided a chance for change.

The spiralling defence budgets of the two super-powers and their commitments across the globe have left them both over-extended and imposed substantial economic strains. In the new, more optimistic atmosphere, the task of realistically assessing Soviet aims, strengths and weaknesses is no less important. The rhetoric from Moscow has changed greatly for the better – but that is by no means enough.

The judgment that the Western democracies make of Gorbachev will determine their policy-making. He does not look to Europe's millions of voters like a menacing figure. He does not use the old Cold War vocabulary with which we were familiar. In his easy use of the media, in his apparent concern for the things that matter to ordinary citizens in all the Western democracies, in his whole demeanour, he is the smiling face over the fence. The attractive personality of his wife seems to confirm this judgment.

A warmer wind of change has replaced the icy Eastern blast with which we had grown familiar. Or has it? The 'threat' as perceived by millions of European voters has receded. Are they right? If so, how far has it receded, and for how long? What are Gorbachev's ambitions? Who will come after him?

He is certainly alive to the need for change. Since Stalin's death some of his successors have repeatedly urged or contemplated reforms – though on a relatively tiny scale – to make the system deliver more efficiently. Khruschev may have been a man of impetuous behaviour, a leader who allowed the Soviet Union to be humiliated in the Cuban missile crisis; but in his eleven years he planted the seeds of change in the Soviet system without which Gorbachev would scarcely have been able to contemplate his present course. The early Brezhnev reforms of 1966/7 failed because they were restricted to the economy and left untouched the suffocating political role of the Communist Party. The forces of reaction were well entrenched and, inevitably, experimentation ended with the invasion of Czechoslovakia. In Andropov, as befitted a former head of the KGB, a leader emerged who focused on better management and greater discipline in the workplace, and sought to reduce drunkenness and absenteeism.

In one sense Gorbachev is, therefore, only repeating the calls for change that others have made. Among working people it has all been heard before. But Gorbachev's predecessors argued that, with only a little more effort, the system could prove efficient. He has blown away that illusion and told the Russians plainly just how bad things are. The strength of his message is in its starkness; his audience may not like what he is saying, they may fear for their self-interest, but no one has any better ideas. For the time being there is no alternative. Hence *perestroika*: the fundamental reform of the system itself that requires for its success the separation of the Party from the State, the creation of an independent judiciary, the delegation of more responsibility to local Soviets, the accountability of individual management, the establishment of co-operatives and the holding of elections in which non-Party candidates not only stood, but triumphed. There is much else on the agenda. Stalin's excesses are now discredited but Lenin's theories remain largely unchallenged. To bring about reform on so ambitious a scale, Gorbachev has to enlist support wherever it can be found. *Glasnost* is his chosen recruiting agent, called in to overcome the deeply entrenched interests of the Party, the military, the KGB and the ever-present bureaucracy through vigorous and universal debate.

Today there is a discernible presence within Russia of a more consumer-oriented middle class, with its own pressure groups and self-interests: a new generation of opinion-formers. They are well equipped for a debate about their country. But the contradictions and complexities of Gorbachev's position become plainer the longer the debate continues.

Glasnost is meat and drink to the intelligentsia, the students, the media – those who form Gorbachev's obvious constituency. But what of the working people who, distancing themselves from the political message by long custom, know that so far *perestroika* has merely succeeded in reducing their wages? Until recently they could produce indifferent goods and get away with it; now, if products fail the quality controls, they have to be remade for no extra pay. There are fewer goods in the shops than before, higher prices threaten and Gorbachev has even cut down on their vodka. It is not much of a message.

Perestroika, to succeed, must be seen to deliver the results which are so far conspicuously missing.

At this stage, it is easy to predict the worst of all worlds: restructuring without results and an articulate intelligentsia free to point a finger. The architect, lavishly praised for the creative genius of his plan, can quickly become the contractor whose building fails to rise from its foundations.

Gorbachev's only chance is to push on, though it is easy to understand his frustration. At the heart of his problem lies the chaos of Soviet agriculture. He knows that the peasants produce on tiny private plots a quite disproportionate percentage of the output. It is not the energy of the people or the quality of the land that is at fault. It is the system, by which both collective and state farms are told what to grow, even what to plant, with no local discretion. It is the hopeless distribution system that divides areas of plenty from areas of shortage and rationing, and separates products from their markets.

It is said that peasants can fly to Moscow from the south with pomegranates in suitcases and make a profit on the journey. But why should anyone bother to earn more money when, for the most part, there is little to spend it on? The inefficiencies flow through all the processing, storage and distribution systems, bringing to the Soviet Union a critical balance of payments problem.

Far from his rhetoric about competing with Western Europe by the turn of the century, Gorbachev must realize that only by a superhuman achievement coupled with a large measure of luck can he even arrest today's relative decline, let alone catch up with the West. Indeed, in 1988, five years after he came to power pledging that agricultural reform was his first priority, the Soviet Union reported the worst grain harvest in its history. Rather than catching up with the West, Russian anxiety now focuses increasingly on the unfavourable comparison with economies elsewhere in Asia. But the Soviet people have long memories. Many will hesitate to follow Gorbachev's lead for fear of what might follow if the leadership were to change. So the cautious will hold back and the doubtful will continue to frustrate progress by inertia, incompetence or obduracy. The need to strike a balance between liberalization and central control can never be far from the Soviet President's thoughts.

As the centre has relaxed its grip, however slightly, nationalism has shown itself in unrest and rioting in several Soviet republics, and while Gorbachev's response to the riots in Armenia and Azerbaijan in 1989 was less autocratic than would have been that of Stalin or Brezhnev, the replacement and humiliation of the local army and KGB bosses by outsiders were in the classic Czarist tradition. If dialogue in the name of *glasnost* becomes synonymous with dissent in the outposts of the Russian empire, then the new ideas, and the regime that pioneers them, will soon be in serious trouble.

In the longer run, there will be no comfort for Moscow from the South, where a primitive economy, endemic corruption and Muslim fundamentalist fervour seem certain to cause mounting trouble. The western rim of the Soviet Union is potentially even more sensitive – and more immediately so – because from Estonia to Georgia the republics are not Russian and they lie across the routes (and military lines of communication) to the West. That in itself highlights the precariousness of the eight countries of Communist Eastern Europe, whose people have suffered over forty years of Communist government and who look enviously at their flourishing West European neighbours.

Gorbachev, therefore, faces daunting and deep-seated problems. All the historic mistakes, all the political and economic distortions, have come home to Moscow to roost. For three centuries and more, Russia has struggled to try to keep up with the West economically and militarily. When parity was achieved in strategic nuclear weapons in the 1970s, equality as a military super-power was achieved. But the burden of devoting more than 15 per cent of GDP to defence is a crippling one; and military might is not enough. Russian achievements have not proved a model to which other countries aspire. Nor, because of Western resolve, has Soviet military power been converted into political weight in Western Europe. The persistent search for security at any price, ignoring the impact on others, has proved counter-productive.

But Western Europe cannot afford to gloat over the difficulties Gorbachev faces. If he fails, we could again face an economically weak Russia run by insular ideologues obsessed with military power. His failure could sour relations as fast as they have progressed over the last few years. If he succeeds, we will face an economically stronger Soviet Union but also a more open and less militarily dominated society. Paradoxically, therefore, the West must assist in strengthening the hand of the Soviet government to compete more effectively against it in the longer term, confident that Western democracy and economic organization will continue to keep us ahead. This is a harder and more subtle task than we have been accustomed to attempt. It will also be slow.

On the other hand, it is as well to remember how far we have already come.

Gorbachev is a Marxist. His may be the smiling face of Marxism but he is not about to jettison one nineteenth-century ideology to embrace another, that of liberal capitalism. He may be a man we can do business with but, however he may appear, he will never be one of us. His aim is not to abandon competition with the West but to regroup in order to pursue it more effectively. He is also a Russian nationalist. Nothing revealed in his plans reduces in any way the need for NATO to continue its policy of deterrence.

The West has to retain an effective ability to react militarily, not just diplomatically, to whatever circumstances develop. In taking precautions against an unpredictable future, it is prudent to prepare for the worst. There lies the rub. As experience of war in Europe recedes, it becomes more difficult for each succeeding generation to appreciate the need for armaments on the present scale and the cost of keeping them modernized. Public opinion in West Germany today is a particular example of this, and of great concern.

It is not just a matter of being aware of the other side's weapons systems, their numbers and disposition: it is about what a potential opponent is capable of doing. It is not even a matter of what the present rulers may do but of what their successors may contemplate. There may be little popular support for such watchfulness but popular opinion is fickle and frequently wrong. Human beings naturally yearn for peace but from the fact that peace is so obviously in all our interests it does not follow that all nations will therefore pursue it. We should not lose patience with policy-makers who appear over-cautious. The average citizen's interest in the lessons of history rarely stretches back beyond the headlines of last month.

So let us start with the facts and examine both the present disposition of military power in the hands of the Soviet Union and what it will be when Mr Gorbachev has implemented the changes he announced in December 1988.

It is estimated that Soviet spending on defence has increased in real terms by one half since 1970; by comparison, the United States' spending has grown by 15 per cent and that of the European members of NATO by 34 per cent over the same period. Over 15 per cent of the USSR's GDP goes on defence. That is more than twice the percentage of any NATO country and is an indicator of the extent to which Soviet policy and the Soviet economy is dominated by military considerations. At the same time – perhaps less ominously for us and more worrying for the Soviet leadership – it reflects the problem of seeking to keep up in military terms with the more economically successful United States, a struggle which absorbs a larger share of the much smaller Soviet economy.

Soviet ground forces have expanded from 165 divisions during the early 1970s to over 200 divisions today. The increase in defence expenditure has meant a marked improvement in the quality of equipment procured by the Soviet forces. Soviet tank production, which has remained consistently high, has been increased by 25 per cent during the last five years, giving an annual production rate of 3,500 modern tanks. Over the same period Soviet artillery production has been increased from 2,000 to 3,000 pieces per annum, with an increased proportion being of the more mobile and better protected self-propelled type. The Soviet Navy has established a powerful ocean-going fleet of 4 Kiev-class aircraft carriers, some 36 cruisers, 60 destroyers, 30 missile-armed frigates and 200 nuclear-powered submarines.

The Soviet Union has the world's largest and most sophisticated chemical warfare capability, with specialist troops highly trained in deployment of chemical weapons. On the nuclear level, although there is broad parity between the US and Soviet strategic systems, in other nuclear categories the Soviets enjoy considerable superiority (Fig. 9.1). By the mid-1990s virtually the entire Soviet strategic nuclear force will have been replaced by new or modernized systems. Even after the full implementation of the INF treaty, the re-targeting of Soviet ICBMs will provide a devastating 5,000 kilometre capacity.

There are more facts, equally relevant, which must be weighed. In the Atlantic-to-the-Urals area covered by conventional arms reduction talks, NATO has about 16,400 main battle tanks in active units compared with the Warsaw Pact's 51,500, and 14,500 artillery pieces compared with the Warsaw Pact's 43,400. When the reduction in tanks announced by Gorbachev takes effect, the Warsaw Pact will have about 40,000, a continuing superiority of more than two to one. In other words, Gorbachev's offer is nicely couched to have substantial appeal in the West while leaving a very large margin of offensive power in hand.

The Soviet leadership has at last begun to admit that previous estimates of defence expenditure were misleading and has promised more openness. This promise is good: its fulfilment will be better. There is also much talk of reduction of the defence budget but since we do not

Fig. 9.1 *The Nuclear Balance*

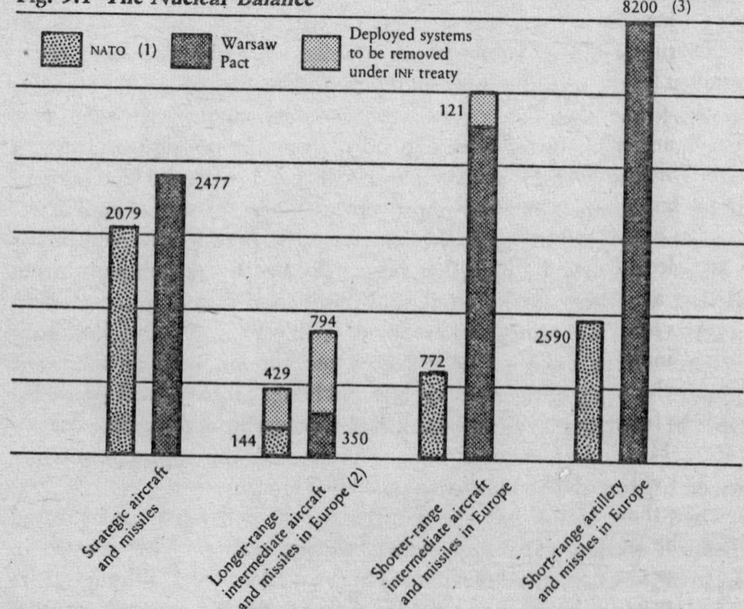

(1) Excludes French systems.
(2) Soviet missiles include 243 SS–20, each armed with three warheads.
(3) Not possible to say what proportion of these systems would be assigned for nuclear operation.
(Source: British Defence Policy 1988–9, MOD)

know the baseline against which any drop in defence expenditure must be measured, any changes here will be difficult to evaluate.

While a gradual shift of resources from the defence sector to the civil economy is essential if Gorbachev's reforms are to succeed, he will not want to force the pace of change and risk antagonizing his military chiefs and their Party supporters. The military balance for years to come will in any case be founded on those equipment modernization programmes already in hand. Reductions in numbers of weapons, which are likely to be concentrated in older, less effective equipment, will not have a marked effect on the Warsaw Pact's capability for high-speed offensive operations; talk about 'defensive concepts' is of little value without substantial changes in numbers and in the balance of equipment – in other words, without a reduction in offensive capability.

To recite these facts is, I hope, to put Gorbachev's striking speech in context. Nevertheless, I welcome the fact that he made it and the opportunity it offers for a much more open dialogue. The West must hope that Gorbachev succeeds and be alert to help him where it can with prudence. But the West's leaders must not underestimate the scale of what he is attempting nor overestimate his chances of success. Should he fail, the likelihood must be that his successor will revert to traditional Soviet attitudes and behaviour rather than take up where he left off.

Glasnost, like any freedom, is no respecter of frontiers. The impact of protest in Armenia reverberates to the Baltic and to the countries of central Europe. Openness has its consequences. Precedents are watched, examples followed. While some strive to keep ahead, others become restive at the thought that they are not keeping up. As the Soviet peoples have more freedom to think the previously unthinkable, it is not surprising that there is an awakening of history and emotion in the lands which lie closest to the West, with their keener awareness of the greater freedoms and higher living standards of the Western democracies. Hungary, Czechoslovakia, East Germany and to a lesser extent Poland will take advantage of their new-found freedom to start questioning their role in the defence of the Soviet Union against a threat from the West, when the West has more to offer than the Russians.

These clear dangers, which threaten a fracturing of the Soviet bloc along its natural fault lines, lend weight to those in the West who argue that Gorbachev is genuinely trying to change his country's posture, rigid as it has been for forty years. The scale of the risks he is taking with his home base deserves, they would argue, a positive response.

For the West, the consequences of Gorbachev's initiatives may prove hardly less profound than for the Soviets, and have already been considerable. The West has preserved an Atlantic alliance and a European cohesion as a direct consequence of the nakedness of the Soviet military threat. Time and again, the Soviets have given ample evidence to justify this concern: in the Berlin blockade, in Hungary in 1956 and in Czechoslovakia in 1968. In the aftermath of the crushing of *Solidarity* and the invasion of Afghanistan, European powers decided to accept Cruise and Pershing missiles, though with reluctance, and even France began to take a more positive view of NATO. So long as Mr Gorbachev can pursue his present strategy, and is minded to do so, he knows that he is scraping away the mortar of Western military cohesion and strategy. This is certainly one of his prime objectives.

For forty years America has led the Western alliance. Fourteen European nations – and Canada – have failed to match the drive and dynamism of American leadership. I often sat in the councils of NATO listening to reasons why this or that footnote had to be added to apparently innocuous texts, to accommodate some remote and largely irrelevant pressure group, and wondered what would have happened if the Americans had not been there to take the lead. The answer is, precious little. So for Gorbachev, as for his predecessors, it will be a high priority to weaken American commitment and leadership, and to weaken the alliance. As long as America leads, he knows that there is serious purpose, and a serious deterrent.

Gorbachev has to take into account a Western Europe which is moving steadily towards an industrial and economic coherence that may create on his doorstep one of the great forces of the twenty-first century. For him, as for so many in the West, the prospect of change – with the uncertainty it brings – may be less welcome than the structure of a divided Europe.

The key to future change in the defence, as in so many, equations is Germany. West Germany is the geographic centre of confrontation with the East, the focal point of the Western alliance. It lies along the central front of any imagined future conflict. The West Germans make the largest contribution to NATO's land forces and are hosts to most of the land and air forces of the alliance. This centrality is not limited to matters of defence: West Germany has the largest economy in the Community and a unified Europe without West Germany is unthinkable. So, the more West Germany can be persuaded to doubt its role in the alliance, the more Gorbachev can relax. The bait he offers is a closer relationship with the Germany behind the wall, as well as a role in the economic regeneration of Central Europe, even of the Soviet Union itself, with echoes of past Russo-German co-operation. It is not conceivable that Russian history would allow Gorbachev to agree to the reunification of Germany but the prospect of it is something on which he can allow the Germans to dwell at no cost to himself.

Gorbachev's timing in the closing months of the Reagan administration was, as usual, impeccable. His speech to the United Nations in December 1988 came in that twilight which bedevils the close season in the four-yearly cycle of American politics, when the reigning President has effectively ended his term but the new one has not taken over. Shevardnadze's declaration in Paris that Russia intended unilaterally to reduce chemical weapons stocks came during the same sensitive period. For the incoming President at least there was the comfort that no one would expect or require him to react instantly. The departure from the scene at the start of 1989 of George Schultz, a bulwark of reliability and restraint as Secretary of State, who understood better than most what the Russians were playing at, seemed from the West's point of view unfortunately timed.

George Bush's response will be based on a number of factors, the first of which will be his assessment of American economic prospects and the speed at which his internal and external deficits can be brought under control. Troops are costly and to cut their numbers in Europe would help to reduce the deficit. Bush knows that, for all the protestations, it is unlikely that any European government will volunteer to make good any American withdrawals. If Gorbachev is seen to proceed with asymmetrical reductions on a significant scale, then there will be a growing temptation for the Americans to take some of their troops home. Bush will have been advised that Gorbachev's initial offers give no military grounds for any American withdrawal but there will be a perpetual temptation to make a partial withdrawal, under cover of the Gorbachev smokescreen, especially as a Democratic Congress presses harder for defence spending to be restrained. Bush's plans for increasing social expenditure, though modest, can only add to these pressures.

Against this, the American people have learned – to their immense cost – of the tragedy that can overtake Europe when America withdraws. The most significant change in American attitudes in this century has been a growing appreciation that it is better to stay and prevent war than to return in order to stop it. On economic grounds alone the logic is unassailable, strengthened by the increasing internationalism of American trade and American corporations. At the outbreak of the First World War, American investment across the world amounted (at current prices) to $5 billion, or 13 per cent of GDP. By 1986, American assets abroad had risen to $1,070 billion or over 25 per cent of GDP. The enormous scale of activities managed by American multinational companies has transformed the perception of an inward-looking America to that of a commercial power whose managers and traders are active throughout the world.

This globalization of markets has its military significance. We are accustomed to seeing the 320,000 American troops based on the continent of Europe with their families as so many pledges of America's commitment. But the hundreds of thousands of American civilians living in Europe or going about their business there have become another bond, and one which every year looks stronger and more permanent.

President Mitterrand can reflect on the changing landscape of European defence with the advantage of the most united public opinion on defence matters in Europe but he must be anxious too. The cornerstone of French foreign policy has been the need to keep Germany firmly committed within an alliance including France, to prevent a return to 1914 or 1939 and, more positively, to provide an alternative to American influence in Europe in a Franco-German-led European Community.

A study of the summit meetings between the French President and the German Chancellor shows the depth of their countries' present relationship. It is quite unlike the relatively brief, formal exchanges which characterize the relationship of Britain with France or Britain with Germany. The French have worked hard to keep the interests of Germany directed westwards. However much we may anguish over the divisive nature of bilateralism within a broad partnership such as NATO or the Community, at least some of the motives which have driven France are ones we would share. The fact that the French pursue their aims in so obvious and dedicated a way may say something for their professionalism and singlemindedness.

Britain is the only European power with a strategic nuclear capability which is within the integrated command of the NATO alliance. This capability consists of the Polaris submarine fleet, shortly to be replaced by the Trident system. Presidents Gorbachev and Bush will be negotiating the reduction by half of their intercontinental missiles just as Britain introduces Trident, and Gorbachev can be expected to use that opportunity to exert pressure on Britain and France to include their nuclear weapon systems in the negotiating process. He will find willing allies in the opposition parties in Britain but will get no change from any present or future Conservative government until circumstances have changed drastically. He can also be expected to pursue an important subsidiary objective: so to sap the will of the European members of NATO as to force a delay in the modernization of European-based short-range nuclear weapons.

One of the difficulties of strong British advocacy of the modernization of short-range nuclear weapons is that such a policy is encountering increasing opposition in West Germany. The more Britain is seen to favour it, the more it will be asked in Germany why foreign countries, anxious to pursue unacceptable policies, are permitted to base troops in Germany at all. As some Russians withdraw from Eastern Europe, this question will be asked more insistently.

So how should British policy be conducted? First we must ascertain whether the game has changed and whether Western Europe's fundamental strategic interests have altered. If so, is that change likely to prove permanent? Beyond doubt Gorbachev has begun a movement to which the West is bound to respond. On the other hand that movement is still in its infancy and its future course is unpredictable.

We must adjust to Soviet policy as it evolves and respond positively to any opportunities for reinforcing the development of more open and prosperous societies in Eastern Europe and in the Soviet Union itself. We must encourage the movement towards reform without appearing to incite unrest or take advantage of change which could slow that reform or even bring it to a halt. At the same time, we have to keep up our guard when 'the threat' appears to be declining. Above all, should the Gorbachev reforms fail, no one should have grounds for blaming the West.

Changes within the alliance will also demand a response. The shift in relative economic power between the United States and Western Europe will require Europe to accept a greater share of the defence burden and the United States to accept that a stronger European pillar must have a stronger voice in alliance security policy. To manage this process of change, we need an institutional framework in which the increasingly powerful and questioning role of Germany can both be welcomed and given expression.

The impact of what Gorbachev is doing is tending to loosen the cohesion of Europe at a time when governments should be seeking closer co-operation for their common defence, not least because of changing American perceptions and priorities. In matters of both foreign and defence policy there remain differences of perspective to be resolved between those participating in NATO's integrated military structure and France outside it; and, even within the integrated structure, between the attitudes of, say, Greece or Denmark and those of the United Kingdom. But the increasing habit of co-operation within the Community will be helpful, and economic and budgetary imperatives will also point towards closer collaboration.

The need for Europe to sustain its defence effort while the superpowers are reducing their own much larger defence budgets will make even more pressing the need to get better value for money from defence expenditure, both by making the best use of increasingly scarce manpower resources and by constraining the spiralling cost of defence equipment.

Britain's interest in managing these changes is founded on our understanding of the indispensable part that the Atlantic alliance has played in maintaining the peace for more than forty years. It must be a prime objective of British foreign policy to preserve and, if possible, reinforce the bonds which hold the alliance together against the unpredictabilities of the future.

The American commitment to Europe is the keystone of the alliance but it does not rest only upon a given number of troop divisions or of any particular weapons system. It consists of the coupling of American self-interest with that of Europe in the defence of the sovereign territory of the nations of the alliance, and that depends upon continuing American leadership of that alliance. This is not to say that Europe will never be capable of defending itself or that one day a concerted foreign policy, and the collective will to back it, may not emerge in Europe. But at present there is no common will among the states of Western Europe to provide for themselves the conventional forces needed to match the potential Russian threat. It would also be destabilizing to the balance of tactical nuclear deterrence if the American contribution were withdrawn.

Difficult though some Europeans find it to accept, it is clear to me that the supreme command of the allied forces must remain in American hands. An American Supreme Allied Commander in Europe (SACEUR), who is in the lonely position of carrying full responsibility if things go wrong, will always be the most powerful advocate for the maintenance of an effective American commitment to give substance to the symbolism of his peacetime task.

It would be that much easier for Washington's military planners to reduce American forces in Europe if those forces were put under the leadership of a European commander, who could never carry the same weight in the Pentagon. Finding a suitable European would in any case be difficult. It is still too vivid a part of recent history for a German to be put in command, however legitimate the disposition of the forces on the central front might make a German claim. Public opinion in France and in the Low Countries, Norway and Denmark is nowhere near ready to accept such a prospect and I doubt if Gorbachev would be able to persuade his people that such an appointment was a fitting response to his overtures for a better tomorrow.

It is a significant advantage that the Americans are apart from the rivalries of Europe, so that defence questions are one step removed from the tensions that may lie ahead as Europe draws closer together. It would be damaging if, for example, squabbles about food mountains or tax harmonization were to provoke disputes about the personalities and nationality of military commanders. The American voice must therefore continue to be powerful both within the ministerial structure of the alliance and at the military level.

For years both Europeans and Americans have at least argued that the alliance would benefit from the stronger voice of a more united Europe. As a result, twice a year, since the late 1960s, beneath the flags and tapestries of some historic building reflecting a past imperial grandeur or sometimes, sadly, in one of Europe's uninspiring modern hotels, Europe's defence ministers meet in the Eurogroup as a prelude to the wider meeting of NATO's Defence Planning Committee. But because France has not been a member of this committee since she left the integrated military structure, her minister is absent. The conversation is full of expressions of good intentions; the practical results seldom live up to them.

France has never left the North Atlantic alliance itself and has always retained a lively interest in defence equipment co-operation, where industrial self-interest overcomes ideological scruples. The result is France's participation in the Independent European Programme Group (IEPG).

More recently, French interest in wider political co-operation, but outside the NATO framework of the Eurogroup, has led to a revival of the Western European Union (WEU) whose membership has also been widened. The WEU was created in 1955 on the initiative of Anthony Eden to do something to fill the gap left by the collapse of the proposed European Defence Community. It provides a forum in which the foreign and defence ministers of member countries can meet in joint session (in NATO, the two ministerial groups meet separately) and this can be helpful since their interests so frequently overlap. It has also played a limited but useful role in co-ordinating the efforts of European navies involved in protecting merchant shipping in the Gulf. But in neither case is its role indispensable. The problem in European defence co-operation is not a shortage of opportunities to exchange views but a surfeit of them. When bilateral EC-related summits are also taken into account, the meetings can come at bewildering speed; and the key to effective military co-operation is the integrated military structure within NATO, not the WEU.

It is therefore tempting – and very British – to be lukewarm towards the WEU and instead to reiterate our traditional Atlanticism. I doubt if this is wise. The credit to be earned with the Americans, who can in any case look after themselves, is limited; while the danger is great that our continental allies will see us, in the defence field as in others, as 'un-European'. The WEU has a limited but distinct value as one of several building blocks in the making of the new Europe – one which has the advantage of allowing debate on a basis of equality among the big four – Germany, the United Kingdom, France and, in economic terms, Italy – and the smaller European countries. We have held reservations based on the divisive consequences for the alliance if WEU were careless of its context but this argues in favour of deeper British involvement, not detachment.

For all that, the only sound foundation for future European security is a close and confident triple entente between France, Germany and the United Kingdom, though that foundation will increasingly come under pressure from the growing strength of Italy and Spain. I recognize that this is difficult for some in Britain to accept. It is felt that a strong Europe could weaken the Atlantic alliance; I believe it will strengthen it and am more concerned that the strength of the Franco-German alliance may diminish Britain's standing with her partners, although recent experience of a more forthcoming French approach to the alliance has allayed these anxieties somewhat.

The Franco-German Treaty of 1963 remains a monument to far-sighted statesmanship. The partnership was sealed only after Britain's persistent refusal in the late 1940s and 1950s to play a decisive role in Europe and it has generated much of Europe's present momentum. Though its continuing health is essential for the health of Europe, it is not enough. It is not surprising that the Europe which Britain allowed – indeed obliged – France and Germany to create without our help failed to take adequate account of British interests, in defence as in other matters. Yet over the years our detachment from the European side of defence was consistent with our distancing ourselves from European policy at large.

There is much that Britain can offer each partner, separately, on which we can build. In the case of the Germans, there is one factor plainly in our favour. Britain plays a more significant role in the defence of West Germany than does France, with more troops and a larger air force on German soil and a more integrated military commitment than France. This has been true since the NATO alliance was founded, and because it has become routine it lacks the novelty which may surround a Franco-German training exercise. Britain sits alongside her German allies in the councils of NATO. The Anglo-German relationship is seen simply as part of the general NATO endeavour, and so it should be. It would be the gravest misjudgment for Britain to weaken its bond with NATO in the hope of competing with France for the attention of the German public. But the Anglo-German relationship still needs to be nurtured. There have recently been some sensible and useful initiatives from the British government to strengthen our bilateral military links with the Germans and to develop personal relationships at both policy-making and military levels.

While some looked with irritation on the Franco-German defence relationship – suspecting it to be more about public relations than substance – many have understood that it has helped to bring France a closer interest in the forward defence of her territory through co-operation with her allies. There is ground for some frustration that this falls short of a complete reintegration into the NATO military framework and that it seems likely to remain the case for the foreseeable future. But second best is better – and could be significantly better – than nothing at all. Provided we can restrain criticism of France's basic position, there is scope for the development of understandings about military action in times of tension or of war which can be of direct benefit to our collective defence effort on the central front and its reinforcement.

If for historical reasons the Franco-German rapprochement has a particular warmth, Britain and France also have in common their roles as Europe's two nuclear powers. Each has always clearly recognized the essentially independent nature of their deterrents. Neither country under their present governments would share or surrender control of those deterrents because what they would lose would be irreplaceable. They would have relinquished for ever control of their ultimate security. But no one doubts that the Federal Republic recognizes the relevance of a French independent deterrent to German security. Indeed Europe and particularly Germany can be reassured by Britain's and France's nuclear deterrents. No one can misunderstand the commitment implied by the presence of British and French forces on German soil. Britain's nuclear deterrent is already NATO-dedicated. What makes increasing sense is to seek to strengthen the relationship between Europe's nuclear powers.

It is clearly right for Britain and France to discuss their individual nuclear strategies. There could well be scope for co-ordination of planning and targeting. There will be no question of joint control of the Trident or the *force de frappe*. It would strike at the fundamental nature of the national deterrent. But neither Trident nor the *force de frappe* will last for ever. Nuclear deterrence is expensive and its weapons and delivery systems take decades to develop. As requirements become clearer for the next systems, to become operational at the beginning of the second quarter of the next century, Anglo-French co-operation in their development would have strategic and industrial symbolism, highly prized alongside the military imperative. The more effective the co-operation, and the more efficient the weapons systems, the more reassurance will be offered to our European allies. I have no doubt that operational control will even then remain national but there seems no reason why research and production costs should not be shared. The circumstances are not directly comparable but it should be remembered that, when President Kennedy concluded the Nassau agreement to provide Polaris to Britain, the same offer was made to France and was rejected by de Gaulle as a threat to French independence. The mounting costs of modern defence technology could lead to a reappraisal of the old arguments.

It will not be considered disrespectful if I say that I have dealt with the members of the NATO alliance who are the most likely to pursue resolute defence policies. If policies change in any of the countries that I have mentioned, there will be no protests to be heard from any of the others.

Defence co-operation is built upon shared strategic interests and a shared view about how they can best be furthered. But the endless, largely unchanging communiques about security policy in Europe's defence ministries exist alongside a different dimension of economic reality, that of running big businesses under considerable pressure.

The consequences of the 1992 single market – a larger market, the impact of industrial mergers on the national industrial base, the need for more competition – have to be addressed. Constrained defence budgets have to absorb steady growth in the cost of ever more sophisticated equipment. The French are in difficulties because a large nuclear weapons programme, a national fighter programme, *Rafale*, and other costly weapons systems have all to be paid for out of their national defence budget. Germany is in the same position as Britain, with a flat defence budget and expensive new projects like the European fighter aircraft and the Franco-German anti-tank helicopter (PAH2), to be funded from within it.

Increasingly, civil spending will determine the pattern of defence procurement as the adaptation of civil products will make available equipment for example in information technology, which is more advanced than the military can afford to develop for themselves. The European Commission will attempt to move into the defence procurement field on the back of their civil industrial programmes. Dual application of products for civil and military use will make this easier. These developments will serve to increase the importance of IEPG in meeting Europe's military requirements more effectively and more economically.

Take a look at the central front, 550 miles stretching from the Baltic to the Austrian border, where the armies of the alliance are concentrated and where the undertakings are absolute. If Mr Gorbachev carries through his announced withdrawals by 1991, the Warsaw Pact, as we have seen, will have 40,000 tanks in the whole of Europe facing some 16,400 NATO tanks. On the central front this will mean 11,500 modern Warsaw Pact tanks (mainly T-80s) facing 6,800 NATO tanks. But the 6,800 break down as follows: the Germans have 3,000 Leopards; the British nearly 700 Challengers/Chieftains; the Dutch have 700 Leopards; the Belgians have 300 Leopards; in southern Germany the Americans have a total of 1,700 M-1s and M-60s, and in the south the French have over 500 AMX-30s.

From this diversity there is no possibility of achieving the military benefits of interchangeable support services. Each contingent requires its own specialist equipment: spares, transporters, ammunition, even fuel. Worse, each of these systems has had to be researched, designed, developed, produced and tested before being brought into service. Worse still, they are all of different ages: not only did they enter service at different times but they will become obsolete at moments when the pressure will be at its greatest to replace them with similarly incompatible systems. Huge vested interests stand behind this process, their actions governed not only by deliberate perversity but by the military and industrial self-interest of each country. Each country's scientific and technological advisers, the production and sales managers in the different national companies, each army's cavalry commanders, all prefer to press for their own brands. Procurement is not governed by the military strategist who works out the operational requirement. Defence directors in the national laboratories have a natural curiosity, which encourages them to push the state of the art beyond the stage reached by their competitors. The chairman of a manufacturing company is preoccupied with work flows and profit levels. The fighting man simply wants the best kit, and wants it today.

In the Ministry of Defence in Whitehall is a document containing lists of countless thousands of items, costed with incredible precision over ten years. It is known as the long-term costing. Virtually all of this equipment will be purchased from British sources or within arrangements convenient to British industry. I have no complaints about this. It is the practice throughout the world. But it indicates the scale of inbuilt inertia and the numbers who are aware of their self-interest. If the American defence programme were organized at state level, defence needs would be analysed and equipment designed in fifty different programmes, reflecting the interests of each state's industrial base. No such nightmare of inefficiency exists on that side of the Atlantic but it does on this. It was to banish this nightmare that the IEPG was set up in 1976, consisting of all the European members of the NATO alliance, including France.

For Britain, as one of the largest European producers of military equipment, there were and remain two broad issues. The first was the near impossibility of maintaining a national manufacturing capability for every type of defence equipment. The cost of research and development of each major weapon is constantly increasing, and the production runs necessary to supply the British armed forces alone are small and therefore relatively expensive. Some of the Ministry of Defence's suppliers – British Aerospace and Rolls Royce, for example – are monopoly suppliers. Often only overseas suppliers offer any competition, as the search for a replacement for the Chieftain tank has shown. Fortunately in other fields, significantly electronics and avionics, a much healthier competition exists. But the Ministry finds itself carrying higher and higher overheads for the development of its own specialized equipment.

The second consideration behind the formation of the IEPG was that, while chances of agreeing common specifications and accepting the need to share costs may be remote, the procurement policies of the USA – rigorously scrutinized by Congress – ensure that American taxpayers' money is spent in America. Only where a European manufacturer has achieved a technological breakthrough which makes his product uniquely attractive to the American armed services will his company be likely to secure a contract. In these cases significant benefits can flow. The American Harrier jump-jet has 50 per cent British content in its engine and frame. But the dilemma remains. How can American co-operation with Europe be balanced when the small companies and small procurement programmes of European countries face gigantic equivalents on the other side of the Atlantic? Co-operation within the Atlantic alliance is very desirable but genuine co-operation will come only when Europe can bring its co-ordinated resources into the common pool.

Since the IEPG was set up in 1976, the separate national bureaucracies of Europe have continued to maintain their separate national procurement systems. None has allowed any effective challenge. In its first seven years, the IEPG members never met at ministerial level and the research directors met only by chance, and too late to discover whose work was being wastefully duplicated by whom. There was no overall strategy, no clear set of options, nothing but a vocal enthusiasm, oft-repeated, for European defence co-operation.

In 1984, as Secretary of State for Defence, I together with my Dutch colleague, State Secretary for Defence Van Howelingen, at that time chairman of IEPG, decided to upgrade the work of the IEPG, convinced as we were that unless we Europeans could learn to work consistently together – in competition but to common specifications – the value of Europe's research and development effort could never match that of the Americans, directed by the Pentagon and by NASA, or of the MITI-sponsored Japanese programmes. I was determined that senior defence ministers should attend IEPG discussions, and with some difficulty this was achieved.

One of the last decisions taken while I was Secretary of State for Defence was to set up, on 1 November 1985, a group 'to make concrete proposals for improving the competitiveness of European defence'. This group consisted of high-powered industrialists, politicians and officials. Britain was represented by Sir Arnold Hall who, as a former Chairman of Hawker Siddeley and Director of the Royal Aircraft Establishment at Farnborough, possessed a unique experience.

The group produced in 1987 a report* in which the first and most

* 'Towards a Stronger Europe', available from the IEPG Secretary, NATO, Brussels.

ambitious recommendation dealt with the creation of a more open and competitive market in Europe. They said that companies should seek groupings, form competing consortia, and that '*juste retour*' should cease to be calculated project by project but rather on the model developed by the European Space Agency, which ensures that, where competitive bidding fails to secure a politically acceptable distribution of the benefits in jobs and cash, an equitable return for each country is achieved by retrospective adjustments over a period of time or within a package of programmes. Contracts should be let on the basis of fixed prices rather than the cost-plus system, where the manufacturer receives his costs plus a guaranteed profit, so that there is little incentive to efficiency.

Particularly significant are the conclusions made by the report relating to small businesses and the vital contributions they can make towards improving the competitiveness of the European defence industry. Our non-European competitors, in particular the United States, attach a high value to small businesses and for three good reasons: small businesses offer the defence industry considerable flexibility, with a wide range of companies providing a rich variety of technical solutions and fierce competition between them; they offer spontaneity and innovation, and the ability to produce good ideas and to translate these into effective hardware; and they offer employment opportunities, creating jobs in high-technology industry. In this context it is particularly encouraging that the British Ministry of Defence spends £1 billion a year with small firms employing less than 200 people.

A number of other recommendations stand out. Industry should play a more significant role in establishing operational requirements, both to moderate the ambitions of armed services chiefs and to maximize the impact of previous and existing technologies and equipment and to freeze specifications. A new drive to standardize components and sub-systems through the agencies of the Commission is advocated, and a central register of bidding opportunities across Europe is recommended, to be maintained by the IEPG. That such eminently sensible suggestions should have emerged ten years after IEPG itself was set up is proof enough of the resistance to necessary change in the national defence establishments of Europe. In some measure ministers had anticipated these recommendations. In 1984 at The Hague we had agreed to one further decision to extend co-operation. As a result I laid down rules in the Ministry that, as part of the procurement process, the opportunities for co-operation had to be considered for each new project and reasons for rejecting such opportunities – if rejecting them was the recommendation – set out in writing.

Britain's objectives are clear. First, we need to achieve the greatest possible output from our own and our allies' expenditure, through progressive standardization of European defence equipment, wherever possible. Second, we should seek to secure for British industry a prime place in the defence manufacturing base in Europe. At the moment Britain and France both keep a comprehensive manufacturing capability in defence; neither can any longer afford it. An encouraging sortie from the national fortresses of defence procurement was made by George Younger, British Defence Secretary, and his French opposite number, André Giraud, in 1986. Recognizing that nuclear programmes, and major projects with profound regional implications such as warship-building, attract intense political interest, the British and French defence ministers agreed to open the rest of their budgets to competition. All production programmes costing less than £100 million and development programmes of less than £50 million now appear on open registers. This may extend to as much as 50 per cent of annual procurement and is therefore a significant increase in competition. A fall-back system for ensuring a *juste retour* still exists but, if the industries of the two countries win contracts of equal value, this will not have to be invoked.

The concept of the open register has been put on the agenda for all IEPG members. By the end of 1989 IEPG should produce its own contracts bulletin which will be freely available to the industries of the other nations. This move implements a ministerial decision taken in Luxembourg in November 1988. This will mirror American practice where a bulletin, 'Commerce Business Daily', is published.

The IEPG has been restructured, with three panels now covering all procurement matters – the harmonization of requirements, research and technology, and the implementation of the Defence Industry Study Report. Another significant step (one which I was never able to achieve) has been the establishment of a dedicated IEPG secretariat. Without such a mechanism to probe the procurement processes within each member state's defence ministry, it is too easy for each to pursue its old nationalistic ways.

Every proposal spells the winning or losing of jobs, of national pride, of military independence. We are not on a level playing field but on a battlefield cratered with inequalities that makes the construction of a fair market a challenge for the most resolute of ministers. It cannot be easy for Spanish or Portuguese ministers to explain a new policy initiative the most likely consequence of which is to switch a deficit with America on arms procurement into an equivalent deficit with the rest of Europe. To them Britain's advocacy of an open market may seem to be solely directed to that end.

The sense of being disadvantaged is familiar to industrialists in every country. What, for example, is the reality of competition for a private sector company such as British Aerospace, which must compete with the nationalized industries of France and Italy in a market place which will offer them perhaps one project in a decade? Rolls Royce went to the wall in 1972 trying to compete, using its own resources, with a civil derivative of a military engine, the CF6, developed by the General Electric Company of America at taxpayers' expense. To reverse the argument, what are the hidden costs of the European airbus in its battle to penetrate the world market place against privately funded American airliners? For those British, French and German industries which are trying to break through the shield with which Congress protects US high technology industry, every step is steeply uphill.

Into this jungle ministers are bound to venture with all the weapons on which they can lay their hands. In the real world – though not in the ideal world of a closer, stronger Europe – their objective is to win, and to win for what are perceived to be legitimate national interests. Winning may well mean stimulating competition in order to harden the bargain but it will not mean buying in the cheapest market if it leaves your own nation powerless to compete again, its industry closed and its capability reduced to subcontracting, because you chose a foreign contractor. The fact that most of those competitive prices will be struck at the margin, once the initial development costs have fallen on to the taxpayers of some other nation, only complicates the judgment. But neither can winning be defined as maintaining a comprehensive national defence capability at an ever higher unit cost than the market place is offering elsewhere.

The faster we can create a competitive European market place the more effectively will we be able to maintain a capacity within European control and under market disciplines of world scale. For Britain to secure a place in that market we need not only a procurement programme that counts at the negotiating table but companies able to form the nuclei of the emerging European industrial base.

In the IEPG, now the main forum for defence equipment collaboration in Europe, we have at last begun the long, immensely difficult process of securing co-ordination from the earliest stages of research to agreement on common weapons programmes. The Europeanization of the defence industries, if it is to be successful, will require the constant and close attention of governments. Strategic interests are too sensitive and only ministers can weigh them against the demands of collective self-interest.

No one should underestimate the difficulties of achieving effective European collaboration. I know the time and effort required to secure even a single – admittedly enormous – collaborative contract. Arriving at the Ministry of Defence in 1983, I learnt that despite the success of Britain's partnership with Germany and Italy in producing the Tornado aircraft, there were proposals for the next generation of fighters to be designed and built in Britain alone. The arguments were venerable, seductive and mistaken: British was better, the RAF would control the specification and British jobs were at stake. And the Germans were about to sign up with the French. I had heard it all before as Minister for Aerospace in 1973 and had decided then that Britain must rationalize and co-ordinate its space programme with those on the continent. From that decision the European Space Agency, after a struggle, was born.

Ten years later the lessons had to be learnt again. It seemed impossible to devise an agreement which would provide Europe with a single aircraft type which European governments would buy in huge numbers and which, for that reason, could be produced at a price to commend worldwide sales among countries anxious to avoid total commitment to one or other of the super-powers. After more than a year of deliberations, the industries of the United Kingdom, Germany, Italy and Spain came together. My prolonged efforts to win round the French did not succeed. The European Fighter Aircraft programme will save the British defence budget £1 billion. It is one of the largest industrial contracts in which Britain has ever participated and the most ambitious co-operative venture in Europe. The French, I believe, now regret their decision to go it alone.

The ready availability at a competitive price of sophisticated American weaponry, thanks to the scale of the American taxpayer's commitment to his country's defence industries, can make a European government's resistance very difficult. As we have seen with the options for a new main battle tank for the British Army, the Americans can always offer an effective weapon earlier, with off-set contracts and the enticing prospect that technological improvements will be paid for. Predictably, finance ministers give such offers powerful backing and all too often service chiefs are attracted by the early acquisition of the latest technology.

The logical response to this American supremacy is not narrow national sentiment but the adoption in Europe of practical arrangements which make military and industrial collaboration both natural and straightforward. That is not advocacy of a 'Fortress Europe' policy but of a gathering of strength in Europe through a combined scale and concentration of R&D that will make co-operation across the Atlantic more real and balanced. We need to develop the concept of families of weapons where the Americans buy one part of the family from Europe and the Europeans another from the United States, as in the planned short- and medium-range air-to-air missiles. Another example is the European contribution to the second and third phases of the Multiple Launch Rocket System (MLRS).

The squeezing of the United States defence budgets that is likely to characterize the early Bush years will make these adjustments both harder and more important. The Congress will be the more insistent that every dollar is spent at home. The danger is in a victory for the protectionist politicians, one of whom, Senator Dixon, in 1988 proposed the Defense Industrial Base Preservation Bill. This Bill if passed would have made it very difficult to sell foreign defence equipment in the United States and would also have been a significant disincentive to trans-Atlantic co-operation.

Europe must also learn to manage its large projects more effectively. Searching for a committee consensus does not make for efficient management. For a single national industry to take the management lead in any programme will never be easy to agree, although there is a logic in a particular country specializing in the production of a particular type of equipment – for example, the Germans in the development of power systems in tanks, the British of the hull and armour. Panavia, the European company which manages the Tornado programme, is a model that could well be followed. There has to be a single management team but a chairman of one nationality can be balanced by chief officers from the other nations so that nationalistic instincts are then reined in and all energies are concentrated on the success of the project. European defence contracts must be managed within structures that ensure the necessary management skills, including the sub-contract level.

Co-operation in equipment procurement is not an end in itself but a means to the end of maintaining effective defence forces in Europe. NATO has been remarkably successful in keeping the peace for forty years. Its effectiveness has rested not only on the strength of the forces deployed by its members but on their ability – albeit with periodic disturbances – to work together and maintain a reasonably united front against Soviet wedge-driving. It has been an unusual partnership, in which the United States has played the dominant part both by its military contribution and through its sway over policy.

In the next phase in its history – now begun – the alliance must discover how to adjust to the changing balance of economic power between America and Europe, and indeed between Europe and the Soviet Union. Effective deterrence will continue to require a mix of conventional and nuclear weapons and the American role in both areas will remain crucial. As the Americans continue to expect a greater commitment by Europe to its own defence, so new generations in Europe will be the more ready to make that commitment if they can also hear a clearer, more competent and authoritative European voice determining the direction in which the alliance develops.

The pace of change is unpredictable and the institutional framework may well remain untidy. The progress of arms control and reduction can enhance the quality of the peace we have enjoyed for more than forty years. It can release resources for more constructive purposes. We must count this an advantage. But as it advances it can diminish resolve and cloud memories of the very policies and resolution that have made it possible. We must continue to persuade younger generations, far removed from that older but more characteristic period of our history, of our continuing responsibility to safeguard what has been won.

Defence policy is not the thing of which miracles are made or where short-term judgments are substituted for the long-range view. The key political tasks in Europe, in the short term at least, will be to counter the increasing unease among the West German people at the burden imposed by the requirements and strategy of the alliance; and to find ways in which the considerable defence capabilities of France can be put to effective use in the common interest of the alliance and of Europe.

A secondary task, but of immense practical importance, is to institute far smoother co-operation among the European partners in joint defence procurement, to produce standardized equipment at less cost and so provide more effective defence within budgets which are likely to be squeezed by new political pressures and the growing cost of modern weapons. The European defence industry is under pressure, and will be reshaped. The British government must play a part in that reshaping or be left a passive spectator.

The British people must decide whether they are content to let the course of events be shaped primarily by Franco-German co-operation and dialogue, welcome as that co-operation is; or whether they believe our deep involvement would serve both Britain and Europe better. In all of this, our commitment to European defence is inseparable from our commitment to Europe itself.

CHAPTER
10

The Future: a Tory Vision

Britain's place in Europe and her relationship with her partners in the European Community will remain controversial and potentially divisive questions for the rest of this century and beyond. The very mention of the word Europe brings a heightened interest in any British audience. Old instincts and new fears clash with the vision of those who argue the benefits of Britain's Treaty commitments. The path ahead is strewn with boulders behind each one of which the forces of resistance lie in ambush for the unwary. The journey will be slower than the more resolute travellers would like, although faster than their would-be dissuaders admit. Nobody should be surprised at such a prospect. Some of the British people's deepest instincts and affections are engaged.

Even the most confident European must, if honest, confess to moments of doubt. The horizons of today's Community – and even its middle distances – are more than a little obscure. If it is hard to see how its institutions may develop over the next decade, it is still harder to foresee what its physical bounds may be, say, by 2007 – fifty years after the signing of the Rome Treaty.

No one wants to get out, and more and more European nations are contemplating with varying degrees of urgency whether they should try to get in. The management consultants will tell you that much of their work concerning 1992 is commissioned by companies based in non-EEC countries which are anxious to establish or consolidate positions in the emerging market. Countries neighbouring the Community are assessing and reassessing the likely impact on their economies of this swelling economy beside them. Applications to join from Morocco and Turkey are on the table. Malta has sought a form of association. Norway may seek before long to reverse her narrow decision taken by referendum not to join. Austria's application to join is planned for 1989. In Sweden the second twinges of doubt are manifest. Will Switzerland hold out? As the hold of Communism becomes feebler, the Central European countries, led perhaps by Hungary or Yugoslavia, may find themselves freer to seek closer economic links with the Community. If popularity is a measure of wealth the Community is thriving.

But which countries should be admitted? There can be only two criteria: successful applicants must be both democratic and European. 'We seek nothing less than all Europe,' Winston Churchill declared as he spread one of his large canvasses before his audience at The Hague Congress in May 1948. 'We welcome any country where the people own the Government, and not the Government the people.'

And to a meeting of the United Europe Committee in London a year earlier he said: 'We seek to exclude no state whose territory lies in Europe and which assures to its people those fundamental rights and liberties on which our democratic European civilization has been created.' Within these confines, every application must be judged by its possible impact on what the Community is already about. The closer an applicant comes to accepting existing policies and structures the better.

The Conservatives, in the European as in other great ventures, have both represented and led the British people faithfully and well. The Party's senior figures have felt and sometimes expressed a wariness of continental entanglements. But there have also been great Conservatives at the forefront of the European movement.

No history of our time can ignore the catastrophic misjudgment of the Conservative governments of the 1930s in their analysis of the unfolding drama of European events. But no Conservative of today can draw anything but pride from the foresight and persistence of Winston Churchill who warned those governments of their folly. He preached an uncomfortable message. He was scorned, distrusted, dismissed as 'a man without judgment'. But he was right and his critics wrong; and he was rewarded in time by his fellow countrymen's recognition of his wisdom and of their debt to him.

Among European citizens at large he came to enjoy unique authority as the man who characterized the British will to fight alone, if need be, to preserve the civilization which had been matured over many centuries by Europe's peoples to the benefit of all mankind. He had held the responsibility for restoring the fortunes of Europe. The Conservative Party can today take inspiration from the grandeur of his vision of Europe in those post-war days – a vision in which a pragmatic gradualism was combined with the most fervent commitment to the ideal of a united Europe in which Britain would play a full part.

I do not have any fresh insight into the controversy about what Churchill would have done to further his European ideas if he had been re-elected in 1945. No one will ever know. By 1951 he was too old and in no mood to challenge Anthony Eden's more sceptical outlook. But his three great speeches on European unity, made between 1946 and 1948 in Zurich, at the Royal Albert Hall in London and at The Hague Congress, set the debate for my generation in our early political years. Those speeches are as fresh and as relevant today as when they first gave hope and purpose to the generations that survived the horrors of the war, inspiring statesmen and helping to confirm in many of the ordinary people of Europe their awakening determination to rebuild their continent to a nobler design.

Churchill in these speeches was often, and deliberately, imprecise. His famous exhortation in Zurich – 'we must build a kind of United States of Europe' – left partisans free to argue, as they have ever since, about whether he saw Britain as one of those United States. But his imprecision was wholly rational: 'In my experience of large enterprises I have found it is often a mistake to try to settle everything at once. We know where we want to go but we cannot foresee all the stages of the journey. . . . We ourselves are content in the first instance to present the idea of a united Europe in which our country will play a decisive part as a moral, cultural and spiritual conception to which all can rally without being disturbed by divergences about the structure. It is for the responsible statesmen, who have the conduct of affairs in their hands and the power of executive action, to shape and fashion the structure.'

If the shape of this structure was for others to plan, Churchill was in no doubt about the scope and reach of this Europe of his dreams: 'It is impossible to separate economics and defence from the general political structure,' he said in The Hague. 'Mutual aid in the economic field and joint military defence must inevitably be accompanied step-by-step with a parallel policy of closer political unity.' Such talk, even from such a man, had already stirred up passionate objections from patriots of narrower vision, in France as well as in Britain. He recognized and reasoned with their fears: 'It is said with truth that this involves some sacrifice or merger of national sovereignty, but it is also possible and not less agreeable to regard it as the gradual assumption by all the nations concerned of that larger sovereignty, which can alone protect their diverse and distinctive customs and characteristics, and their national traditions.'

Churchill's doctrine of a larger sovereignty has been well understood among continental Europeans since 1945 as an effective antidote to the narrowness and timidity which national sentiment can engender. Their very pride in their own past histories, their determination to exert continuing influence in a world of multinational companies, of vast currency flows, of military and economic super-powers, of global threats to our environment, has taught them that they can enjoy a greater measure of sovereignty together than apart. They want to be in charge of events and not submerged by them. They want true sovereignty tomorrow, not merely the memories of what it meant yesterday.

I believe that the rising generation will understand and adopt the Churchillian view. But for many of my generation, although the practical arguments for Europe have carried them far, a psychological barrier remains – a difficulty in warming to the idea of closer political union with continental Europe and an uneasiness in contemplating a partial merger of sovereignty which, unlike Churchill, they are inclined to see as loss, not gain.

The British are not alone in this struggle to acquire a sense of belonging. The Pyrenees are to Spain what the Channel is to Britain, and Spain has also experienced the distraction of great national interests far from Europe. But most of Spain's empire slipped from her hands a century before Britain's and her people, unlike most of the British, share with the core of the present Community – the strongest of the European states who drew up the Treaty of Rome – the bond of their Roman Catholic faith.

The belief in national sovereignty – of supreme authority – has always been in a high degree illusory, even under absolute rulers. Why does it endure? Sovereignty is an emotive word because it links two ideas which appeal to every citizen's sentiment, the ideas of national independence and of national strength and influence; and by linking them suggests that neither can survive without the other. However deep-rooted, this belief is mistaken. In our interdependent world, and particularly within an increasingly convergent European Community, it is a barrier to understanding. Sovereignty can be impotent. A man in the desert is free and sovereign. He is beyond the reach of any alien authority, but he is powerless. To have value, sovereignty must be capable of being used.

The reality of power changes with the nature of society. Groups of human beings once huddled around their cave or behind primitive stockades, proud of their independence, loyal to others in their group and reliant on their collective strength – their local sovereignty – to control natural forces and restrain their enemies. As men wandered further by foot, then by coracle, carriage, ship or aircraft, so the circle of their loyalties gradually widened. The strength of common loyalty is no less intense: it merely extends to wider frontiers. As Edmund Burke put it: 'To love the little platoon we belong to in society is the first link in the series by which we proceed to a love of country and mankind.'

'Good fences make good neighbours' is a very British sentiment but it is only a partial truth. Among nations, frontiers observed have indeed helped to keep the peace. But, where peace is secure, then frontiers unmanned and barriers lowered allow other great benefits – cultural and spiritual enrichment, material increase – to be shared and to multiply. We recognize the tension and passions, the loves and hatreds, the bitterness and jealousies which have been stirred up wherever the frontiers of allegiance or of religion have been forcibly changed. But we observe, too, how rival, apparently conflicting loyalties can sometimes be brought together to create a greater strength. This is what gives Europe its potential and its citizens the ground for their hopes.

New combinations do not destroy ancient loyalties. As British citizens, we salute a British monarch and respect the union flag. But these objects of our loyalty are of recent enough origin and were not adopted without controversy. There were Scots in 1707 (there are some today) who believed that the passage of the Act of Union was a betrayal. The Welsh proclaim their ancestry with as much pride now, 400 years after the union the English imposed upon them, as they would have done before it. Nothing of the national spirit of the Scots or the Welsh has been lost.

And how long is it since the rival kingdoms of England savaged each other in the name of petty sovereignty and local patriotism? Tell a

Yorkshireman that he is British and no one will swear greater loyalty. But tell him that he is part of a merger with the House of Lancaster and you rekindle the passions of the Wars of the Roses.

The passions of clan and country are not far beneath the skin. We cling to what we know and feel safe with, the convictions and often the prejudices of our parents. This is the real world of politics. In the 1990s as in the 1950s the builders of the European Community must do their work on ground which is trenched and pitted by the pride, ambitions and emotions of many nationalities. Among these builders will be statesmen who will wrestle with the challenge of change and seek to guide people through it; and, sadly, there will be politicians who will exploit the discomfort of change and work on the fears of those who feel they must resist it.

The twentieth century has brought change at a pace and on a scale beyond all previous human experience. It is easier to talk to one's friends in Australia today than it was to one's relatives at the other end of the village street a hundred years ago. We see national armies drawn together more closely than ever before to form alliances on a trans-national scale. Some companies today are richer than the average nation state and their strategies are often more influential. The transmission of the written and spoken word, nationwide and worldwide, becomes every day more rapid and efficient. But man's instinctive distrust of unexplained change and his distaste for the unfamiliar remain, and there is a new and growing fear – a perfectly rational fear – of the anonymity, remoteness and seeming carelessness of the modern world's ever larger concentrations of power.

I have said that the British people have grasped the practical arguments for Europe, and I believe that they have; but it is also clear that their grasp is not yet as firm as that of other nations in the Community. We have seen it before. We faltered in our first approach to the Community. We adopted its treaties late. We then spent the late 1970s and early 1980s fighting, as we were forced to do, for our financial burden to be lightened. It is not surprising that, among some on the continent, this history leads to a questioning of our European credentials, so that a word of caution spoken in London may sound like apostasy in Bonn. We have found persuasion harder. We argued for a practical step-by-step development of Europe; we had to accept the more legalistic, structured advance of the Single European Act.

In the continuing discussions about completing the internal market,

Britain is likely to seek exceptions in more cases than other members of the Community. That will not rupture our relations with the other eleven; it will merely delay the closing of the gap which has for so long denied us a leading and influential role. It is not essential that taxes should be harmonized within a completed market; but if Britain wants to place herself in the most favourable position within that market, she will acknowledge that deals have to be struck and compromises worked for, and conduct herself accordingly. It is not essential for Britain to get rid of frontier posts. But if taxes are harmonized, smuggling for the ordinary citizen loses its appeal.

I cannot believe that these are reefs upon which Europe could ever founder. Immediately important, they are historically trivial and they will be worn away by successive generations, impatient with the lack of political will or skill to give effect to the familiar and relatively simple conception of one market. If politicans appear hesitant about the next step in the making of Europe, that hesitancy will soon appear in the boardrooms and banking parlours. To pick and choose from the constituent parts of Europe's programme, to dine *à la carte*, is to risk quenching the enthusiasm that British managers must display if the opportunity of 1992 is to be grasped.

Commercially, perhaps the most dangerous infection of this kind is Britain's continued stand against the pursuit of closer monetary arrangements in Europe. No one in Europe really sees this as necessitating the sudden conjuring up of a central bank or a single currency, let alone the transference to the Brussels bureaucracy of national economic policy-making. But British coyness will stir competitive spirits in Paris and Frankfurt to do all in their power to weaken, for their own gain, the financial pre-eminence of the City of London. The more British politicians are heard questioning the need for European convergence in one field, the more they will discourage progress in fields where they want it.

For Britain, as for her partners, Europe is only an opportunity, not a guarantee. It is certainly not a promise underwritten by continental largesse. Until the distant day when economic union may make rivalries pointless, continental exporters will still be out to win at British exporters' expense. The battle will be relentless.

The disruptions and re-orientations of the newly deregulated market place will produce changes in the 1990s more disturbing and demanding than those of the 1980s. For Britain to have a ghost of a chance every sinew must be stiffened. Too many doubts, however patriotic their expression may sound, will foredoom the country's efforts. Vision and a single minded urgency are going to be demanded.

The debate in Britain today has ceased at last to be a debate about the fact of British entry. Few reputable politicians in Britain now question British membership of the European Community or maintain with any credibility that there is an alternative. For the Conservative government, Margaret Thatcher proclaimed Britain's European destiny in her speech at Bruges. In 1988 too, the British Labour Party decided to remove the leg-iron with which, alone among the Community's Socialist parties, it had chosen to shackle itself – and tried to shackle the country – during our first fifteen years of membership. Neil Kinnock formally signified Labour's decision to drop hostility to Europe from its programme – a recognition that such hostility now earns very few votes. The TUC did a U-turn at its conference in September 1988 and now claims to be a supporter of Europe 1992. I note their conversion.

In part this reflects a sense of despair of Labour ever winning power in Britain, so they have decided to back another lost cause: that of socialist corporatism. They will find that the belief that Europe offers an alternative route to socialism is a delusion. They may seek to replace the old argument about Europe right or wrong with a debate over Europe right or left, but events will out-run them.

Throughout the world socialism is in retreat; capitalism is in advance and eveywhere more competitive. Only capitalism in Europe can withstand the competition that we will continue to face from the rest of the world.

The Europeans look to the logic that will carry us on through the market place to which we are already committed. They seek to explore the efficiencies and disciplines of co-ordinated economic policies and a common currency. The history of the 1950s is proof that nothing will stop or divert them, queasiness among the British least of all.

So the British people and government are left with two choices. The first is to play a leading role, seeking to influence the changing institutions and laws of Europe on lines which further British interest, or which at least do us no harm. The second choice is to settle for a two-speed Europe, with Britain bringing up the rear, more sure of what we are against than of what we are for. The leadership of Europe's second eleven is ours for the taking: there are twelve member countries in all, it should be remembered, and the rest are all content to fill the ranks of the first eleven. There is, as I see it, only one proper basis for any country's foreign policy: self-interest. Plainly it is in Britain's interest to seek to influence and participate in the growth and deployment of the European Community's steadily increasing power.

But let us weigh these choices more closely. What are the arguments for a minimalist approach? First, it is easier to sell to a domestic political audience. There will always be those who will applaud the 'sock it to 'em' defence of today's interests with yesterday's phrases. National leaders like to be seen battling for national interests, and public opinion likes to see them do it. Second, it enables progress to be made at the margin, unperceived and therefore with minimal controversy. The more gradual and discreet the successive steps by which realism moves the country closer to its European neighbours, the less the risk of stress and tension. The public mood can change as practice changes. As intra-European trade increases, as the frontiers open, as mergers proceed and young people's careers progress within a more mobile Europe, it can be argued that the attitudes of new generations will adapt to a progressive and tranquil Europeanization. With luck, what is controversial today will be in demand tomorrow or the day after.

There is nothing ignoble about this cautious approach. At every step, legitimate national interests will be at stake. Each of the twelve member nations has interests for which its elected leaders will fight; and, although in the end compromise will resolve the most bitter battles, each knows that the harder he fights the more satisfactory that compromise is likely to prove. It is therefore to be expected that each country will approach the new Europe with a greater or lesser degree of caution.

But there are penalties to be incurred by a grudging approach. Coolness communicates itself as rapidly as warmth. Politics today is boundary-free. Every capital has its foreign correspondents, every newspaper its foreign pages. Every negative speech by a senior politician on European affairs, delivered in ringing nationalist tones to a domestic audience, is heard abroad and can have damaging consequences. Every hostile speech provokes at best despair, at worst contempt. The French and Germans, at every sign of British aloofness, draw closer together. The smaller countries of the Community will continue to look for leadership to the driving energy of France or Germany if Britain has little to offer. Profoundly they want Britain to play the fullest part of which she is capable. Many of them see an active British presence as the Community's best guarantee against narrowness or lopsidedness. Even in France, there is an understanding that tomorrow's Europe will either be largely a Franco-German community – less Atlanticist and more protectionist – drawing on a more centralized tradition of government; or a more outward-looking, open-trading, Atlanticist Europe which Britain's historical experiences and world view will have helped to shape. In the latter event, the small countries know that they will be in less danger of being squeezed by their larger neighbours. Jacques Chirac's concept of a web of alliances based on the French will encounter the balancing influence of the British.

Our fellow Europeans want us to travel their road, but they will no more allow us in the 1990s than in the 1950s to frustrate their ambitions. In the last resort, we are free to decide for ourselves the level of our contribution. No armies will cross the Channel to force us to keep faith. If we march with our friends we will further our cause and theirs. If we dawdle or drop out they may spare us no more than a regretful shrug.

I see nothing to counter the repeated evidence of British history that we are at risk from any assemblage of power in continental Europe from which we are excluded. Today the risk of our exclusion or partial exclusion comes only from ourselves. The way to prevent it is to commit all our national energies to the enterprise of Europe – to persuade ourselves that Britain's national interest will be served only by the determined building up of a stronger, closer Community.

Churchill urged his audience at the Albert Hall on 14 May 1947 'to promote the cause of United Europe, and to give this idea the prominence and vitality necessary for it to lay hold of the minds of our fellow countrymen, to such an extent that it will affect their actions and influence the course of national policy'. No hesitancy there, and little room for doubt that he saw the European adventure as one in which British minds and strengths would have to be unreservedly committed.

If he looked for fervour from the British, then it must be said that they have yet to show it. If he looked for a change of heart in Britain, an abandonment of our long habit of seeing our neighbours (as they indeed saw us) as strangers, with different values as well as different tongues, he might have seen in our generation the beginning of such a change. But if what he hoped for most was a settled conviction by the British that the cause of European unity was their own cause, then I believe that the fervent hope of Britain's greatest modern European – forty years on – has been fulfilled. Our destiny, he would say, lies with Europe.

Index

ABCC, 107
Acheson, Dean, 10
Act of Union (1707), 211
Action Programmes on environment (EC), 163–4
Adam, Robert, 4
Adenauer, Konrad, 9, 12
Advisory Committee on Science and Technology (1987), 152
Afghanistan, 178–9, 187
AFL–CIO, 86
'Agricultural Policies, Markets and Trade 1988', 47–8
agriculture, 46–57, *see also under individual countries*
Agriculture Act (1947), 46
Agriculture Council, 31
Air Pollution from Motor Vehicles Directive (1988), 169
Airbus, 119
Aircraft Production, Ministry of, 137
Alcuin, 2
Algeria, 179
Alps, 160
American Enterprise Institute, 86
American Federation of Labor and Congress of Industrial Organizations (AFL–CIO), 86
Amery, Leo, 87
Anderson, Mark, 86
Andropov, Yuri, 176, 181
Anglo-Saxons, 2
Arabic language teaching, 129
Aral Sea, 173
Areas of Outstanding Natural Beauty, 165
Ariane space programme, 117
Armenia, 182, 187
Asia, 61
Association of British Chambers of Commerce (ABCC), 107
Athenaeum Club, London, 156
Augustine, St, 2
Australasia, 61
Austria, 22, 208
Azerbaijan, 182

Balfour Report (1929), 138
Baltic Sea, 159, 173
Bank of England, 89, 92, 100, 102, 105
banking, 56, 63, 88–93, 100–2, *see also under individual countries*
Banque Nationale de Paris, 101
Barclays Bank, 101
Barfield, Claude, 86
Barlow Clowes, 105
Basic Research Credit, 149
Basic Research in Industrial Technologies for Europe (BRITE), 118
BBC, 7
Bede, Venerable, 2
Belgium, 104
Benelux countries, 9
Berlin, 8, 187
Bevin, Ernest, 10–11

'Big Bang', 61
Boniface, St, 2
Boots, 77
Boston, USA, 171
BP, 84
Bretton Woods system, 91
Brezhnev, Leonid, 176, 180, 183
BRITE, 118
British Aerospace, 169, 198, 202
British Broadcasting Corporation, 7
British Rail, 121
Brundtland report, 167–8, 176
Brussels, Treaty of, 11
Brynmill Park, Swansea, 155
budget (EC), 38–57; and Britain, 40–3
Bundesbank (West Germany), 72, 90
Bundesrat (West Germany), 35
Bundestag (West Germany), 33
Bureau Européen des Unions de Consommateurs, 63
Burke, Edmund, 211
Bush, George, 48, 86, 171, 176, 189, 190
Business/Education Task Force, 135
Butler, Richard Austen, 15, 137, 139

Callaghan, James, 16, 68, 71, 127
Calvin, John, 4
Canada, 61, 84, 87, 187
Canning, George, 5
CAP *see* Common Agricultural Policy
Caspian Sea, 173
Castlereagh, Robert Stewart, Viscount, 5
Catherine the Great, Empress of Russia, 4
Catholicism, 3, 210
CATS, 133
CBI *see* Confederation of British Industry
Cecchini, Paolo, 77–8
Celts, 2
Certificate of Pre-Vocational Education, 140
Chamberlain, Neville, 82
Channel Tunnel, 58, 81, 120, 121, 122
Channon, Paul, 122
Charlemagne, 2
Charles, Prince of Wales, 168
Chatham House, 72, 74, 86
Chernenko, Konstantin, 176
Chernobyl, 160, 172–3, 175
Chevenement, Jean-Pierre, 85
China, 59
Chinese language teaching, 129
Chirac, Jacques, 69, 216
Christian Democrats (West Germany), 69
Christianity, 2, 2–3
Churchill, Sir Winston, 7, 10, 11, 87, 208–10, 216
Clarendon Royal Commission on the Public Schools, 136
CNAA, 133, 151
Coca-Cola, 59
Cockfield, Lord, 54, 76–7, 79, 81, 101
Cockfield plan, 79–82
Colet, John, 3
Columba, St, 2
COMETT, 131–2
'Commerce Business Daily', 201
Commerce, Chambers of, 135
Common Agricultural Policy (CAP), 38, 46–7, 49–52, 55, 57, 158, 166
Commonwealth, 5, 6, 10, 11, 15, 67, 102
Communist Party (France), 7
Communist Party (Soviet Union), 180, 181
Community in Education and Training for Technology (COMETT), 131–2
'Competence and Competition' (NEDO), 153
Confederation of British Industry (CBI), 96, 107, 109, 129, 135, 150
Conservative governments, 40–1, 139, 208
Conservative Party (UK), xiii, 11, 72, 82, 90, 208, 209
COREPER, 17
'Cost of Non-Europe, The', 77
Council of Economic Advisers (USA), 86
Council of Education Ministers, 128
Council of Europe, 11
Council of Foreign Ministers, 31
Council for Industry and Higher Education, 149
Council of Ministers, 31–4, 35; and Delors committee, 89; formation, 16–17; powers, 19, 24, 25, 31; resolution on education, 126

Council for National Academic Awards (CNAA), 133, 151
Countryside Commission, 165
Cranford Community School, 131
Credit Accumulation and Transfer Scheme (CATS), 133
Crédit Agricole, 101
Crédit Lyonnais, 101
Crickhowell, Lord (formerly Nicholas Edwards), 160
crime, international, 80–1
Cripps, Sir Stafford, 11, 12
'Crisis of British Industry, The' (*The Times*), 136
Crosland, Anthony, 127
Cruise missiles, 175, 176, 187
currency, 90–1
currency markets, 72–3
Customs and Excise, Department of (UK), 38, 107
Czechoslovakia, 181, 187

Dainton, Sir Frederick, 138
Danes (early), 2
DARPA, 65
de Ferranti, Basil, 33
de Gasperi, Alcide, 9
de Gaulle, President Charles, 7, 12, 13, 22, 49, 59, 67, 196
defence, 178–206
Defence Advanced Research Projects Agency (DARPA), 65
Defence Industry Study Report, 201
Defence, Ministry of (UK), 60, 116, 178, 179, 198, 200, 203
Defense Industrial Base Preservation Bill, 204
Deloitte Haskins & Sells, 105
Delors, Jacques, 18, 88–9, 92
Denmark: defence 192; environment, 161, 176; foreign language teaching, 130
Deutsche Bank, 101
Development of Inventions Act (1948), 137
Devlin, Lord, 107
Devonshire Royal Commission on Scientific Instruction and the Advancement of Science (1872–5), 138
Diana, Princess of Wales, 168
DIN system, 109
Directorate General of Defence Quality Assurance, 124
Disraeli, Benjamin (Lord Beaconsfield), 125
Dissenters, 5
Dixon, Senator, 204
Dock Labour Scheme, 122
DTI *see* Trade and Industry, Department of (UK)
Dukakis, Michael, 170
Dunkirk, 4

'EC, The: Progress or Decline?', 74–5
ECCTIS, 132–3
ECOFIN, 31
Economic and Social Committee (of EC), 18, 131
'Economics of 1992, The', 78
economics, 58, 75
Economist, 91
ecu, 90, 91
Eden, Sir Anthony (later Earl of Avon), 11, 193, 209
education, 126–54; core curriculum, 127, 131; credit transfer, 132–3; expenditure on, 128, 146–50; foreign language teaching, 128–31; links between higher education and industry, 150–4; science and technology, 136–7; teacher in-service training, 134; vocational training, 138–53
Education Acts: 1902, 136; 1918, 137; 1944, 137, 139; 1986, 134
Education, Board of (UK), 137
Education, Ministry of (France), 130–1
Education Reform Act (1988), 127, 131, 134
Education Resolution (1974), 128
Education and Science, Department of (UK), 129, 134, 142
Education and Science, Secretary of State for, 151

Educational Counselling and Credit Transfer Information Service (ECCTIS), 132–3
Edwards, Nicholas (later Lord Crickhowell), 160
Eliot, T. S., 2
Employment Bill (1988), 18
Employment, Department of (UK), 106, 142
Employment, Secretary of State for, 151
EMS *see* European Monetary System
'Engineering: Our Future' (Royal Commission Report), 138
Engineering and Technology Programme, 151
English teaching (as foreign language), 130
Enlightenment, 4
Enterprise in Higher Education initiative (1987), 151
environment, 155–77; and action programmes, 163–4; EC policy, 162–4; of general concern to European nations, xiii, 160–1; and green capitalist, 170–1; and green consumer, 168–9; and industry, 169–70; international meetings on, 176; pollution, 158–60, 163, 165–6
Environment, Department of the, 116, 121, 156, 160
Environmental Impact Directive (1985), 166
Erasmus, 3
ERASMUS, 131–2
ERM *see* Exchange Rate Mechanism
ESA *see* European Space Agency
ESPRIT, 118
Estonia, 183
'Eurangos', 19
EUREKA project, 117
Eurogroup, 193
'Europe – Open for business' campaign, 97
European Agricultural Guidance and Guarantee Fund, 38
European Bank, 76, 88–92
European Coal and Steel Community, 9–10, 11
European Commission, 9, 17–20, 24, 70, 101, 103, 111, 197
European Communities Act (1972), 21
European Community: formation and membership, 10–14
European Community Action Scheme for the Mobility of University Students (ERASMUS), 131–2
European Council, 17, 31; meeting of, Hanover (1988), 58; and Luxembourg (1985), 76
European Court of Human Rights (Strasbourg), 20
European Court of Justice (Luxembourg), 18, 20–1, 164
European Currency Unit (ecu), 90, 91
European Defence Community (proposed), 11, 193
European Development Fund, 40, 55
European Environmental Bureau, 160
European Fighter Aircraft programme, 119, 203
European Free Trade Association (EFTA), 12, 22
European Investment Bank, 40
European Launcher Development Organization, 117
European Monetary Co-operation Fund, 71
European Monetary System (EMS), 16, 70, 71, 72–4, 90
European Parliament, 18–20, 23, 25–7, 33, 131; members, 33–4
European Scientific Research Organization, 117
European Social Fund, 52
European Space Agency (ESA), 117, 118, 119, 200, 203
European Strategic Programme for Information Technology (ESPRIT), 118
exchange controls, abolition of, 60, 76, 103
Exchange Rate Mechanism (ERM), 70, 71, 91

FAST, 118
Fatstock Marketing Corporation, 38
Federal Reserve Bank (USA), 63

Federal Vocational Training Act (West Germany, 1969), 141
Feldstein, Martin S., 85
Felixstowe, 122
Figaro, Le, 130
finance, 100–5
Finance, Ministry of (Belgium), 38
Financial Services Act, 103, 105
Financial Times, 72
Finland, 22
Finniston, Sir Monty, 138
First World War, 136, 137, 189
'Flow of Candidates in Science and Technology into Higher Education, The' (Dainton enquiry, 1968), 138
Folketing (Denmark), 33
Fontainebleau agreement (1984), 43–4
Ford Motor Company, 59
Forecasting and Assessment in Science and Technology (FAST), 118
Foreign Office (UK), 15, 37, 109; second minister (proposed), 37
Fowler, Norman, 108
France, 215–6; agriculture, 46–7; banking, 104; defence, 179, 187, 190, 192, 193–7, 194–6, 201, 202, 206–7; education, 6, 127, 130, 134, 146, 147, 153; environment, 159, 175; expansion, 67; foreign language teaching, 130; insurance, 104; relationship with Britain, 3, 5, 7, 10–11; research and development, 113, 117; and Revolution, 5; unemployment, 69; vocational training, 140, 143
Franco, Francisco, 69
Franco-German Treaty (1963), 194–5
Free Democratic Party (West Germany), 47
French Revolution, 5

G7 meeting (Paris, 1988), 176
GATT, 48, 84, 86
General Agreement on Tariffs and Trade (GATT), 48, 84, 86
General Electric Company, 64, 202
General Motors, 59
Georgia (Soviet Union), 183
German language teaching, 130
Germany, East, 9, 187
Germany, West, 215–6; after Second World War, 8–10; agriculture, 46–7; banking, 104; currency, 72, 90; defence, 11, 184, 188, 190, 191, 192, 194, 194–7, 202, 203, 204, 205–6, 205; education, 6, 127, 130, 134, 147, 153; environment, 159, 174; environmental pollution, 159; expansion, 67, 69; foreign language teaching, 130; *Länder*, role of, 134, 141; and NATO, 11–12; relationship with Britain, 3–4, 7, 15; research and development, 113, 119; unemployment, 69; vocational training, 140–2, 143
Giraud, André, 201
'Glass-Steagall rules', 102
Glaxo, 169
Goethe, Johann Wolfgang von, 3
Goodison, Sir Nicholas, 94
Gorbachev, Mikhail, 22, 87, 172–4, 179–89, 190, 191, 197
Gorbachev, Raisa, 180
Great Exhibition (London, 1851), 136
Greece, 9
Greeks, ancient, 2
Green Consumer Guide, 168
Green Consumer Week, 168
Green parties, 161, 173

Hague, The, congress at (1948), xii, 11, 208, 209, 210
Hall, Sir Arnold, 119, 199
Handel, George Frederick, 4
Harrier jump-jet, 199
Hawker Siddeley, 119, 199
Hazardous Waste Inspectorate, 165
Heath, Edward, 13
Helsinki agreement on human rights, 180
Heritage Coasts, 165
High Authority, 9, 10
Hill Samuel, 99
Hitachi, 143
Hitler, Adolf, 6, 9, 10

Holland, 3, 4, 69–70; defence, 192; environment, 160, 176; foreign language teaching, 130
Honda, 66
Hong Kong, 85
House of Commons Foreign Affairs Select Committee, 23
House of Lords, 29
Howe, Sir Geoffrey, 60, 73
Hume, David, 4
Hungary, 187, 208

IBM, 64, 65, 131
ICI, 84
IEPG *see* Independent European Programme Group
Imperial College of Science and Technology, 136
Independent European Programme Group (IEPG), 193, 198–9, 200, 201, 203
India, 5
Industrial Training Boards, 139
Industry Year (1986), 135
INF Treaty, 178
information technology, 64, 146
Information Technology Skill Shortage Committee, 146
Inland Revenue, 77, *see also* taxation
insurance, 102–3
Integrated Mediterranean Programmes, 53
International Association for the Evaluation of Educational Achievement, 138
International Court of Justice (The Hague), 20
International Monetary Fund, 68
International Stock Exchange *see* Stock Exchange, London, 105
Investment Services Directive, 104
Ireland, 2
Irtysh, River, 173
Italy: agriculture, 46–7; defence, 194, 203; environment, 159; industry, 9; insurance, 104; relationship with Britain, 4; unemployment, 69

Japan, 61–6; agriculture, 48; banking, 101, 104, 106; defence, 199; and global markets, 59; insurance, 102; research and development, 113, 118; standards compared with Europe, xii; technology, 64–6; trade and industry, 22, 83, 85–8, 107, 110, 117, 119; vocational training, 140, 143
Japanese Development Bank, 66
Jenkins, Roy, 70
JET nuclear research project, 128
Job Creation Programme, 139, 140
Johnson, Christopher, 91
Joint Research and Development Act (USA, 1984), 66
Joseph, Sir Keith, 133

Kennedy, John Fitzgerald, 196
Keynes, John Maynard, 7
KGB, 181, 183
Khruschev, Nikita, 180
King, Tom, 142, 156
Kinnock, Neil, 214
Kohl, Helmut, 69
Korea, 85
Korea, South, 86
Korean War, 11

Labour Force Survey (1984), 142–3
Labour governments, 40, 67–8, 96, 127, 138
Labour Party, 23, 67, 127, 214
Large Plant Emissions Directive (1988), 165
Lawson, Nigel, 72, 86
Lenin, V. I., 181
Liberal government (1907), 136
Lloyds Bank, 91
Local Employer Networks, 135
Locke, John, 3
Loi Monory (France), 84
Lomé Convention, 40, 54, 56
London, City of, 100, 103, 104, 170–1, 213
London money market, 61
Louis IX, King of France, 91
Luther, Martin, 4
Luxembourg, 35, 103, 201

Luxembourg Compromise (1965), 22, 23, 59

M25 motorway, 122
Macdonalds, 59
Machiavelli, Niccolo, 3
Macmillan, Sir Harold (later Earl of Stockton), 12, 67
Malta, 208
Manpower Services Commission (later Training Commission), 139, 142, 151
Manufacturing Systems Engineering Programme, 151
Marin, Manuel, 133–4
Marshall, General George, 8
Marshall Plan, 8, 10
Massachusetts, 35
Massachusetts Institute of Technology, 146
Medical Research Council (formerly Medical Research Committee), 137
Mediterranean Agreements, 55
Mediterranean Programme, 56
'Mergers Policy' (DTI), 111, 112
mergers and takeovers, 109–12
Merlin Ecology Fund, 170
Messina, xii, 12
milk quotas, 51
Ministry for International Trade and Industry (MITI, Japan), 66, 119, 199
MITI, 66, 119, 199
Mitterrand, François, 69, 128, 190
MLRS, 204
Monnet, Jean, 8–9, 10, 11, 12, 13, 126
Montebello declaration, 174
Montesquieu, Charles-Louis, de, 4
More, Sir Thomas, 3
Morocco, 208
MSC, 139, 151
Mulroney, Brian, 84
Multiple Launch Rocket System (MLRS), 204
Muslim fundamentalists, 183

Napoleon I, Emperor of France, 5, 127
Napoleon III, Emperor of France, 127
Narjes, Karl-Heinz, 85
NASA, 199
Nassau agreement, 196
National Chemical Advisory Committee, 136
National Economic Development Office (NEDO), 153
National Farmers Union, 45
National Institute Economic Review, 143
National Institute of Economic and Social Research, 147
National Nature Reserves, 165
National Parks, 165
National Physical Laboratory, 136, 137
National Research Development Corporation (1949), 137
National Rivers Authority, 160
NATO (North Atlantic Treaty Organization); and defence, 174, 176, 184, 185, 187, 190, 191–8; Defence Planning Committee, 193; and EFTA, 12; and European co-operation, xiii; foundation, 8; and rearmament of Germany, 11–12
Nature Conservancy Council, 165
NEDO, 153
New York money market, 61
New York State, 35
Newton, Sir Isaac, 3
Nippon Telegraph and Telephone company, 143
Noisy-le-Roi, 130
Non-Associated aid programme, 55, 56
Normans, 2
North Atlantic Treaty Organization *see* NATO
North Sea, 159; ministerial conference, 166; oil, 97
Norway, 22, 176, 192, 208
Nuffield French language teaching scheme, 129

Ob, River, 173
OECD, 47–8, 63, 169, 176
OEEC, 11, 12
oil prices, 63–4, 70–1, 73

Omnibus Trade and Competitiveness Act (USA, 1988), 85–6
Open University, 132
Organization of Economic Co-operation and Development (OECD), 47–8, 63, 169, 176
Organization for European Economic Co-operation (OEEC), 10, 12

Palmerston, Henry John Temple, 1st Viscount, 5
Panavia, 204
Paris International Exhibition (1878), 136
parliament (Belgium), 33
Parliament (UK), 25, 28–30, 76
Peat, Marwick and Mitchell, 38
Pennsylvania, 35
Pentagon (USA), 65–6
Pershing missiles, 175, 176, 187
Personal Equity Plan, 84
Pétain, Henri, 10
Petrovsky, V. F., 172, 174
Philips, 64, 83
'Plant a Tree' Year, 157
Poland, 187
Polaris missiles, 190, 196
Polytechnics and Colleges Funding Council, 151
Prestt, Ian, 156
privatization, 96
Privy Council, 137
Public Expenditure White Paper (1989), 43

quangos, 19

RACE, 118
Rafale, 196
Reagan, Ronald, 48, 145, 178, 188
Red Army, 179
Reformation, 2, 3
Regional Development Fund (EC), 39, 52–3
regional imbalance, 123–4
Regional Research Core Concept (Japan), 66
research and development, 66, 112–9, 149
Research and Development in Communications Technologies for Europe (RACE), 118
Rhine-Danube canal, 120
Rhode Island, 35
Rhodes, 167
Robbins Report, 150
Rolls-Royce, 169, 198, 202
Rome, Treaty of: amended by Single European Act, 76; environmental policy, lack of, 162; and establishment of EC, xii, 12; objectives and commitments, 16, 19, 21, 22, 23, 58, 74, 79, 102, 126, 207; participating states, 210; provisions of, 19, 22, 25
Rostov, 173
Rothschild Customer-Contractor Requirement Boards, 116
Royal Aircraft Establishment, Farnborough, 199
Royal Commission (1884), 136
Royal Commissions, 138
Royal Dutch Shell, 82
Royal Society for the Protection of Birds, 156
Ruskin College, Oxford, 127

Sainsbury, Hon. Timothy, 124
Sainsburys, 168
Salisbury, Lord, 136
SALT II, 178
Samuelson Royal Commission on Technical Instruction (1884), 138
'Saving the Ozone Layer' (conference, 1989), 171
Scandinavia, environment, 160
Schmidt, Helmut, 69
Schuman, Robert, 9
Schuman Plan, 9, 10
Science and Engineering Research Council, 151
Scientific and Industrial Research, Department of, 137
Scientific Instruction, Select Committee on (1868), 138

Scotland, 1, 2, 3, 4, 146, 211
Scottish Conservative Conference, 73
SDI, 65, 117
Second Banking Directive, 101, 104
Second World War, 6, 8, 10, 137
Select Committee on European Legislation (House of Commons), 28–30
Select Committee, House of Commons (1868), 136
Sellafield, 165
Seneca, xi
Shaftesbury, Lord, 82
Shakespeare, William, 3
Shell, 84
Shevardnadze, Eduard, 171–2, 174, 188
Shrewsbury School, 155
Schultz, George, 189
Siemens, 64
Single European Act (1986), 17, 22–5, 33, 54, 58, 76, 101, 162–3, 164, 212
single market, 76–88, 167–9
Sites of Special Scientific Interest, 165
Skill Improvement Programme (proposed), 144
Smith, Adam, 4
Social Democrats (West Germany), 69
Social Fund (ED), 38
Solemn Declaration, 23
Solidarity, 87
Soviet Union, 7, 8, 9, 59, 91, 160; defence, 178–89, 179–88, 205; environment, 171–6
Spain, 210; and defence, 194, 203; insurance, 104; research and development, 119; unemployment, 69
Spanish language teaching, 130
Speer, Albert, 9
Spens Report (1939), 137
Sputnik launch, 65
Stalin, Josef, 180, 181, 183
standards and regulations, technical, 109
Standing Committees on European Documents, 29–30
Stock Exchange, London (International Stock Exchange), 94, 103, 142
Stock Exchange, Tokyo, 105
Stockholm Conference (1972), 162, 167, 176
Strategic Arms Limitation Talks (SALT), 178
Strategic Defence Initiative (SDI), 65, 117
Sweden, 22, 153, 208
Switzerland, 22, 159, 160

Taiwan, 85, 86
Tangier, 4
Tax Reform Act (USA), 149
taxation, 77, 79–80, 81, 96, 124–5, 144, 149–50
Teaching Company Scheme, 151
Tebbit, Norman, 97
Technical Education, Royal Commission on (1867), 138
Technical and Vocational Education Initiative (TVEI), 135
technology, 64–6
TELETEXT, 133
Tesco, 168
Thames, River, 159
Thatcher, Margaret, 171, 172, 176, 214
third world, EC aid to, 55–6
Thomson, 64
Thorn-EMI, 64
Times, The, 36
'*Times, The*, 1,000', 62
Tokyo money market, 61
TOPS, 139
Tornado aircraft programme, 119, 203, 204
Tory Party (18th century), 4
'Towards a Stronger Europe' (report), 199–200
trade, 96–100, *see under individual countries*
Trade, Board of, 15
Trade and Industry, Department of (DTI), 96–7, 104, 109, 111, 116, 135, 151
Trade and Industry Select Committee report on Information Technology (House of Commons), 146
trade unions, 96, 127
Trades Union Congress (TUC), 214

Training Commission (formerly Manpower Services Commission), 139, 142
'Training for Employment' (White Paper), 108
Training and Enterprise Councils (TECs), 108
Training Opportunities Programme (TOPS), 139
training programmes, privatization (proposed), 108–9
transport, 120–2
Transport, Department of, 120
Treasury (UK), 115, 160
Trevelyan, George Macaulay, 136
Trevi group, 81
Trident missiles, 190, 196
TUC, 214
Tugendhat, Christopher, 49
Turkey, 208
TVEI, 135

unemployment, 52, 69–70, 96, 122–3, 139
Unilever, 82, 84
United Europe Committee, 208
United Europe meeting, 7
United Nations, 174, 176, 188; Conference on the Human Environment, 162; Environment Programme, 172; International Conference on the Environment (proposed), 172
Universities Funding Council, 151
USA: agriculture, 47, 48, 182; Air Force, 65; banking, 101, 101–2, 106; Congress, 25, 26, 34–5, 150, 178, 198; defence, 12, 179, 187–90, 192, 192–3, 198, 198–9, 199, 200, 203–4, 204–5, 205; education, 146, 149, 152; environment, 171, 176; industry, 110, 117; insurance, 102; relationship with Britain, 6, 14, 15; relationship with Europe, 8, 10–11, 13, 192, 196; research and development, 113, 118; Senate, 35–6; Senate, as model for EC system of control, 34–7; standards compared with Europe, xii; technology, 65–6; trade, 22, 61–6, 85–7; Treasury, 86
USSR *see* Soviet Union

Van Howelingen, J, 199
Venice, 157
Versailles, Treaty of, 6, 7
Vietnam, 179
Virginia, 35
Voltaire, François Marie Arouet de, 4

Waldegrave, William, 167
Wales, 2, 211
Warsaw Pact, 185, 186, 197
Werner Report (1970), 70
Western European Union (WEU), 11, 193–4
Whig Party, 4
Wildlife and Countryside Bill (1981), 156
William I (the Conqueror), King, 2
William III, King, 4
Wilson, Sir Harold, 13
Wimpy, 59
Wolfenden, Lord, 155
worker participation, 82–4
World Bank, 56
World Commission on the Environment and Development, report, 167–8, 176
World Health Organization Conference, 176

'Yes Minister', 32
Yorkshire, 212
Young, Lord, 18
Younger, George, 201
Youth Opportunities Programme, 140
Youth Training Scheme, 140
Yugoslavia, 9, 208

Zurich, 209